Degunking for eBay Sellers with Time Limitations

Time-constrained degunking also applies to selling on eBay. If you are selling products and trying to improve your business, here are some different tasks that you can perform if your time is limited.

Fifteen-Minute Degunking

If you have a very short amount of time—less than half an hour, say—you should focus on these two simple but results-oriented activities:

1. Find some quick ways to get more of your sales listings online (Page 135).
2. Create a free About Me page that supports your eBay selling activities (Page 100).

Thirty-Minute Degunking

If you only have thirty minutes or so, I recommend you perform the fifteen-minute degunking plan listed above and then complete these tasks to help you improve your selling activities:

1. Boost your feedback rating so that you can build a good reputation that will attract more business (Page 94).
2. Update your auction headings so that they attract more attention (Page 136).
3. Choose better keywords to help buyers find your items (Page 161).
4. Cross-promote multiple items you have for sale (Page 165).

One-Hour Degunking

If you have an hour to degunk your sales activities, you can go a little deeper, improve your reputation as a seller, and promote yourself a little more. Here are the tasks to focus on:

1. Perform the thirty-minute degunking plan.
2. Improve your presentation by cleaning up and talking up your items (Page 158).
3. Improve the quality and quantity of your auction photos (Page 141).
4. Clean up the payment process for your customers (Page 143).
5. Gather six to ten items from your home that you can sell on eBay (Page 186).

Three-Hour to Half-Day Degunking

Because you now have a little more time to degunk your selling strategies, with this plan you'll be able to:

1. Perform the one-hour degunking tasks.
2. Research the merchandise you plan to offer (Page 152).
3. Streamline your shipping process (Page 170).

4. If you have a store or site, make sure it is listed on Google (Page 163).

5. Gather up some special gifts and personal notes to improve your customer service (Page 174).

6. Research items that are the most popular to sell on eBay (page 189).

Spare Moment Degunking

There may be times when you are doing something around the house or with your computer and you discover that you have a few minutes to spare. To this end, I've created my Top Twenty list of degunking tasks that you can perform. These tasks do not need to be performed in any specific order. Simply select a task and perform it to help you get better at buying or selling on eBay.

Twenty Useful Degunking Tasks

1. Track and organize your sales activities with eBay (Page 112).

2. Reduce unsolicited e-mail that you receive as a result of your eBay activities (Page 79).

3. Save searches that you conduct frequently (Page 38).

4. Respond to negative comments that can hurt your reputation (Page 95).

5. Place smarter bids by comparison shopping to learn the value of what's being sold (Page 59).

6. Learn how to keep from being cheated by a buyer (Page 238).

7. Provide incentives for customers who purchase multiple items from you (Page 209).

8. Degunk your current auction descriptions (Page 126).

9. Add more and better photos to your auction listings (Page 141).

10. Use the eBay discussion boards to get an answer to one of your nagging problems (Page 86).

11. Improve your shipping plan before you sell an item (Page 148).

12. Learn how to recognize and avoid dishonest bidders (Page 74).

13. Fund surplus, overstock, and other cut-rate merchandise to sell (Page 198).

14. Research completed auctions to get a better idea of how well certain items are selling on eBay (Page 154).

15. Create complex searches with degunking operators (Page 35).

16. Adjust your bidding strategy to better match the type of auction that you're in (Page 62).

17. Manage your auctions and schedule multiple sales with Seller's Assistant (Page 122).

18. Learn how to apply some tips to attract collectors (Page 157).

19. Watch an auction closely so that you can place a last-minute bid (Page 115).

20. Recognize warning signs so you can avoid transactions that go sour (Page 226).

The Degunking 12-Step Program

Here is the basic 12-step degunking process that you should follow to fully degunk your eBay activities:

1. Clean up and optimize your computer and your eBay registration data, and create shortcuts to help you wade through eBay's crowded Web site (Chapter 2).

2. Create and save your favorite searches, and learn to search all of eBay—not just auctions (Chapter 3).

3. When buying, apply the best tactics for increasing your winning percentages and place smarter bids by comparison shopping (Chapter 4).

4. Improve your communications with buyers and sellers to improve your chances of winning bids and selling more items for bigger profits (Chapter 5).

5. Build up positive feedback by making easy purchases, and market yourself to develop a good reputation (Chapter 6).

6. Organize your My eBay page and use eBay's automation features to watch sales, manage auctions, and automate email responses (Chapter 7).

7. Spruce up your auction descriptions and learn to use a well-organized template and provide lots of personal detail about what you sell (Chapter 8).

8. Find sales help when you need it and spend time and money marketing your sales through keywords and multiple categories (Chapter 9).

9. Learn to streamline your shipping process, improve your shipping schedules, over-pack what you sell, and add personal notes and gifts that will improve customer satisfaction (Chapter 10).

10. Select the best inventory to sell and research what's valuable and what's in demand on eBay (Chapter 11).

11. Sell what you know, plan ahead for big seasonal sales, and develop techniques to encourage repeat customers (Chapter 12).

12. Avoid disputes by providing refunds, spelling out requirements clearly, and following a set schedule for approaching nonresponsive buyers and sellers (Chapter 13).

Degunking for eBay Buyers with Time Limitations

To get the full benefits of degunking, I highly recommend that you complete all of the main eBay degunking tasks in the order that they are presented. Performing all of these tasks will require a bit of time. If you want to approve your buying activities and win more bids but your time is limited, here are some suggestions for valuable degunking tasks you can perform in the time you *do* have—whether it's fifteen minutes, one hour, three hours, or a half day.

Fifteen-Minute Degunking

If you have a very short amount of time—less than half an hour, say—you should focus on fine-tuning how you have eBay set up:

1. Clean up your eBay configurations and set up shortcuts to save a bunch of time (Page 20).
2. Get rid of cookies and temp files that can waste your time (Page 15).
3. Streamline how you view eBay (Page 25).

Thirty-Minute Degunking

If you only have thirty minutes or so, I recommend you perform the fifteen-minute degunking plan listed above and then the following tasks to better locate the best deals on eBay:

1. Use filters and special sorts to make your eBay searches more specific (Page 32).
2. Search outside of eBay to get more complete information about the products you want to purchase (Page 41).
3. Uncover bargains by looking for typographical errors and bad sales schedules (Page 52).

One-Hour Degunking

If you have an hour to degunk your eBay activities, you can focus more on your bidding techniques so that you can win more auctions. Here are the tasks to focus on:

1. Perform the thirty-minute degunking plan for eBay buyers.
2. Install special software that lets you search quickly for feedback, individual sellers, and sales categories (Page 45).
3. Synchronize your clock with eBay (Page 56).
4. Place smarter bids by comparison shopping to learn the real value of what's being sold (Page 59).

Three-Hour to Half-Day Degunking

Because you now have much more time to degunk your buying techniques, with this plan you'll be able to:

1. Perform the one-hour degunking tasks.
2. Study the competition by using some eBay search tools (Page 61).
3. Learn how to bid at the last second of an auction (snipe) and win (Page 64).
4. Learn how to use the technique of proxy bidding to increase your chances of winning (Page 68).
5. Use smart Dutch auction strategies to effectively buy multiple items (Page 69).
6. Learn how to protect yourself from dishonest bidders (Page 74).
7. Learn how to bid on and follow auctions with your cell phone or other wireless devices (Page 89).

Greg Holden

PARAGLYPH
P R E S S

President
Keith Weiskamp

Editor-at-Large
Jeff Duntemann

Vice President, Sales, Marketing, and Distribution
Steve Sayre

Vice President, International Sales and Marketing
Cynthia Caldwell

Production Manager
Kim Eoff

Cover Designers
Kris Sotelo

Degunking™ eBay

Paraglyph Press, Inc.
4015 N. 78th Street, #115
Scottsdale, Arizona 85251
Phone: 602-749-8787
www.paraglyphpress.com

Paraglyph Press ISBN: 1-932111-99-9

Printed in the United States of America
10 9 8 7 6 5 4 3 2 1

PARAGLYPH
P R E S S

The Paraglyph Mission

This book you've purchased is a collaborative creation involving the work of many hands, from authors to editors to designers and to technical reviewers. At Paraglyph Press, we like to think that everything we create, develop, and publish is the result of one form creating another. And as this cycle continues on, we believe that your suggestions, ideas, feedback, and comments on how you've used our books is an important part of the process for us and our authors.

We've created Paraglyph Press with the sole mission of producing and publishing books that make a difference. The last thing we all need is yet another tech book on the same tired, old topic. So we ask our authors and all of the many creative hands who touch our publications to do a little extra, dig a little deeper, think a little harder, and create a better book. The founders of Paraglyph are dedicated to finding the best authors, developing the best books, and helping you find the solutions you need.

As you use this book, please take a moment to drop us a line at **feedback@paraglyphpress.com** and let us know how we are doing—and how we can keep producing and publishing the kinds of books that you can't live without.

Sincerely,

Keith Weiskamp & Jeff Duntemann
Paraglyph Press Founders
4015 N. 78th Street, #115
Scottsdale, Arizona 85251
email: **feedback@paraglyphpress.com**
Web: **www.paraglyphpress.com**

Recently Published by Paraglyph Press:

Small Websites, Great Results
By Doug Addison

A Theory of Fun
For Game Design
By Raph Koster

Degunking Your Email, Spam, and Viruses
By Jeff Duntemann

Perl Core Language Little Black Book
By Steven Holzner

Degunking Windows
By Joli Ballew
and Jeff Duntemann

Degunking Your Mac
By Joli Ballew

3D Game-Based Filmmaking: The Art of Machinima
By Paul Marino

Windows XP Professional: The Ultimate User's Guide,
Second Edition
By Joli Ballew

Jeff Duntemann's Wi-Fi Guide
By Jeff Duntemann

Visual Basic .NET Core Language Little Black Book
By Steven Holzner

The SQL Server 2000 Book
By Anthony Sequeira
And Brian Alderman

The Mac OS X.2 Power User's Book
By Gene Steinberg and Pieter Paulson

Mac OS X v.2 Jaguar Little Black Book
By Gene Steinberg

The Mac OS X.2 Jaguar Book
By Mark R. Bell

Monster Gaming
By Ben Sawyer

To all the eBay members who have shared
their knowledge and experiences with me:
thanks for welcoming me into your community.

ॐ

About the Author

Greg Holden has been hunting down and reselling collectibles, oddball items, and antiques of all sorts for much of his adult life. Greg has written more than 25 books on computers and the Internet, including *How to Do Everything with eBay* and *How to Do Everything With Your eBay Business,* by Osborne-McGraw Hill, and *Internet Auctions for Dummies* and *Cliffs Notes Guide to Buying and Selling on eBay*, both published by Hungry Minds. He is acknowledged as being one of the top book authors and experts writing about eBay. He is the owner of Stylus Media, which specializes in technical writing, publications management, and desktop publishing.

Acknowledgments

When you join eBay, you join a community, and you quickly learn that you need to work with other people in order to get things done in a gunk-free way. This book worked the same way. Keith Weiskamp and Steve Sayre helped get the book off the ground and contributed a good deal of editorial help along the way. So did copyeditor Judy Flynn and reviewer Cynthia Caldwell. Thanks to all of them for helping to get this book done on time.

Thanks also to my agents at Studio B, Neil Salkind and Lynn Haller, for helping bring this and other projects my way.

The text of *Degunking eBay* was made considerably more valuable thanks to the cooperation of a number of people, including PowerSellers Melissa Sands and Kimberly King. My friend Liz Krause helped by providing merchandise from her basement, and Scott Wills helped with photography. Behind the scenes, my assistants Ann Lindner and Ben Huizenga provided invaluable help with editing. Finally, thanks to my daughters Lucy and Zosia, for inspiring me and keeping things in perspective by reminding me what's really important.

Contents at a Glance

Contents

Chapter 8
Sprucing Up Your Auction Descriptions 125

Chapter 9
Strengthening Your Selling Strategies 147

Introduction

You're in heaven: you've found eBay. You've discovered some fantastic bargains. You have just purchased a stuffed animal like the one you loved so much as a child. You've even started to sell a few things and make some pocket money. You are beginning to realize that eBay might not just be an amusement or a way to make a few extra bucks but a real source of significant income that can really change the quality of your life. Not surprisingly, you start to spend more time on eBay. You make an effort to learn how to buy and sell; you start placing bids on more items that you think are bargains. You put more items up for sale and start visiting garage sales to find more items to sell on eBay.

But things don't go according to plan. Your closet, your attic, and your garage are still a mess. You can't spend enough time after work or on weekends to get all the sales online that you want to. Many of your items go without bids or for only a few dollars, making the time you spend on shipping and packing unprofitable. You've also got problems finding items to sell: you spend hours scouring resale shops and flea markets for bargains, only to come up with a few trinkets. (You begin to wonder if all the people who used to sell their bargains this way are now on eBay—and in fact, they probably are.) You are consistently outbid on the things you really want to buy. Increasingly, it seems like there are fewer and fewer bargains on eBay. You begin to seriously ask yourself the question: what have I got to do to sell successfully on eBay?

Without good planning and some common sense, it can be difficult to find bargains to buy and sell profitably on eBay. The main problem is that there are more and more people trying to do exactly what you are doing, and those people are getting smarter about building their eBay businesses. You need to learn how to work better and smarter to keep up with the competition. You know that there are instructions and tutorials for beginners; you've seen them, and you may have even taken a course or two. There are also a ton of books for eBay beginners.

The problem is that while it's easy to get started, you need to take a leap and go beyond the beginning stage. You don't have the luxury of gradually learning how to be successful on eBay. You need to *degunk* your eBay activities now. You need to create better sales listings, bid smarter, learn how to avoid being ripped-off, find better items to sell, improve your shipping and customer service, boost your feedback rating and get rid of negative comments, develop profitable relationships with reliable sellers, and generally use eBay more efficiently. That's what *Degunking™ eBay* will do for you.

You don't need a new PC or new software. You also don't need to quit your "day job" and start selling full-time on eBay—not yet, at least. You might want to take that big step down the road, but the point is that you don't need to do that just now. You could hire a trading assistant to sell on eBay for you, and you could take your items to one of the many storefronts that are springing up to sell your stuff on eBay for you. But that won't help you generate real income on a steady basis, and it won't help you control your business if you're series about building your eBay sales. You can improve your eBay business yourself— you only need to know how with a set of techniques that experienced sellers have known and tried themselves. That's why I wrote this book.

Degunking eBay is not just another book on how to get started with eBay. This book is an easy-to read and concise guide showing you, step-by-step and in plain English, how to improve the way you buy and sell on the world's leading auction site. I'll show you how to streamline how you navigate eBay, how to avoid trouble, how to organize and systematize your eBay sales, and how to handle a host of other situations you won't want to discuss with your closest friends.

Why You Need This Book

Over the years, I've written a number of books about eBay, and I've bought and sold hundred of items on the site myself. More importantly, I've talked to numerous PowerSellers and others who have used eBay to their advantage. By taking their best insight and adding in a lot more from my own experience, I can convey many words of wisdom to you so you don't have to spend months or even years figuring it out yourself.

eBay has been around long enough so that the strategies for success are well known. You don't need to be a pioneer or reinvent the wheel. You just need to learn how to be a smart eBay user. If you want to degunk (or clean up) the way you use eBay, you can do this by taking advantage of this book's unique features:

√   An easy-to-follow 12-step degunking process that you can put to work immediately (see Chapter 1).

√   Explanations, in everyday language, of how to buy and sell more effectively on eBay.

√ Details on how to save time and boost efficiency with the help of auction sales tools, both on eBay and the Internet.

√ Unique "GunkBuster's Notebook" features in every chapter to help you reduce clutter in your home and in your eBay transactions.

√ Suggestions on how to communicate better with other eBay members so you can find answers, get support, and resolve any problems you might encounter.

√ Instructions on how to find what you want on eBay more quickly.

√ Strategies for packing and shipping that eliminate problems and attract positive feedback.

√ Insiders' tips and techniques for preparing auction descriptions that attract bidders and buyers.

How to Use This Book

Degunking eBay is structured to cover all the basic activities you're likely to perform while using eBay. The first part examines aspects of using eBay that apply to everyone—buyers and sellers, casual users and everyday experts. You'll learn how to tune up your PC so you can connect to eBay more quickly, how to get the clutter out of your eBay searches, and how to bid more effectively. After these introductory chapters, you'll learn about topics that will help you use eBay on an everyday basis: communicating better, improving your image and feedback rating, and using eBay's own services for members.

The second part focuses on topics of interest to those who want to sell either part- or full-time on eBay. You'll learn how to write better descriptions, advertise and manage your sales, pack and ship effectively and efficiently, and purchase the inventory you need to resell at a profit. Finally, those who want to sell full-time on eBay will learn how to run a business on the auction site, how to degunk problem transactions, and how to follow the example of PowerSellers who've made eBay a regular source of income.

TIP: *You can skip around the book to find the topics that interest you most. But if you read Degunking eBay from beginning to end, you'll be following the proven 12-step Degunking process that will systematically streamline your eBay activities and help you use the site more effectively.*

A Note on Evolving eBay

One of the beautiful things about the Web and the Internet is that everything can be easily changed. Nothing is written in stone. For authors like me, that's both a blessing and a curse. On one hand, there are always new resources to explore. On the other, the moment you fix a URL or a product name on paper, it has the potential to change or move to a new location.

eBay is no different. It's constantly changing its organization. Much of the time, it makes changes in response to feedback from members. Sometimes, it takes away resources that members like me have grown accustomed to and come to love. The point, for you, is not to panic when you check out a page and it has moved, or when you look at a page like the eBay home page or the Search: Find Items page and it seems to be slightly different. As this book reminds you, it's the way you approach eBay that's important—not the details of what something is named and where it's found. eBay is constantly evolving, so just go with the changes. It's what a dynamic, online marketplace is all about!

The Degunking Mindset

The more you learn about degunking your eBay activities, the more you'll realize that degunking is a mindset, not just a set of technical skills. The degunking mindset applies to much more than eBay: you can use the same approach to degunk your computer, your Web browser, and your PC. Rather than simply being a set of processes that you follow when you want to sell a lot of items on eBay, the degunking approach is a disciplined one that is designed to help you manage your PC and your online experiences. If you follow the basic steps outlined in this book, you'll keep your home in order, your PC will keep humming smoothly, and you'll win more bids and sell more stuff on eBay. *Degunking eBay* will make your time on the world's most popular auction site more time-efficient, more productive, more profitable, and certainly more enjoyable.

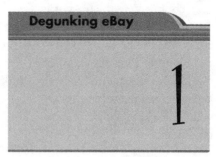

Why Is eBay All Gunked Up?

Degunking Checklist:

√ Make sure you understand the four basic processes you can apply to degunk your eBay activities.

√ Learn about the main causes for eBay gunk.

√ Make sure you understand that the best way to get the most out of eBay is to have a degunking strategy and stick to it.

√ Consider degunking your own home to help you get rid of what you don't need.

√ Learn the eBay degunking 12-step program and put it into practice.

E-commerce—the buying and selling of goods and services on the Internet—works because it is quick and easy and because you have a great deal of control as the customer. eBay is without a doubt the most successful marketplace on the Internet and one of the most successful online businesses in the world. Therefore, you'd logically think that it must be one of the easiest to use and best organized. In other words, you'd think that you could always find what you are looking for and you would not have to waste much time when you're buying and selling your goods. Think again.

Because you've picked up this book, you probably realize that not only can eBay get really gunked up, but all of your related buying and selling activities can get gunked up as well. Remember the last time you searched for a popular category of items and you had to sort through over 1000 listings just to find what you were looking for? Have you ever needed to burrow through hundreds of categories and subcategories just to locate the best one in which to list your auction? Or have you been trying to auction off so many products lately that you can't even keep track of your sales? You also probably know that you can waste a lot of time if you don't really know what you are doing and you have a "gunked up" buying or selling strategy. Perhaps you haven't even put much thought into how you could improve your auctions and thus the same old techniques that you've been using since the beginning haven't really been working for you as well as they should. These days, individuals and businesses all over the world depend on eBay for all or part of their income. Gunk on eBay or gunk associated with your eBay activities isn't just an inconvenience; you could be losing a considerable amount of business. Rest assured: You're not alone in your frustration!

You've come to the right place because I'm here to help you develop a program that really works for getting the most out of eBay. Whether you are a buyer, seller, or both, I'll show you how you can save many hours of your valuable time and a significant amount of money. In this chapter I'll explain how eBay can get really cluttered and inefficient and how your own buying and selling strategies can get gunked up as well. In the second part of the chapter I'll introduce my unique degunking strategy for getting the most out of using eBay. I've been an eBay buyer and seller since its very early days, and I've learned a number of techniques that can really help you do things like remove all of the clutter that gunks up your eBay searches, spruce up the descriptions for the products you auction, improve your buying and selling techniques, degunk your shipping and customer service procedures, and much more. I'll present some of the important questions that you need to consider to help you understand how your eBay activities are getting gunked up, and then I'll introduce you to the degunking 12-step program that this book is based on.

Although there are a variety of eBay degunking tasks that you can perform, I've designed this book so that you can get the most out of it by following the tasks in the order presented. If you stick with the strategy that I'll be presenting, you'll get the best results.

What the Experts Know

Those techie types called Webmasters and geeks know how to keep their computers running smoothly while using the coolest features on the Web. And those individuals with the coveted title "eBay PowerSeller" know how to cut down on search times and remove the roadblocks and clutter that can prevent you from making a good income and big profits on eBay. The good news is that you can also learn to do the same things. But until now, no one has put all of the techniques into an easy-to-follow book like this. What I'm about to show you is really not that hard. My eBay degunking approach is divided into four key areas:

Basic eBay degunking 101: The focus here is to take care of all of the eBay housekeeping chores so that you can get the most out of eBay whether you are buying or selling. I'll help you focus on using the right browser, getting rid of the gunk it has already accumulated, and then configuring it to prevent gunk from piling up on your PC in the future. But that's just the beginning. I'll help you degunk the way that you connect to eBay and navigate through the cluttered maze of features. eBay has grown so quickly that many users miss out on using the more useful and productive features because they simply can't find them. I'll also help you focus on preventing scripting errors and on optimizing eBay for the best performance. Finally, we'll spend important time degunking eBay searches so that you can really get through the clutter and find the important stuff you need. Part of my goal in all of this is to help you get your PC in shape so that it helps you efficiently complete your eBay activities. If your computer is organized and degunked, eBay and the rest of the Internet will naturally run more smoothly. Searching and logging on to eBay can go more quickly with a few simple degunking procedures, too.

Degunking your basic eBay activities: The tasks in this area are designed to help you become both a better eBay buyer and a better eBay seller. Here you'll learn how to really degunk and improve your bidding techniques so that you can win more auctions and get more mileage for your dollars. I'll also show you how to degunk your communications with other eBay users so that you can reduce the junk e-mail you receive, avoid fraudulent messages, and get more done in a shorter amount of time. As you get involved with more auctions, the amount of communications that you can receive from other eBay users can increase exponentially, so understanding how to keep your communications organized and clutter free is a very important early step. Another important degunking task that we'll focus on involves cleaning up your image on eBay so that buyers and sellers will really want to do business with you. Finally, you'll learn how to degunk the basic eBay software and services so that you can optimize and better track your activities.

Degunking your selling techniques: Your success depends on developing a gunk-free selling system. You can use special software to automate the process of creating sales listings. You can also design templates so that you can list items much faster and spend more of your time building your business and looking for items to sell. Early on I'll show you how you can quickly spruce up your auction descriptions by doing things like telling stories, focusing on the unique features of your products, and improving your photos. I'll also show you how to streamline the payment process. Once you increase your sales, you can build up your feedback rating, which will encourage more customers to bid on or purchase what you have to sell. In no time at all, you'll have a regular source of income from eBay. Another important area we'll focus on is how to degunk your shipping and customer service. This is an area that many eBay users often overlook. That's a big mistake because one of the most important aspects of eBay is customer service.

Improving your eBay business: The more you use eBay, the more serious you'll get about wanting to build up a business with which you can have fun and make money. Here, you'll learn how to really focus on what you do best and clean up and maximize your activities. You'll learn how to increase your profits, how to provide incentives for repeat customers, how to degunk your pricing and improve the incentives that you offer, how to better organize your eBay Store, how to deal with problem customers, and much more. I'll even provide you with a set of proven degunking tips from eBay PowerSellers.

Understanding How You Got So Gunked Up

You didn't necessarily do anything to get gunked up. You used the Web and you made a few purchases on eBay. Before you knew it, your house was overflowing with junk—I mean with the valuable collectibles you so painstakingly and carefully purchased! Your browser is now overflowing with unwanted temporary files. Your e-mail inbox is bloated with eBay communications (and even spam), your hard drive is cluttered with programs, photos, and product descriptions, and you probably can't keep track of all of the products that you are buying and selling. Let's examine how so many eBay members end up in this predicament—and how to get out of it.

Back in 1995, when eBay first started under the name AuctionWeb, the site *was* simple and virtually gunk free. It was relatively easy to use because the system was so simple. There were only a few hundred users and a single discussion board, which eventually came to be known as the eBay Café. There weren't even any photos to accompany auction listings—at least, not in the beginning. Writing product descriptions was easy because you didn't have to compete with so many other sellers, and buyers could easily find what they were looking for because the offerings were limited.

But eBay has really changed since its humble beginnings! These days, many of the estimated 8 million people who buy and sell on eBay each day find the site to be cluttered and time consuming to use. They spend a lot of time searching for products and trying to get through all of the different categories that are provided. For some users, just trying to keep track of all of the clutter that fills the eBay pages is a full-time job! This is compounded by the fact that there are over 150,000 people who have a full-time job of buying and selling products on eBay. There are also currently tens of millions of registered members around the world and over 12 million items listed on eBay every day.

If you are wondering how eBay can get so cluttered, you should consider the two general sources for all of the gunk that we experience:

√   *eBay is complex.* eBay has become one of the most complex and busy sites on the Internet. In addition to millions of members, it has accumulated a decade's worth of gunk. With 26,000 sales categories, it can be hard to find what you want or advertise sale items in the right place. eBay itself places bits of data called *cookies* on your computer so you don't have to log in all the time. It displays animated advertisements. Its affiliated marketing companies track how members use the site. Special scripts executed on eBay's servers enable you to edit and crop your photos on your screen, spell-check your auction descriptions, and perform many other functions. All of these files and programs make accessing and navigating eBay a slow and difficult process for many users.

√   *You might be your own worst gunk magnet.* That's right. You, the individual eBay user. Just surfing the Web on a regular basis loads you down with temporary files that your browser stores on your system. Your computer is loaded down with programs called *spyware* that track your activities without your knowledge. Your computer may have insufficient memory, and your files are scattered all over your hard disk. If you sell a lot of products on a regular basis, you probably have hundreds of old product descriptions lying around, and I won't even nag you about the hundreds of old digital photos that are likely clogging up your PC! And despite being in a hurry to find that rare collectible or sell that precious widget, you don't use eBay's site efficiently.

Rather than cleaning out all the gunk you already have around the house, you buy more gunk, much of it stuff that you don't need. You try to put items that people won't buy up for sale. You take too long to put items up for sale. And your product descriptions probably aren't working for you as well as they could.

The good news is this book can help on both of these fronts. I can help you improve your experience on eBay by showing you how to identify where the gunk comes from and learn to get rid of it. In this book, I'll identify some of the common sources of gunk that mess up eBay, related to both software and the way you buy and sell. If you use eBay more efficiently, you can sell more, you can save money by buying smart, and you can degunk your own surroundings in the process. With the expertise you gain, you can even move on to degunking other people's basements, attics, and corners, and you can create your own eBay business to provide a source of part- or full-time income. The reality is that the better you get at degunking, the more money you can make!

Gunk Hunting on eBay

By this time you're probably asking yourself where all of the gunk that's described in the preceding sections actually comes from. After all, if you can identify the source, you stand a good chance of removing that gunk. Right?

Just think of all the hardware and software components that have to work properly—and work together—when you search for something or place a bid on eBay. First, there's your computer, which needs to literally be up-to-speed as far as its processing capability. It also needs to have enough memory. Then there's your Internet connection, which has to be functioning correctly, and your browser, which needs to have something called *cookies* enabled and needs to be a fairly recent version. (Find out more about browser requirements in Chapter 2.) Then, there's all the stuff around your house, which is gunking up your daily existence.

Those are things on your end that you can control. On the other end of the connection, eBay's site needs to be functioning well enough to receive millions of visits and requests for information each day—and it's a very complex resource, as mentioned in the preceding section. The sales descriptions you view need to be accurate and to the point rather than cluttered with unnecessary information. But as you know already, there are literally millions of listings on eBay, and eBay's sales categories are hard to "drill" through in order to find just what you want.

These problems impact your success on eBay in a number of ways. Problems with your computer make it difficult to log on and make you spend more time on the site; so do inefficient searches. You fail to find what you want. When you do find it, you don't win it. Slowdowns affect how many sales you can put online at any one time; the slower you sell, the more cluttered your house remains. Worse, you end up with sales that don't attract any bidders or buyers at all. You are left to scratch your head wondering, "What can I do better?" Some answers are given in the sections that follow.

Computer and Browser Gunk

This is the starting place because everything we do with eBay comes through our Web browser and our PC. Every time you use eBay, you're likely downloading and collecting all kinds of junk without even realizing it. You'll get temporary files, tons of e-mails, spam, and other junk that can slow you down. Over time you'll find that your browser runs more slowly, as does your operating system. Consider the gunk as dirt that clouds up your lens and makes it hard to do anything quickly. Some of this gunk (and the related problems that you experience) can be caused by the following:

√   Using a browser that isn't eBay friendly

√   Having a browser that gobbles up too many cookies and gets bloated

√   Using a browser that can't properly handle scripts and style sheets

√   Accumulating too many temporary files on your PC

√   Not having a system to deal with all of the eBay-related e-mails and spam you receive

Clutter around the Home

In addition to your computer, your home or office can also quickly become a gunk magnet the more you use eBay. This is something I probably don't even need to point out too strongly, but I will just because you might need a friendly reminder! From your buying and selling activities, you probably have closets (and maybe even a garage) full of stuff you've accumulated that is just gathering dust. (Or perhaps this stuff has made it into your house and you're tripping over it on a daily basis!) To make matters worse, you probably think all of this stuff is important because you think you'll soon be selling it on eBay and thus you are reluctant to throw anything out. If you are really bothered by this junk, you could take stock of all the things that are cluttering up your basement, your attic, your garage, and your closets. Pick out 10 items and put them up for sale on eBay. (Just think about how good it feels to clean out your closet and throw away all of the stuff you don't need.) Once you've gotten the hang of making money on eBay and have cleaned out your own house, you might just be inspired to clean out other folks' houses, too.

Inefficient Searching

Recall that I told you that there are over 26,000 categories to list products under on eBay. This means that eBay has more categories than the actual products most stores have to sell. If you took the time to look at each category, you'd find that there are a myriad of products just hiding out, lost in all of the clutter. With so many products and categories, a typical search will display so much information that it could take you days to properly review it all. If you don't know what eBay gunk is yet, I can now tell you that this is the genuine item. Because of this gunk, you probably spend more time searching through eBay listings than performing any other activity. Now imagine how much time you could save if you learned better ways to search and navigate through all of the clutter to find the really important stuff.

Developing a Bad Image

The worst kind of eBay gunk, the kind that can hurt you, is bad feedback from sellers or buyers. This is the kind of gunk that separates the losers from the winners. With so many people using eBay, the feedback system helps create an efficient marketplace and one that also helps foster a system of trust. Without it, eBay would be like the Wild West and you wouldn't likely be able to trust anyone you buy a product from or sell a product to. But the feedback system can really hurt you as a buyer or seller if you don't know how to use it properly and you let your image get all gunked up.

Badly Run Auctions

With so many great products available on eBay, the last thing you want to do is waste your time getting involved with auctions that are badly run. eBay is good at cracking down on people who misbehave, but it's hard to watch over 8 million people. Sellers who aren't concerned about behaving badly have learned how to manipulate the eBay system to create all kinds of junk: auctions that are rigged, auctions that offer illegal products, auctions that have phony customers who are skilled at bidding up the prices at the last minute, and so on. If you've used eBay often, you've probably already been a victim of some type of scam. Gunk like this really hurts the vast majority of honest eBay buyers and sellers. Fortunately, there are things that you can do to protect yourself, and I'll be showing you how later in this book.

Poorly Written or Misleading Product Descriptions

We are all guilty of this sin. In our haste to get our products into an auction, we leave out some of the important details, forget to include a good photo, or exaggerate a little more than we should. Poor product descriptions really contribute to the sea of eBay gunk because they make it difficult for buyers to select the products they really want. In a store, you can look at and often touch the item you are interested in. With eBay, you have to rely on what you read or see. When eBay sellers post descriptions that are poorly written or misleading, this creates a "chain of junk" effect that wastes time and money. A customer might be misled and purchase a product and then have to return it. This in turn creates more gunk in the form of negative feedback being posted. This is why it is important to learn how to perfect the art of writing and posting product descriptions, as you'll learn in this book.

Selling on eBay Inconsistently and without a Plan

If you don't have a good plan for what you are doing, you can really gunk up your eBay business. The most successful sellers are those who have a focus and stick to it. They develop a reputation for selling certain types of items and their customers know that their expectations will be met. The opposite of this is a business or seller that generates a lot of gunk that clogs up eBay with products that customers don't want to purchase or products that customers will likely complain about. The nice thing about eBay is that anyone can quickly set up shop and start offering goods for sale. But this also contributes to eBay's unfortunate side: it can become a big source of gunk because of sellers who perform badly.

Poor Customer Service

Have you ever won on auction and then had to wait weeks to receive your product? Or have you experienced difficulty just getting the person you purchased a product from to respond to your e-mails? Proper communication and good customer service are essential to good eBay business. Unfortunately, some people have different ideas about what is good customer service and their lack of attention to detail can really gunk up your eBay experience.

The Strategy behind Degunking

The key to having success with eBay is learning how to get organized, reduce clutter, and develop buying and selling strategies that can greatly maximize your time. Degunking both eBay and your buying and selling strategies isn't difficult as long as you have a strategy and dedicate a little time to following it. You might at first feel like you don't have time to invest, but if you don't, you'll continue to use eBay inefficiently and waste time and money.

The basic strategy behind degunking eBay is based on how eBay operates in the first place:

√   How eBay users communicate with each other to facilitate the buying and selling process

√   How eBay organizes auctions

√   How sellers and buyers are assigned feedback ratings

√   How different types of auctions operate

√   How eBay provides unique features such as personal Web pages to help both buyers and sellers

√   How eBay handles bidding problems and disputes with users

√   How eBay supports different payment programs

√   How eBay provides options and services for sellers who want to set up their own businesses

eBay works best when all the buyers and sellers take a "good neighbor" approach. eBay itself tries to keep the guidelines and rules as simple as possible and expects that users will do their best to police their activities.

Important Questions to Ask Yourself

As you perform buying and selling activities on eBay on a regular basis, you need to ask yourself some of the following questions:

√   Am I getting too much e-mail related to my eBay activities?

√   Is my PC getting too cluttered from all of the files and other junk that I've been collecting?

√   Does it seem that I'm spending more time than I need to trying to find products to purchase?

√   Am I having trouble finding the best categories for my auctions?

√   Am I losing too many auctions because my buying strategy isn't as effective as it needs to be?

√   Am I getting negative feedback related to eBay activities that is hurting my ability to buy and sell products?

√   Do I have procedures that automate my product listings and other selling-related activities?

√   Am I wasting time sending out products and dealing with customer support issues that could be saved if I had a better system in place?

The Degunking 12-Step Program

Here is the basic 12-step degunking process that you'll follow in this book:

1. Clean up and optimize your computer and your eBay registration data, and create shortcuts to help you wade through eBay's crowded Web site (Chapter 2).

2. Create and save your favorite searches, and learn to search all of eBay—not just auctions (Chapter 3).

3. When buying, apply the best tactics for increasing your winning percentages and place smarter bids by comparison shopping (Chapter 4).

4. Improve your communications with buyers and sellers to improve your chances of winning bids and selling more items for bigger profits (Chapter 5).

5. Build up positive feedback by making easy purchases, and market yourself to develop a good reputation (Chapter 6).

6. Organize your My eBay page and use eBay's automation features to watch sales, manage auctions, and automate email responses (Chapter 7).

7. Spruce up your auction descriptions and learn to use a well-organized template and provide lots of personal detail about what you sell (Chapter 8).

8. Find sales help when you need it and spend time and money marketing your sales through keywords and multiple categories (Chapter 9).

9. Learn to streamline your shipping process, improve your shipping schedules, over-pack what you sell, and add personal notes and gifts that will improve customer satisfaction (Chapter 10).

10. Select the best inventory to sell and research what's valuable and what's in demand on eBay (Chapter 11).

11. Sell what you know, plan ahead for big seasonal sales, and develop techniques to encourage repeat customers (Chapter 12).

12. Avoid disputes by providing refunds, spelling out requirements clearly, and following a set schedule for approaching nonresponsive buyers and sellers (Chapter 13).

Ready for Degunking?

The most difficult part of degunking eBay and degunking your buying and selling tasks involves dedicating a little time. As the book progresses and we look at the different techniques, I'll point out how just much time you'll likely need to perform different tasks. The first degunking tasks will be the ones that will likely get you the most results in the least amount of time. My approach will be to show you not only how to fix things but how to get yourself on a little maintenance program so that your computer always runs well and you can sell on eBay regularly without unnecessary delays. If you're new to the world of degunking, don't worry. It's much easier than putting together a barbecue grill in the backyard with those ridiculous instructions they provide. (What language do they write those things in anyway?)

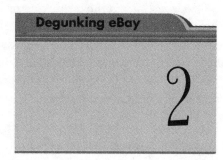

2

eBay Housecleaning 101

Degunking Checklist:

√ Degunk your PC and desktop to streamline how you navigate eBay.

√ Learn how cookies, temp files, and other gunk can slow you down.

√ Clean up your eBay configurations and set up shortcuts to save a bunch of time.

√ Find out about the dangers of fake eBay sites.

√ Update your software to navigate eBay more quickly.

√ Learn why certain content on the eBay site disappears.

√ Streamline how you view eBay.

O ur first step in the degunking process involves performing a set of house keeping chores. But don't worry, because these chores are easier and more fun to do than cleaning your kitchen at home. eBay housekeeping is a little like cleaning and maintaining your office space at work. If you let things pile up, you won't find important things, you'll waste time, and you might even miss an important opportunity.

What exactly is eBay housecleaning? It involves all of the background and often hidden things that you might not be aware of but can impact how you connect up with and use eBay. These would include things that you can do on your PC directly, things that you can do online at eBay, and things that you can do at your home or office. On your PC desktop, it is properly setting up your browser, getting rid of cookies and temporary files you don't need, fine-tuning your computer setup, and organizing your e-mail system. On eBay, it is fine-tuning your eBay connections, optimizing your eBay settings, configuring your eBay navigation features, and so on. Finally, the things that you can do at your home or office include organizing all of your stuff and getting rid of all the clutter you have so that you can have the right products to sell on eBay.

My goal is to help you quickly get your eBay universe together. We have a lot of ground to cover, so let's get started.

Degunk Your PC and Desktop

Don't worry, I'm not going to give you too many housekeeping chores to perform with your PC. I simply want to focus on a few things that you can do to help you use the Internet and eBay more effectively. Entire books have been written on cleaning and improving the performance of PCs, and if you are interested in this, I recommend you pick up a copy of *Degunking Windows* (Paraglyph Press, ISBN 1932111-84-0) if you are interested in fine-tuning Windows XP or *Degunking Your PC* (Paraglyph Press, ISBN 1933097-03-5) if you want to take care of all of your hardware-related issues.

Using eBay on a regular basis puts a bit of strain on your PC. You'll likely accumulate a number of temporary files, e-mails and spam, cookies, and other gunk you don't need. Fortunately, this stuff is easy to get rid of, and once you get rid of it, you can keep it away by performing some maintenance tasks every so often. In addition to the gunk you gather, gunk collected by your PC can slow it down if you don't set up your PC properly.

Say Goodbye to Temporary Files

Whenever you surf the Web and use services like eBay, you download image and text files to your computer. These visuals don't just appear on your monitor; by default, the files are stored on your hard disk, and for good reason. With the files stored on your hard disk, your browser can display them more quickly than if it had to download the files from a remote Web server (that is, if the content hasn't changed since your last visit). But if you don't clean them out periodically or change the default settings, you can end up with many megabytes' worth of temporary files that slow down your system. And a slowed-down system will slow down eBay. If you don't believe me, open Internet Explorer and follow these steps:

1. Click Tools and choose Internet Options.

2. On the General tab, click Settings. The Settings dialog box opens.

3. Write down the current location of the Temporary Internet files folder and notice how much disk space is currently being allocated to the temporary files your browser accumulates. The number of megabytes listed in the box next to "Amount of disk space to use" is the maximum space those files can consume (see Figure 2-1).

4. For now, click OK twice to close Settings and Internet Options.

5. Open Windows Explorer and navigate to the folder that was listed in Settings as the location of the temporary files. Scroll down and make note of just how many files there are (see Figure 2-2).

    These temporary files do have a purpose: they speed up revisits to pages you view frequently. But some of the files, such as the cookies (described in the following section), might be preventing you from performing some functions on eBay. In subsequent chapters, you'll learn how to control how many

Figure 2-1

Your browser can accumulate many megabytes' worth of temporary files.

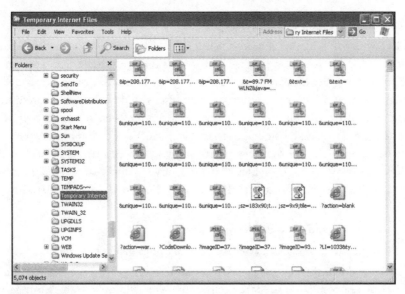

Figure 2-2

A cluttered folder full of temporary files can take memory from other applications.

files are saved and how to clear out this folder periodically to keep your system humming along happily.

Zap Those Cookies

These innocent sounding things are, well, not always so innocent. Cookies are designed to help Web sites you visit keep track of your activities. For example, if you visit a particular shop through eBay, the shop might store a cookie on your PC to keep track of your preferences and the pages that you visit. Usually cookies are harmless, especially if you keep a medium or higher level of security. But if you get a lot of them, they can gunk up your PC and your Web browser could run slower.

What does a cookie look like? You won't typically see them, but they are bits of digital data (files) that are stored on your PC as text documents. Like so many Web sites you visit, eBay uses cookies. When you revisit the site, eBay checks for the presence of the cookie and determines that you have already signed in. Some users don't like the idea of remote Web sites placing files on their computers and they have configured their Web browsers to block all cookies.

In order to remove cookies from your computer, you can do one of two things:

√   Install a program that's designed to delete them automatically, such as Cookie Crusher (**www.thelimitsoft.com/cookie**) or Cookie Pal (**www.kburra.com/cpal.html**).

√   Use your browser's own controls to delete cookies.

If you use Microsoft Internet Explorer, follow this short set of steps:

1.   Choose Internet Options from the Tools menu.

2.   On the General tab, click Delete Cookies.

3.   Click OK to close Internet Options and return to your browser window.

If you use Netscape Navigator, do the following:

1.   Choose Preferences from the Edit menu.

2.   In the Preferences window, click the arrow next to Privacy & Security to display the subcategories beneath it.

3.   Click Cookies. The Cookies preferences appear.

4.   Click Manage Stored Cookies to display the Cookie Manager window.

5.   Click Remove All Cookies.

6.   Click OK to close Cookie Manager and OK to close Preferences, and return to the Navigator window.

You can, of course, change your browser's settings for accepting cookies. But you might make it impossible to log in to eBay if you do so. eBay basically forces you to accept cookies from its site. To allow cookies from eBay while denying them from other sites, in Navigator's Cookie Manager window you can click the Cookie Sites tab to list sites like eBay from which cookies are allowed. In Internet Explorer, open the Privacy tab in the Internet Options dialog box, and click Edit to open the Per Site Privacy Actions dialog box. (You might have to move the Privacy slider to a setting other than Accept All Cookies to make the Edit button clickable.) Follow the instructions in Per Site Privacy Actions to allow cookies from eBay while blocking them from other sites.

NOTE: *Cookies, frankly, aren't the most dangerous security threat associated with eBay. That honor goes to e-mail messages that attempt to scare you into giving out your personal information. Typically, you get a message claiming that you have been suspended from eBay and you need to reregister. The problem is that, as part of your supposed reregistration, you have to provide a social security number, checking account number, credit card number, and just about everything but your mother's maiden name. Don't respond to any e-mail requests that ask for your User ID, password, or other information; forward such messages to spoof@ebay.com, and keep your data private.*

GunkBuster's Notebook: Is the eBay Home Page Missing?

Occasionally, if you go to the eBay home page but you haven't yet signed in or you haven't registered with a User ID and password, you'll see the page shown in Figure 2-3 instead of the more familiar home page.

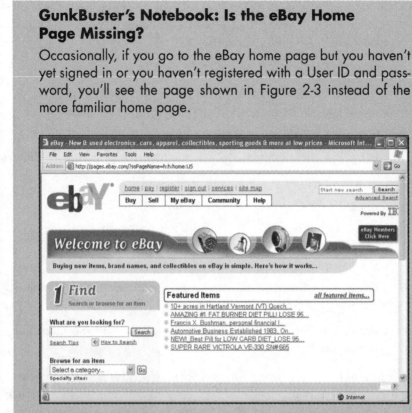

Figure 2-3

This version of the home page appears to visitors who aren't signed in or registered.

To keep this page from appearing every time you revisit the site, you need to make sure your browser accepts cookies. In Internet Explorer, choose Internet Options from the Tools menu, click Privacy, and choose a setting such as Low or Accept All Cookies by moving the slider. In Netscape Navigator, choose Preferences from the Edit menu, click the arrow next to Privacy & Security, click Cookies, and choose one of the three options for accepting cookies other than the "Disable cookies" option.

TIP: When you sign in on eBay, check the box labeled "Keep me signed in on this computer unless I sign out." You won't have to keep signing in if you want to visit My eBay or perform other functions. But be sure you log out when you're not at your computer so that others don't use your account to make purchases on eBay without your approval.

Bookmark Favorite Categories

Chances are you visit the same sales categories over and over again—perhaps not all the time, but at certain times when a piece of merchandise has "grabbed" you and you can't get it out of your mind. If you are looking for a particular kind of shoe, for instance, you visit the same parts of eBay several times a week to see if one has come up for auction. The obvious way to revisit favorite sales categories on eBay is to create a set of bookmarks or favorites that you can access easily from your browser's menu bar: You go to the category opening page (for instance, the Men's Shoes subcategory) and choose Add Favorites from Internet Explorer's Favorites menu or Bookmark This Page from Netscape Navigator's Bookmarks menu. Continually choosing categories from your Favorites or Bookmarks menu gunks up your Favorites or Bookmarks menus.

You have to take the time to organize your bookmarks, and they can quickly grow and become unwieldy. As an alternative, eBay has also added a Favorites section to the bottom of its home page. If you have identified favorite sellers or searches in My eBay as described earlier in this chapter, you can access those options from the drop-down lists shown in Figure 2-4.

Figure 2-4

You can access favorite sellers or categories from the list at the bottom of eBay's home page.

NOTE: *Although I added several favorite searches to My eBay, as you can see from Figure 2-4, the searches did not appear in the Shortcuts to My Favorites section.*

Customize Your Links/Personal Bar

Another way to use your browser to navigate eBay is to take advantage of its Links (Internet Explorer) or Personal (Netscape Navigator) bar—a toolbar you can customize with links to your favorite Web pages. Both toolbars come with their own default buttons, but you can delete them and replace them with links to pages on eBay that you visit frequently, such as My eBay, the Search: Find Items page, or a favorite category opening page. To remove a button on either the Links or Personal toolbar, right-click it and choose Delete from the short-cut menu that appears. To add a button, drag a page's URL from the Address bar directly atop the Links or Personal toolbar. When you release the mouse button, the new shortcut is added. Netscape Navigator's Personal bar is shown in Figure 2-5.

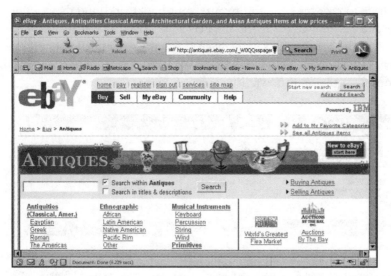

Figure 2-5
Set up browser toolbar links so you can revisit your favorite pages on eBay.

NOTE: *Navigator's Personal bar is divided into two sections. You can add and delete buttons in only one of those sections—the one labeled Bookmarks.*

Degunk Your eBay Configurations

Connecting to eBay is usually a snap. But over the years, I've run into some problems that would have caused me to tear my hair out, if I had any to tear. Some of those problems had nothing to do with eBay. Other times, software that is designed to work with eBay has trouble connecting. Some examples are described in the sections that follow.

Avoid Fake eBay Sites

When you type Web page URLs, you have to get the characters just right. A typo can give you a generic "The page cannot be found" message or, worse, a site that has been cleverly designed to look like eBay but is in reality a fake.

You are also directed to fake eBay Web pages by e-mail messages that tell you that you need to verify your registration information or that your eBay account has been suspended for some reason. A link included in the body of the e-mail message directs you to update your registration information by going to a page like the one shown in Figure 2-6. This page looks legitimate because it uses the eBay logo and that of the e-commerce certification service Truste, but it's not!

When you go to such pages, you are prompted to enter a new User ID and password—and, possibly, personal information such as your checking account number, credit card number, and the like. If you receive such a message, don't

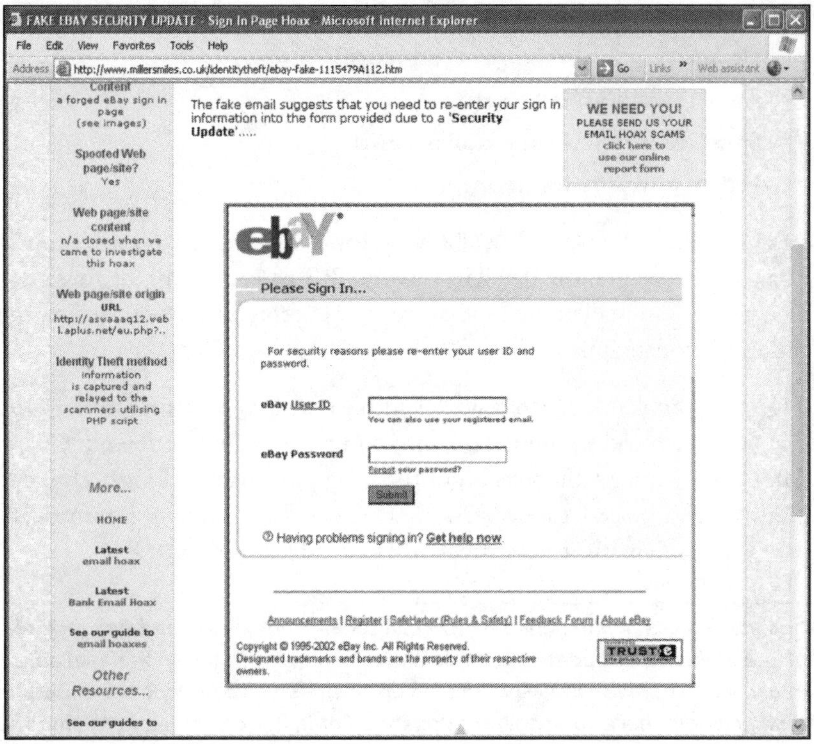

Figure 2-6
Don't submit information to "eBay" as a result of an e-mail message.

respond to it; instead, forward it to **spoof@ebay.com**, an e-mail address that has been set up especially to uncover such fraudulent sites. *eBay will never ask you for your personal information by e-mail!*

CAUTION: Identity theft is a huge issue on the Web these days. It was discussed earlier in connection with e-mail, but it pertains to other communications as well: never provide personal information or information about your eBay account via e-mail to anyone, ever. Never respond to an e-mail that claims to be eBay and that asks for your personal information. Beware of spam claiming to be eBay.

Update Your Software and URLs

Any software that depends on making connections to eBay will run into problems once in a while. eBay, like virtually all other Web sites, is not static. Pages are moved around and addresses are changed periodically. It's very common for software that depends on making interfaces with eBay's database to suddenly malfunction and need to be updated because eBay has moved its search pages around, created new categories and subcategories, or instituted other organizational changes. If you use the auction creation software provided by the following auction services, you might need to update it periodically:

√ HammerTap (**www.hammertap.com**)

√ Andale (**www.andale.com**)

√ SpareDollar (**www.sparedollar.com**)

√ Vendio (**www.vendio.com**)

After installing eBay's toolbar, a browser toolbar designed to connect quickly to eBay (described in more detail in Chapter 7), I had problems logging into eBay. I eventually uninstalled the toolbar and had to reinstall a newer version that had more up-to-date links.

The same problem occurred with Turbo Lister, a free auction description tool that you download and install on your computer (also described in Chapter 7). After a few months, the version of the program I had no longer connected to eBay. I then installed a new version, which is configured to automatically update itself as new information becomes available.

TIP: When you access online services, you can receive automatic updates and avoid many of the problems of updating your software manually. Services are available that you can use with your Web browser, and it's up to the service provider to update you as needed so you don't have to search for updates. For instance, instead of using the free Turbo Lister software, you can pay a monthly fee to use a program like Seller's Assistant, which eBay makes available online as a service. (See Chapter 7 for more details.)

GunkBuster's Notebook: Interference from BFAST

For a period of several weeks, I kept getting detoured on my way to eBay. Whenever I entered the usual URL, **www.ebay.com**, in my browser's Address box, my browser wouldn't take me to the familiar eBay home page. Instead, it went to the generic Windows "that address could not be found" page. At the top of the page, in the Address bar, a URL resembling this one was visible:

```
http://service.bfast.com/bfast/

click?=bfmid=34567ck498sah23&siteid=489472363
```

What is bfast.com? It's the URL that corresponds to BFAST Express Services which, in turn, is a part of Be Free, Inc., a marketing company based in Massachusetts. Be Free works with marketing partners to redirect visitors to its servers or to the Web sites of its client advertisers.

What does this have to do with eBay? In 2001, according to a search engine called Refer-it (**www.refer-it.com**), eBay partnered with Be Free to start up an affiliate program: Be Free would track clicks from affiliate Web sites that lead visitors from those affiliates to eBay's Web site. Any time someone registers as a result of that click-through, the affiliate would earn $5.

The problem apparently plagues Internet Explorer but not other browsers such as Opera and Netscape Navigator. To solve the problem, I did two things: I ran a shareware program called Ad-Aware by Lavasoft (**www.lavasoftusa.com**) which removes traces of the information that bfast.com leaves on my computer. I also had to manually remove cookies I had received from bfast.com. This is how to do it:

7.1. Open Internet Explorer and choose Internet Options from the Tools menu.

8.2. On the General tab, click Settings under Temporary Internet Files.

9.3. When the Settings dialog box appears, click View Files.

10.4. When the Temporary Internet Files dialog box appears, click Name to sort the cookies by name, and delete any that contain bfast.com.

11.5. Close Temporary Internet Files, and click OK to close Settings and OK again to close Internet Options.

TIP: *Ad-Aware is an extremely useful application for removing spyware from your computer. Spyware includes cookies and other applications that track your activities, often without your knowledge. You can download a trial version of the program at www.lavasoftusa.com/software/adaware/.*

Unblock Content that "Disappears"

One of the many useful functions performed by software like Norton Internet Security and the Google toolbar is the ability to keep banner or pop-up ads from appearing on Web pages. Norton Internet Security, in particular, has the ability to detect and block banner ads: instead of the ad, you see a blank space and the generic word *advertisement*.

On rare occasions, antivirus software mistakes genuine content for advertisements. It has happened that the eBay LiveHelp link on the site's home page has apparently disappeared due to antivirus software, and eBay users are left wondering where it went. LiveHelp is a feature that enables eBay members to exchange interactive chat messages with eBay staffers. If you encounter this problem and you use Norton Internet Security, you can exempt eBay from ad blocking by following these steps:

1. Double-click the Norton Internet Security icon in your Windows system tray or double-click the program icon to open the application.

2. Double-click Ad Blocking.

3. When the Ad Blocking window appears, click Advanced.

4. When the Advanced window appears, scan the list of Web sites presented in Web Contents Options for **www.ebay.com**.

5. If you see eBay.com in the list, single-click the site's name to select it. If you don't see ebay.com in the list, click Add Site, enter **www.ebay.com**, click OK to add it, then click www.ebay.com to highlight it (see Figure 2-7).

6. Click Add, and enter the URL for the Live Help icon: **http:// ebay.doubleclick.net/clk;8188303;9130450;e**.

7. Click OK twice to return to the Norton Internet Security window.

You might want to enable Ad Blocking for the "real" ads that appear on eBay, including the ads for current movies that have begun to turn up on the site's well-traveled home page, although they have nothing to do with auction sales.

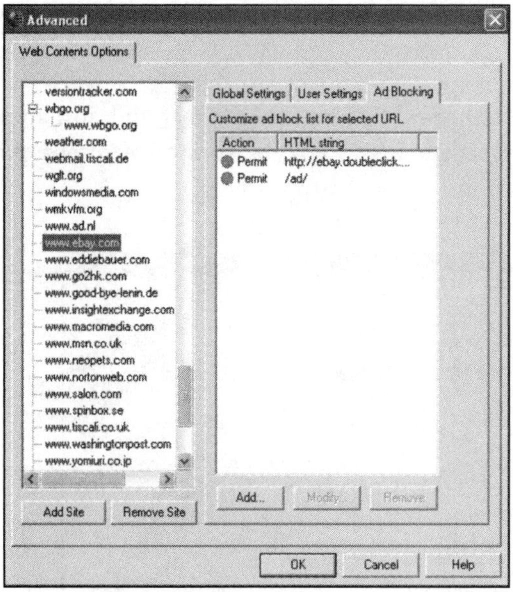

Figure 2-7
You can turn ad blocking on or off for eBay or
other Web sites if you use Norton Internet
Security.

Streamline How You View eBay

How do *you* use eBay? Chances are you go to the home page and immediately
search for something. Searching is, I suspect, one reason why visitors remain on
eBay's Web site for nearly one and three-quarters of an hour each time they
visit. But searching isn't the ultimate goal: it's only a way of getting to the goal
of buying something, selling something, or getting valuable information about
the worth of collectible items. The problem is that there's such a wealth of
merchandise on eBay that it can be hard to find just what you want right away.
If you can cut down on your search time, you can spend that time bidding or
preparing items for sale. The following sections present ways to streamline eBay's
wealth of information in order to focus on what you really want.

NOTE: *The amount of time a Web site can hold visitors is referred to as its "stickiness." The figure about eBay's
stickiness comes from Neilsen/NetRatings: **www.nielsen-netratings.com/pr/pr_040616.pdf**.*

Getting More out of the Site Map

A site map plays an important role in helping visitors to navigate a large-scale
Web site. By presenting a list of all (or virtually all) of the site's pages, it gives

visitors an idea of the scope of the site and enables them to find what they're looking for.

You access eBay's site map either by clicking the <u>site map</u> link just above the navigation bar or by going directly to **http://pages.ebay.com/sitemap.html**. The page full of links shown in Figure 2-8 appears.

Figure 2-8
eBay's site map is a good, though crowded, gateway to much of its information.

The site map is plagued by a couple of problems. First, it doesn't include all of the pages on eBay. It's impossible to include all auction sales because they are starting and ending continually. All of the About Me Web pages and eBay Stores have changing inventories too.

---

*TIP: You can search eBay's database of About Me pages by going to the About Me login page (**http://pages.ebay.com/sitemap.html**), clicking Other member pages, and entering the member's User ID in the About Me section of the Find Members page. To search eBay Stores, go to the Stores home page (**http://stores.ebay.com**) and enter the name of the store you want in the box beneath the Find a Store heading.*

The bigger problem with the site map is the fact that it's so very, very crowded. Scrolling through the three columns full of links for that one section you want can be tedious and time consuming. You can cut down your search time in a couple of ways.

Take advantage of your browser's Find command. While the site map is displayed, press Ctrl+F. Alternatively, you can choose Edit | Find (on This Page) if you use Internet Explorer or Edit | Find in This Page for Netscape Navigator. In any case, a Find dialog box appears (see Figure 2-9). Enter the item you're trying to find—say, Rules & Safety, the PowerSeller program, or the Feedback Forum. Click Find, and your browser will jump to the chosen keywords and highlight them.

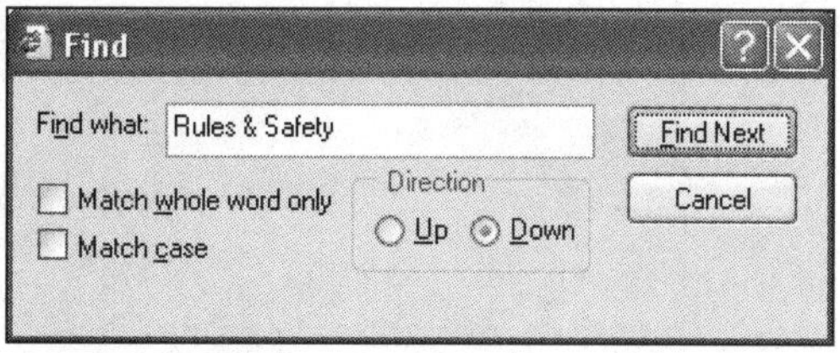

Figure 2-9
Use your browser's Find function to jump to the
eBay link you want.

The other way to make the site map more usable is to pull out the pages you use most frequently and group them in a set of Favorites (Internet Explorer) or Bookmarks (Navigator). You can also customize your browser's Links bar so that the pages you want to find most frequently are just a click away.

Use Themes to Get Better Organized

You're likely to turn to the site map in order to find eBay's very useful Themes page (**http://pages.ebay.com/themes.html**). One of the easiest-to-overlook organizing pages on eBay, Themes is a set of categories or activities that can speed up the often laborious process of burrowing into eBay to find a type of item. For instance, if you're looking for a gift for someone who loves country-and-western music, clothing, and culture, you wouldn't necessarily find it in the site map or even on the Buy page (**http://hub.ebay.com/buy**). (Buy, by the way, is an extensive list of top-level categories.)

The Themes page, shown in Figure 2-10, is a stripped-down list of general sales categories. If you are looking for a gift for a friend who loves country-and-western, you can search under the Occasions or Cultures headings, for instance.

Using eBay's Global Sites

Those of us who surf eBay from the U.S. are lucky. When U.S. residents search for items on eBay's main U.S.-based Web site, they can browse items being sold in the U.S. as well as those listed in the U.K. and Canada. But if you have some

Figure 2-10
Themes give you another option for "drilling down" into eBay's sales categories and subcategories.

proficiency in a foreign language, you can find many more available items being sold in eBay's many sites around the world.

Searching eBay by country is another way of narrowing down the millions of auctions and fixed-priced sales being held at any one time. It's also a way of evading the competition. If you are fluent in Spanish, for instance, you can shop eBay's site in Mexico. Even if you speak only English, you can go to the Advanced Search page and search for "Items Available to" your country as explained in the following tip. You'll turn up some items you wouldn't necessarily locate by sticking with your default options. For instance, I'm continually searching for an antique Waterman Patrician fountain pen. I didn't find any when I searched in the U.S., U.K., and Canada. When I enlarged the search results to include all sellers who would sell to the U.S., I turned up the pen shown in Figure 2-11, which was being offered in the Netherlands.

You'll find links to each of eBay's overseas locations at the bottom of the home page. At this writing, 23 sites were available outside of the U.S., including Argentina, Brazil, Hong Kong, Italy, Korea, Switzerland, and Taiwan.

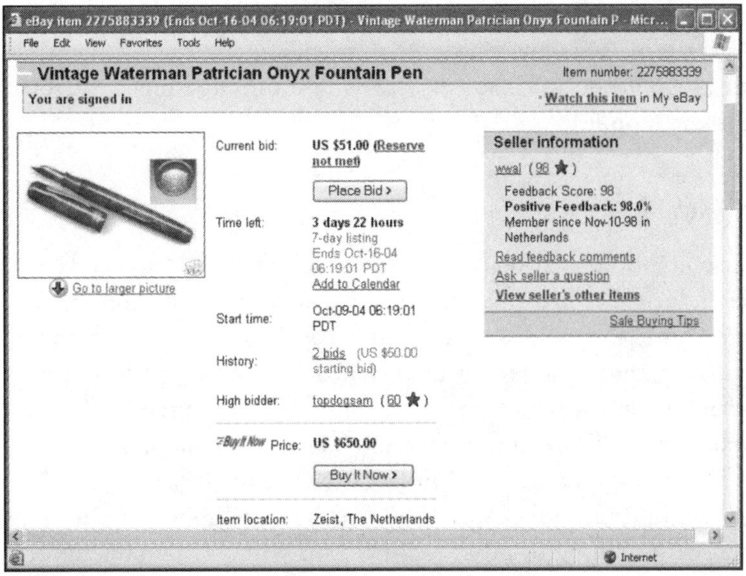

Figure 2-11
You can focus or enlarge search results by specifying location options on the Advanced Search page.

TIP: You can enlarge your search to include non-English-speaking countries by clicking Advanced Search, scrolling down to the More Search Options link, and going to the Location section. Click the button next to "Items available to," leave United States selected (or your own country, if you live elsewhere), and click Search. You'll get a wider range of listings in English, including those in European countries such as the Netherlands. For the widest possible range of search results, click the button next to "Items located in," choose Any Country from the drop-down list, and click Search. You'll get results drawn from eBay locations all over the world; the listings will be in many different languages.

Getting Organized at Home

Before you can sell anything on eBay, you have to get organized. This can be harder than actually putting items up for auction: it means clearing out shelves, rummaging through drawers and boxes, unclogging closets, and delving through your basement to see what sort of merchandise you can sell.

As demonstrated on the television shows that illustrate how people's lives can change when they clear out their clutter and get their living spaces in order, cleaning can be an exciting thing. It's especially good when you can set aside potential sales items, do research on those items, and clean them up so you can photograph them. That's what you need to do: take an inventory of what you have, evaluate what might sell on eBay by doing research, and putting those sales items online. (See Chapter 11 for more on choosing what to sell and doing research on it.)

Summing Up

This chapter introduced you to the concept of housekeeping on eBay: cleaning out the hidden files that pile up over time, and tuning up the hardware and software that enable you to connect to eBay. First, you learned about a few things like temporary files and cookies that you need to clean out of your computer so you can access eBay and other Web resources more efficiently. Next, you learned about overcoming some problems you might have connecting to eBay and ways to revisit your favorite parts of eBay more quickly. Then, you learned different ways to navigate eBay's voluminous Web site so you can find the auction listing or other resource you want. It's all a matter of getting organized, and that applies not only to eBay but to your situation at home too. If you can clean out the clutter in your own home, you'll find merchandise to sell, and you'll also improve your immediate physical surroundings. That's what eBay is all about, after all: degunking the process of buying and selling so you can improve your day-to-day life.

Degunking Your eBay Searches

Degunking Checklist:

√ Make eBay item searches more specific by filtering and sorting.

√ Combine search operators to restrict or enlarge a search.

√ Create complex searches with degunking operators.

√ Save searches you conduct frequently.

√ Search completed auctions to research prices and products more effectively.

√ Install special software that lets you search quickly for feedback, individual sellers, and sales categories.

What's the single thing you do most often when you visit eBay (after you log in, of course)? You almost certainly do a search for something that's up for auction. You might be searching for something to buy or checking on one of your own auctions to see how the bidding is going. Or you might be searching for a buyer or seller or an eBay Store that has what you want at a fixed price. To do just about anything on eBay, you have to search for it first.

You probably know what it's like to misplace something and not be able to find it, or to have to scour through a cluttered basement looking for a single tiny object. If you have shortcuts such as labeled boxes or designated shelves to look through, you'll find that precious object more quickly. In the same way, you can focus your searches on eBay so you don't have to look so long and hard. If you can find just what you want amid the millions of sales items available each day on eBay, you'll save both time and money. If your searches are done more efficiently, your whole experience of buying and selling on eBay is going to jump to a new level. This chapter will show you how to degunk the process of searching eBay—how to focus your searches so you don't have to wade through dozens of pages of search results before you find the bargain you want.

Make Your Searches More Effective

A normal search on eBay is almost certain to be gunked up. eBay's search utilities are sophisticated, and they allow millions of people to look through ongoing sales in a given day. But most of those people don't use all the capabilities those search utilities have. They simply click in one of the search boxes, either on the home page or on an auction description page, and they use a keyword or two, such as "G.I. Joe," as shown in Figure 3-1.

They quickly get 6, 10, 20, or more pages of items related to their search terms. If their desired object is a popular one, such as a collectible G.I. Joe or Barbie doll, they can spend up to an hour browsing through the search results. Most of those results are gunk. Only a few are likely to be what they are seeking.

Making your searches more specific (and then more effectively sorting through the results) is a basic degunking technique that eBay members frequently overlook. By putting together search terms that are designed to locate exactly what you want, and saving those searches so you can access them quickly each time you want to look for something, you speed up the process of shopping, comparing prices, researching other buyers and sellers, and carrying out the many other activities that go into using eBay wisely.

Figure 3-1
Entering keywords in one of eBay's search boxes is only one of several options available to you.

TIP: One way to make your searches more useful is to expand the goals of your search. Beginning eBay users only search to find specific collectibles or household items that appear to be bargains. Advanced users search in order to do price comparisons. They want to know if an item is really a bargain or not; they want to set a reserve price for a sale; they want to see who is getting a good price for a sales item so they can analyze why that seller's items attract more bids than those of the competition. In other words, you don't have to be planning to buy something in order to do a search for it. Knowledge about a market for a particular item is valuable information.

Combine Search Terms

The first and easiest way to search is to simply enter more search terms in one of eBay's search boxes. By entering more terms, you tell eBay to conduct a more specific search. You can refine the search even more by following the steps described in the next section.

Choosing Between "All" and "Any"

If you want to specify searches that include all your search terms, you should use eBay's Search: Find Items page. Click the Search button in the eBay navigation bar (or click Search in the eBay toolbar) to access this page, which you see in Figure 3-2.

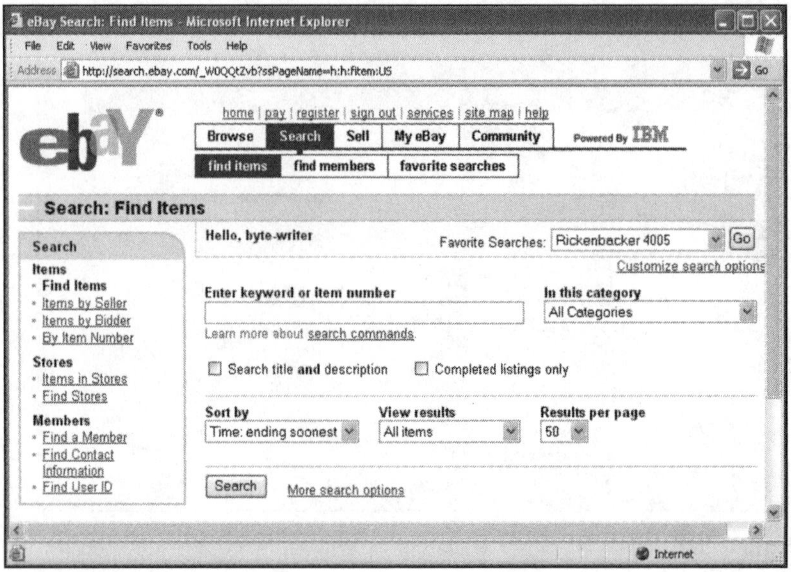

Figure 3-2
eBay's Search: Find Items page gives you more tools for focusing your searches.

If you enter your search terms in the Enter keyword or item number box on the Search: Find Items page, eBay will do its stuff and look for what you want, but it will assume that you only want to find certain things:

√ Currently active sales
√ Sales that contain all of your search terms in the title

Suppose you do a search on Search: Find Items for "G.I. Joe" and you come up (as I did) with 2,990 items ranging from G.I. Joe action figures to a set of G.I. Joe cartoon DVDs, fleece clothing, a toy jeep, comic books, and more. Here's how to get more control over your search: click the Back button to return to Search: Find Items. Then, click the unobtrusive little link More search options to access a souped-up version of the search page. You can enter your search terms in the Enter keyword or item number box as before. But the additional search tools enable you to choose one of four options from the drop-down list beneath this box:

√ **All of these words.** This is the default option; it looks for matches that contain all of the search terms. If you are looking for an action figure and enter the terms G.I. Joe action figure, you'll get a narrow set of results: these are sales that have all four of the words in the title. (I came up with 108 listings.)

√ **Any of these words.** This option will bring you a wider set of search results; eBay will find current sales that contain any of the words in the title. If your search terms are "G.I. Joe," for instance, you'll find every sale that contains the word *Joe,* including "Joe Smith," "Joe Boxer," "Old Black Joe," and many more. (I came up with a whopping 32,300 items for a simple "G.I. Joe" search.)

√ **Exact phrase.** Choose this option when you want to find an exact combination of words; make sure you have the spelling exactly right before you click Search.

√ **Exact match only.** This option is even more restrictive than Exact phrase. It takes into account not only the keywords you have entered, but any other criteria you have chosen, such as a specific sales category.

You might think that the "Any of these words" option is guaranteed to bring you many more search results than you want, even though I've been emphasizing that you need to find ways to narrow and focus your search results. "Any" can be a useful option in some cases. For example, suppose you want to find more than one variation on a type of item, such as a Barbie doll house and a car. Enter the words "Barbie doll house car" in the search box, then choose Any of these words option (see Figure 3-3).

If you do choose the Any of these words option, you won't necessarily end up with a bloated, unfocused search. You can still gain a measure of control by entering terms you want to leave out in the Exclude these words box.

CAUTION: *Common words like the, and, and or are included in searches; don't include them when you choose "Any of these words" or you'll end up with thousands of search results you don't want. Only use and and the if they are integral parts of the item you're looking for, such as records by the group Tommy James and the Shondells. In this case, though, you might want to choose "Exact phrase" rather than "Any of these words."*

Use Special Degunking Operators

The advanced version of eBay's Search: Find Items page does a pretty good job of letting you set up relatively complex searches. You can search for a group of terms and then exclude some words. But some eBay users turn searches into an art by setting up long and complex series of search terms. They come up with combinations of search terms that can't easily be accommodated in the search

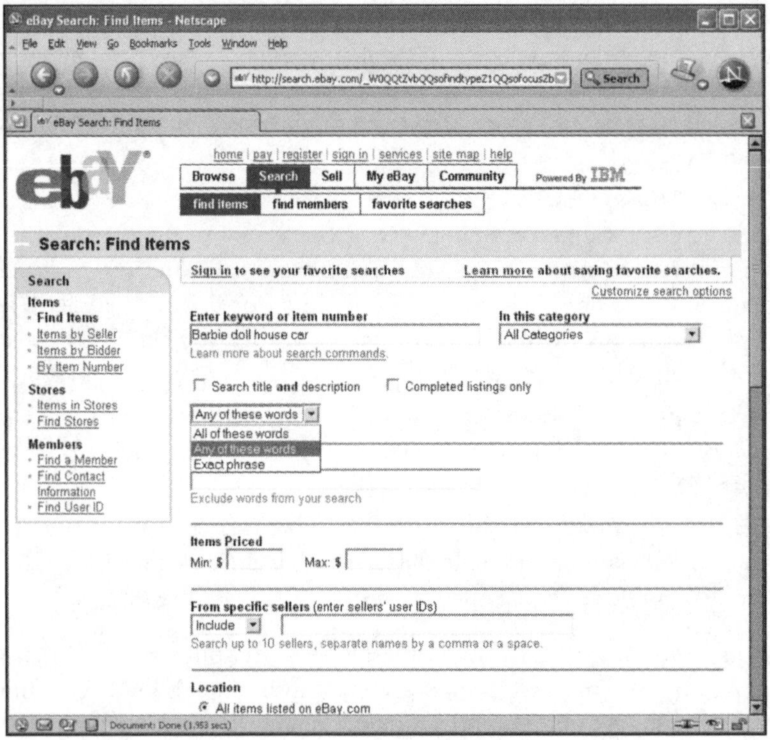

Figure 3-3
Choosing the Any of these words option enables you to find variations on items.

page's boxes. They have to be typed manually using special operators—which, for the purpose of this book, I'll call *special degunking operators* because they let you refine and control searches.

All of eBay's search tools, including the search box on the home pages and in the Search: Find Items page, recognize the use of special characters that help you control how a search is done. Many savvy eBay experts use characters like the plus sign (+) to combine more than one search term and the minus sign (–) to exclude terms that are not needed. For instance, by entering the following terms, you tell eBay to search for seat covers for 1999, 2000, or any later model of Volkswagen Passat (and not seat covers for any kind of Volkswagen, only the Passat) and floor mats but not leather ones:

```
"Volkswagen Passat" (1999,200*) floor mat mats -leather
```

Here, the quotation marks around *Volkswagen Passat* are used to locate exactly that combination of words (not Volkswagen Beetle, Jetta, or other models). The terms *1999* and *200** are placed in parentheses so that the search will find one date or the other. The asterisk is a wildcard operator: it causes the search to find all listings with 2000, 2001, 2002, and later dates in the title. A listing of frequently used search operators is shown in Table 3-1.

Table 3-1   eBay's Special Degunking Operators

Operator	Example	What It Does
minus sign (-)	word1 -word2	Excludes the term preceded by the minus sign.
asterisk (*)	199*	Finds any terms that begin with the characters preceding the asterisk; the asterisk can stand for any character.
quotation marks	"word1 word2"	Finds exactly the terms contained in quotation marks.
parentheses	(word1,word2)	Finds one term *or* another

Once you start to use search operators, you'll probably like them. Many experienced users create complex searches that combine multiple operators. You can find some examples, and get more tips and comments about eBay's search functions, on the Search discussion board (**http://forums.ebay.com/db1/ forum.jsp?forum=80**).

Improve Completed Auctions Search Results

You have probably searched through eBay's database of completed auctions to research completed sales prices. However, by filtering completed search results, you can get even more targeted information. This, in turn, gives you more accurate price information to help you make future pricing decisions. Follow these steps to improve your completed search results:

1. Click Search in the eBay navigation bar.
2. Check Completed Items only.
3. Enter your search terms in the Enter keyword or item number box.
4. Click Search.
5. When the search results page appears, click the link Refine Search next to the Search button.
6. Refine your search by adding more terms in the Search: Find Items page when it reappears with your original search terms entered. You can exclude search terms, enter a price range, or search for items near you based on your zip code.
7. Click Search again.

TIP: *eBay buyers and sellers highly value the ability to search for items located in their immediate vicinity. They have the chance to view such items in person or even pay for them and pick them up in person. Entering your zip code should narrow the search to your immediate area, but comments on the Search Discussion Group indicate that it isn't always reliable.*

Save Your Favorite Searches

Once you have constructed a complex search, you'll .save time with future searches by saving the search terms. eBay lets you assign a name to your search and save it in a list of searches. Using a saved search is like dialing a speed-dial number on your cell phone. First, you assign the frequently conducted search number a name. Then, you go to your My eBay page to redo the search whenever you need to. Why enter as many as 100 characters every time you want to find something? Clicking on a saved search only takes a fraction of the time.

To save a search go to the Search: Find Items page or any search box. Enter your search terms and, when the results appear, click the link <u>Add to Favorites</u> that appears in the yellow area just above the results. When the Add to My Favorite Searches page appears (see Figure 3-4), click the button next to Create a new search or Replace an existing search. In addition, you can check the box next to Email me daily for… if you want eBay to send you a message whenever an item appears that matches your search criteria.

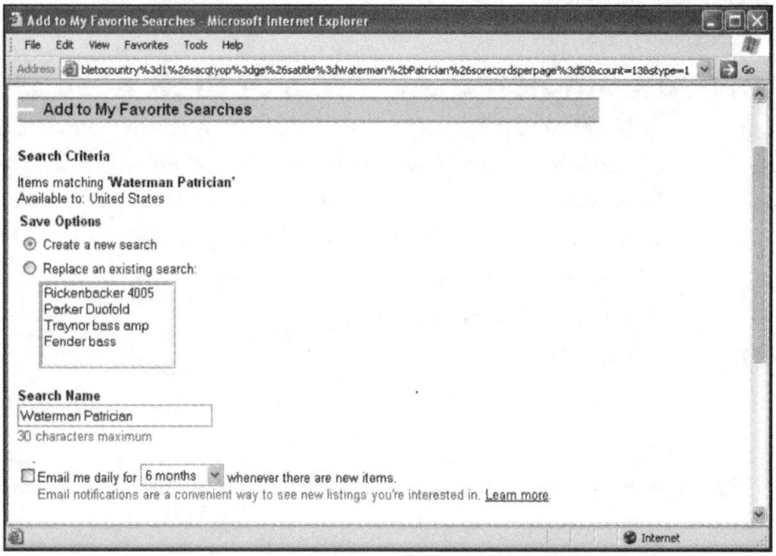

Figure 3-4
You can save a search and have eBay notify you when items you're looking for appear.

TIP: You can go a step beyond simply saving searches with a program called Bay Prospector (www.bayprospector.com). This application lets you save searches in an organized "tree" format that resembles Windows Explorer's layout of folders and files (see Figure 3-5).

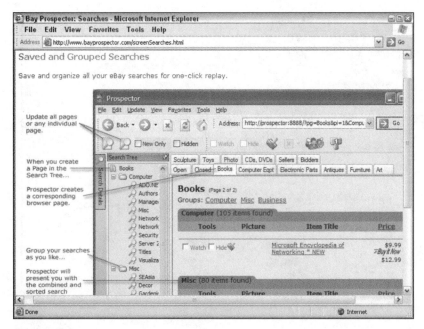

Figure 3-5
If you need to save lots of searches and organize them, try this non-eBay application.

TIP: *The Standard version of Bay Prospector costs $25, while the Professional version costs $39. The Professional version includes a tool that enables you to snipe (place last-second bids on auctions). The program requires Windows 98 or later to run; the Macintosh OS is not supported.*

Filter Search Results

Degunking is all about not accepting the search results you are given by default and taking steps to improve the precision of your searches. Whenever possible, resist the temptation to immediately click on the titles of individual sales; instead, filter or sort them to make them more accurate. Let's next look at some techniques for refining your search results.

Browse through Matching Categories

When you receive a set of search results, don't overlook the options in the yellow left-hand column (see Figure 3-6). They enable you to find more specific, focused results using the results initially found by eBay.

The options are easily overlooked because your impulse is to start scanning the items listed in the search results. But if you take a minute or two to try the

Figure 3-6
Matching Categories and Search Options make it easier to find what you want.

following tools, you'll cut down on your search time and probably uncover items you didn't see in the initial search results:

√ **Matching Categories.** This area of the left-hand column lists the category within eBay where the search results are found. Click the category name to connect to the category opening page. By browsing the category, you might be able to locate items that didn't show up in the search results due to misspellings by their sellers. For instance, if you search for "Packard hubcap" and the seller lists the item as "Packard's hubcaps," it will be listed in the category but not turn up in your search results.

√ **Search Options.** Check one of the boxes in this section to winnow down the search results:

√ **Items listed with PayPal** selects only those items whose sellers accept payments through the electronic payment service PayPal.

√ **Buy It Now items** isolates those sales items that have a fixed Buy It Now price. They may or may not also be offered at auction.

√ **Gift items** is virtually meaningless; it selects only those items whose owners have paid an extra fee to have a gift item icon next to them. Many other items may be suitable as gifts, but they may not have gift icons next to them.

√ **Items listed as lots** describes items that are offered in quantity.

√ **Completed listings** shows only sales that have already ended.

√ **Listings** lets you display only items offered at sales starting today, ending today, and ending within five hours.

√ **Items priced** lets you single out the current price (a bid price, a starting bid, or a Buy It Now price) based on a range you specify.

Once you have checked the criteria you want to use to filter the search results, click the Show Items button at the bottom of Search Options. The options you saw before are narrowed accordingly. Be sure to click Customize at the bottom of the Search Options section to degunk your filtering even more. Delete the search options you use the least and arrange the ones you use most frequently. You can also add two options that don't appear by default: **Items listed in US $** and **Multiple item listings** (see Figure 3-7).

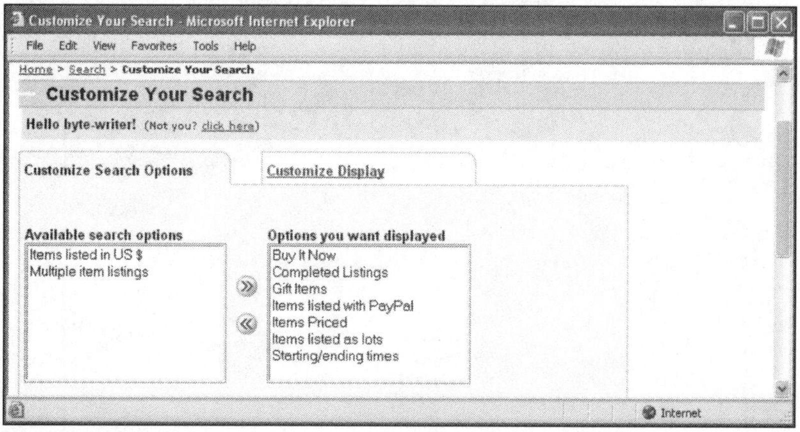

Figure 3-7
Customizing your search options helps you focus your results even more.

GunkBuster's Notebook: Search Outside of eBay

eBay isn't the only place to search for items that have been sold on eBay. Several organizations enable anyone to access eBay's database of completed auctions. Often, you can get far more extensive and useful information on one of these sites than on eBay itself.

Here's an example: Suppose you are looking for a hubcap from a desirable antique Packard motor car. You can search through eBay's completed auctions and come up with less than 10 listings. But if you search through Andale (**www.andale.com**), a site that provides a variety of auction-related services and software, you get a far more extensive set of listings. Table 3-2 shows a comparison of the completed auction data.

Table 3-2   Completed Auctions: Andale versus eBay

Data	eBay	Andale
Number of search results	9	39
Start date	August 24	July 23
End date	September 5	August 6
Completed sales	3	27

eBay provides more recent sales information, but Andale provides data over a slightly longer period (14 days, compared with 2 for eBay) and with many more sales descriptions. Andale makes it ridiculously easy to search eBay's database. There's a search box right on its home page: Enter your search terms, click Go, and in a few seconds, you have extensive search results like the ones shown in Figure 3-8.

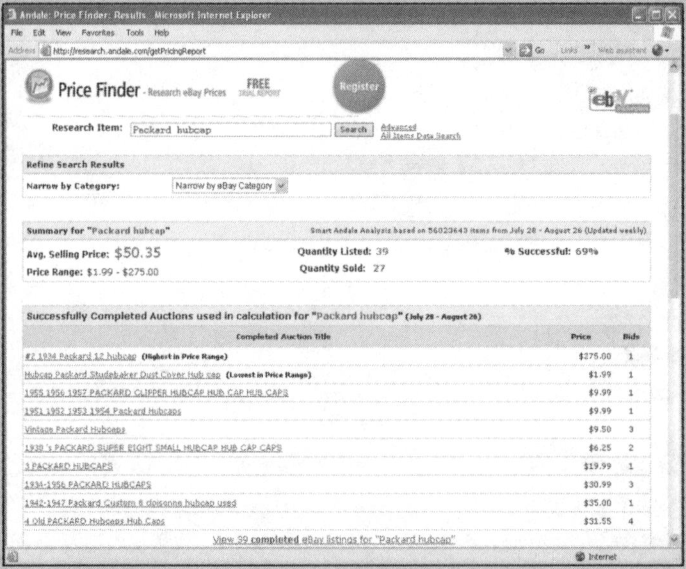

Figure 3-8

For extensive eBay search results, it pays to look outside of eBay.

If you sign up for an Andale product called Price Finder (which costs $3.95 per month, with the first month free), you can get extensive reports that include sales data over a period of several months. To find out more, go to the Price Finder home page (**www.andale.com/research/res_quickstart.jsp**).

Try Analysis Software

You can also download and run a program that searches eBay's database, analyzing current or completed sales. The advantage of installing your own software is control: You configure the program the way you want, you operate it when you want, and you uninstall it when you don't want to use it anymore.

A program called DeepAnalysis by HammerTap and an eBay software product (an application that you have to download and install) called My Auction Search lets you search eBay's completed auctions. Find out more at **www.myauctionsearch.com/support.htm**. You can also try a program called HarvEX/Turbo-Sniper (**www.xellsoft.com/HarvEX.html**).

Find Anything You Need

Most of the time, you search for good deals on eBay. But you can speed up your use of the site by searching for many other things, too. You can look through mountains of feedback comments to find the few you want, you can locate individual buyers and sellers, and you can shop through the wares offered in eBay Stores, which are established by experienced sellers as a way to offer many items at fixed price rather than at auction.

Searching Feedback

If you have been selling on eBay for any length of time, you have probably accumulated dozens or even hundreds of individual feedback comments. It pays to know what others have said about you so you can protect your reputation. If you disagree with a customer's comment, you can post an explanation or clarification, and you can even get negative feedback removed (as described in Chapter 6). You may want to investigate the comments about someone with whom you want to do business. If a seller has hundreds or even thousands of positive feedback comments, you may want to focus on only the negative ones. You can find neutral or negative comments in a flash. Follow these steps:

1. Click Search in the eBay navigation bar to connect to the Search: Find items page.

2. Click Find a Member.

3. Type the person's eBay username in the Enter User ID of member box, then click Search.

4. When the feedback comments appear, scan the quick summary at the top of the page. You might see a feedback summary like the one shown in Figure 3-9, with more than 1,000 feedback comments to look through.

5. If you want to find the negative or neutral comments buried in this sizeable pile of feedback, you have two options: use eBay, or use an outside auction

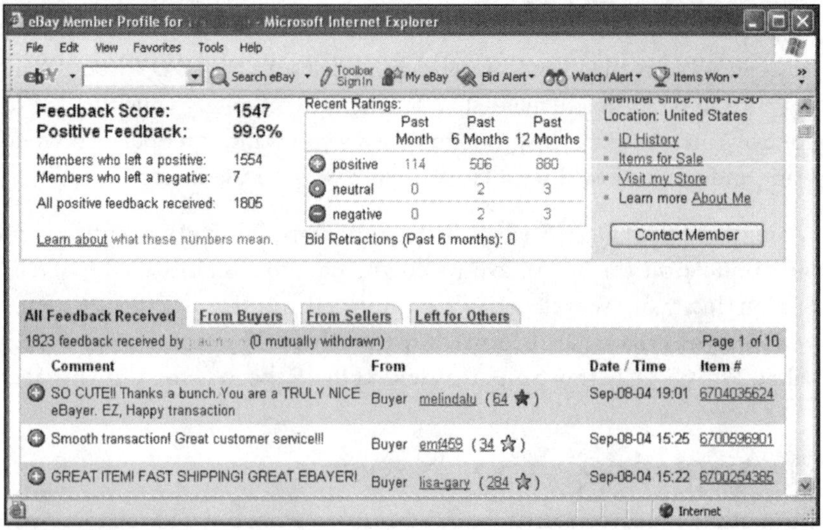

Figure 3-9
Sorting through lots of feedback can be time-consuming.

service. These steps are based on using eBay's gunky system, in which case you have to look through page after page of feedback to find the comment you want. Scroll down to the bottom of the first feedback page, and choose 200 from the Items per page drop-down list. The page refreshes so that 200 feedback comments are shown at once. By displaying 200 items per page, you have fewer pages to look through.

6.   Scroll through each page looking for a gray "neutral" or red "negative" icon. It's a decidedly gunky way to find feedback, but you'll eventually uncover what you want.

In the GunkBuster's Notebook "View Feedback with BayCheck Pro," I'll show you a more efficient way to search through feedback.

NOTE: *Because the ratio of positive to negative comments is so high, you might think that the negative comments are irrelevant. Nevertheless, some buyers or sellers might be curious about those few comments and why they might have occurred given the member's stellar record otherwise.*

GunkBuster's Notebook: View Feedback with BayCheck Pro

I don't understand why eBay doesn't make it easier for members to search through other members' feedback. To degunk such searches, you have to turn to a program like BayCheck Pro by HammerTap. You can try the program free for 30 days, then purchase it for $19.99. All you have to do is enter the User ID of the eBay member you want to research and click the Check button in the BayCheck Pro toolbar and you get a detailed summary of that person's activity on eBay. The data includes any changes of User ID, items currently for sale, and feedback. Click the Feedback received tab and you can view the member's current feedback. You can choose to have BayCheck Pro display up to 500 comments at once from the Comments per drop-down list (see Figure 3-10).

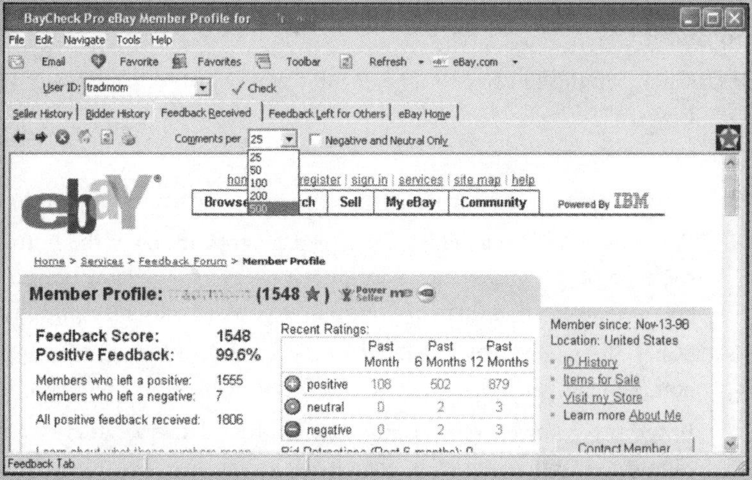

Figure 3-10
This program makes it easy for you to view a large number of feedback comments and sort out the negative and neutral ones.

Once you have BayCheck Pro installed and you have an eBay member's feedback displayed, it's easy to sort out the negative or neutral comments. Just check the box next to Negative and Neutral Only in the Feedback Received or Feedback Left for Others column. The negative/neutral comments will be displayed and the positive ones eliminated.

CAUTION: *Don't take negative or neutral comments at face value. The person leaving the comment may or may not have had legitimate reasons for leaving the "gray mark" or "red mark" on the member's record. Consider the feedback comments as a whole when deciding whether or not to do business with a person.*

Searching for Sales Categories

eBay has thousands of categories of merchandise. What's more, it is continually creating new categories and rearranging subcategories to make merchandise easier to find. Browsing through the complete list of sales categories that appears when you click Browse in the toolbar shows just how gunky the system is. How, for example, do you find the perfect category or subcategory in which to sell something?

There is a special search tool that you can use, but it is difficult to find unless you have attempted to sell something. Follow these steps and I'll show you how to find it:

1. Click Sell in the eBay toolbar. (Don't worry; we won't actually sell anything now.)

2. Click Sell Your Item.

3. Sign in with your User ID and password, if you are prompted to do so.

4. When the Choose a Selling Format page appears, click the button next to the type of sale you want to conduct, or leave the default option (online auction) selected and click Continue if you are only researching.

5. When the page entitled Sell Your Item, Step 1 of 5: Category appears, congratulate yourself: You've found the well-hidden category search tool!

6. Enter a word or two in the Enter keywords to find a category box shown in Figure 3-11, and then click Search.

7. A list of all the categories in which the specified item could be sold appears in a new window entitled Find a Main Category. Scan the list. Notice that the categories are ranked to indicate how many items are sold in each category. For instance, Figure 3-12 shows all the items on eBay in which hubcaps have been sold. A full 67 percent of all the hubcaps sold on eBay have been sold in the first category on the list, so you should probably pick that category if you want to sell (or buy) a hubcap. Don't overlook the other categories, though, as they might contain some hidden gems that won't come up on searches because of misspellings or other problems.

The list of categories that appears after such a search is most valuable when deciding where to list an item for sale. You can list an item in more than one

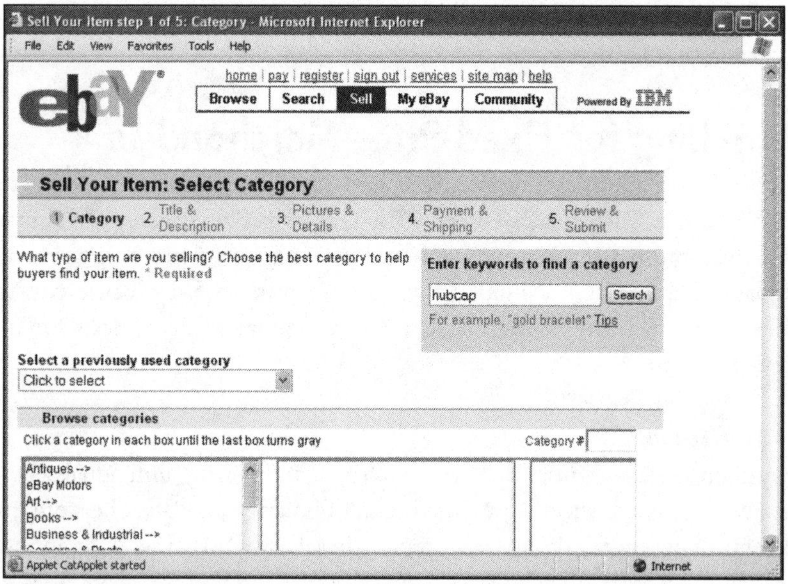

Figure 3-11

This box enables you to search eBay's sales categories by keyword.

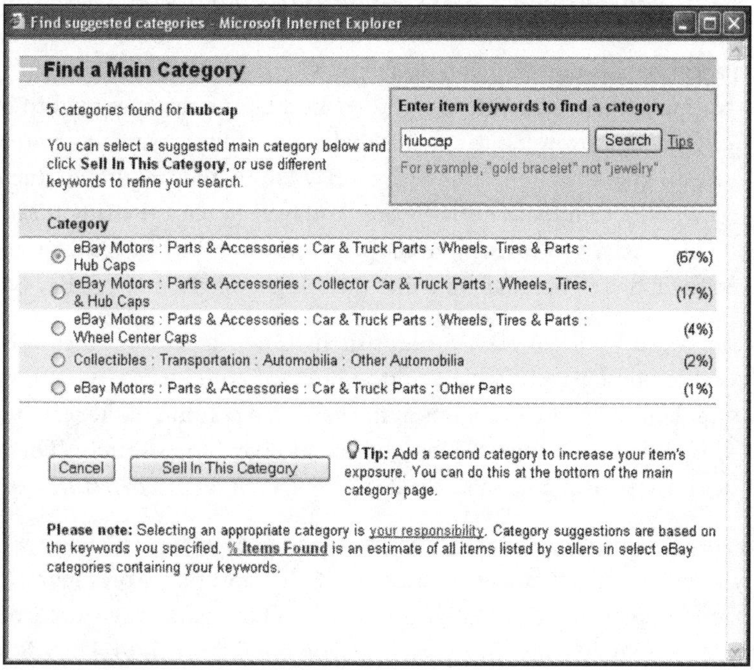

Figure 3-12

Categories listed in search results are ranked by popularity.

category, and it pays to pick the most likely ones to maximize page views and bids (see Chapter 9).

Searching for Fixed-Price Merchandise

Auctions have traditionally been the best-known type of sale conducted on eBay. But fixed-price sales—sales with Buy It Now prices—give buyers an attractive option. What's attractive is that you can buy something immediately, without having to get caught up in bidding wars that can cause you to pay more than you really wanted to. Let's next explore some options for finding fixed-price sales.

eBay Stores

eBay Stores—sales venues that are established and run by individual sellers and offer items at fixed prices—are growing in popularity on eBay. The store managers tend to be knowledgeable and reputable sellers who know a lot about what they sell. eBay Stores give buyers a way to browse and buy merchandise instantly, without getting caught up in competitive bidding. They also give buyers a way to buy more items from sellers they trust and have dealt with previously.

One way to search for stores is to go to the eBay Stores home page (**http://stores.ebay.com**) and enter a search term in the search box shown near the top of the page. Use this option if you don't know exactly what you want and don't have a particular seller in mind. eBay Stores home page searches tend to be exceptionally gunky, however. First of all, the default results present you with traditional auction sales that are not hosted in eBay Stores, they're just conducted by members who happen to *have* eBay Stores. You have to click the Buy It Now tab at the top of an eBay Stores search result (see Figure 3-13) to see fixed-price sales. But even then, there's no guarantee that the sales items are part of eBay Stores.

How can you degunk an eBay Stores search? One suggestion: After you do a search on the home page, click the button next to Store Inventory Only, which appears just beneath Search Options in the left-hand column of the search results page. (This option only appears after you do an eBay Stores search.) Then click Show Items to narrow down the results to the contents of actual stores.

Here's another, radically different idea: Visit the sales of buyers and sellers you already know and trust. If any of those sellers has an eBay Stores icon next to their name, click it to go to that person's store. Then search the store from the box on its own home page. An example is shown in Figure 3-14. The advantage is that you give more business to a seller you like, your chance of encountering fraud is very low, and you build up an ongoing connection with a seller.

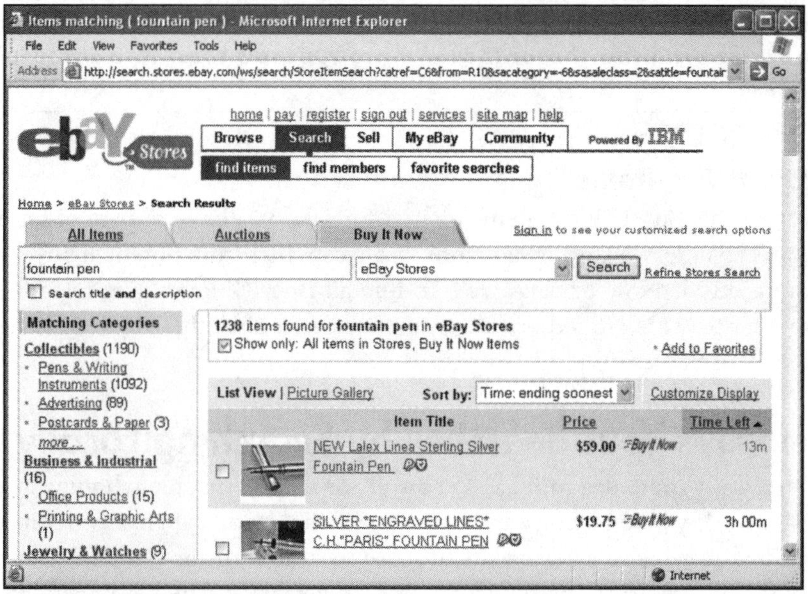

Figure 3-13

eBay Stores home page searches tend to be gunked up.

Figure 3-14

You can search an individual eBay Store's sales category.

TIP: Once you become a repeat customer, you can ask for discounts. You can ask the seller to ship several items at once to save on postage costs or ask for a discount on a bulk purchase.

Buy It Now Items

Not all the Buy It Now items offered for sale on eBay are part of an eBay Store's inventory. Many are auctions that accept bids from potential buyers and have a Buy It Now price as well. To find all Buy It Now items, regardless of whether they are offered as part of an eBay Store, click the Buy It Now tab at the top of the search results page.

Improve Your Searches by Searching Locally

Often, it's a good idea to find local buyers or sellers—people who live in your own area. If you're buying a big item that's difficult and expensive to ship, such as a motor vehicle, it makes lots of sense to deal with someone in your own geographic area. You can inspect the item in person, and pick it up and pay for it personally.

Buyers can find sellers in their own area by entering a zip code in the Items near me section of the Search: Find Items page. After entering the zip code, choose a distance from the adjacent drop-down list labeled "within." Choosing an option tells eBay to search within 10 miles, 25 miles, 50 miles, and so on.

Searching Internationally

Usually, when you search eBay, you search only for sales within your own home country and within countries in which the same language is spoken. For members in the U.S., that means you'll also see some sales listed in Canada, Australia, and Great Britain. If you scroll down to the bottom of a page of search results, you will see the following link:

`See all items` including those available from non-English speaking countries.

Click this link and you instantly enlarge your eBay search to include the many countries in which eBay has separate auction sites. You see them listed at the bottom of the home page; they include Argentina, Australia, Brazil, China, France, Germany, Hong Kong, India, Ireland, Italy, Sweden, Switzerland, and Taiwan, among others.

You can also search eBay's international sites by clicking Search in the navigation bar, clicking More search options, and scrolling down to the Location section of the search page. You have two options here:

√ **Items located in.** These are items whose sellers live in a specific country. Whatever country you choose, make sure the seller will ship to your part of the world.

√ **Items available to.** This option enables you to search for items that are available only to buyers from a specified country. Select your own country from the Items available to drop-down list.

The options are important because some sellers don't want to go through the extra trouble, such as customs requirements, that can be associated with shipping to another country. You might find a rare Maori cloth in New Zealand, but if the seller won't ship to your country, you can't purchase it on eBay.

Looking Up Other eBayers

One aspect of being a proficient eBay buyer or seller is the ability to communicate with other eBay members. The more friends you have on eBay, the more people you can turn to for advice. The faster you can find people, the quicker you'll solve that problem that's been bugging you. For instance, if you are concerned about a seller and you want to make sure he or she can be trusted, you can surf around the Web to one of the many sites that perform "background checks" and discover whether the individual has a criminal record. You can also contact buyers or sellers who live in your area so you can get a look at an item for sale in person or pick it up personally with your car.

It's easy to find a seller on eBay as long as you have that individual's User ID. Once you have written down their User ID from an auction description or other page on eBay, follow these steps:

1. Go to the Search: Find Items page by clicking Search in the eBay navigation bar or doing directly to **http://search.ebay.com/ws/search/AdvSearch?sofindtype=13**.

2. Click Find a Member. When the Search: Find a Member page appears, enter the User ID in the appropriate box and then click the button next to the information you want: the member's feedback profile, About Me page, or User ID history.

3. Click Search. The information should appear if it is available. If the member doesn't have an About Me page and you check that option, you won't see it.

TIP: The User ID history can help you degunk transactions that might turn out to be problematic. If you find that a member has changed their User ID frequently, it's a warning sign. That member may be trying to conceal a bad reputation resulting from fraudulent or dishonest behavior.

You might want to get someone's contact information if you haven't been able to reach them through eBay's internal messaging system. If a week or two has passed since the end of your sale and the high bidder or buyer hasn't responded, don't sit and wait. Click Find Contact Information and look up the address and phone number so you can reach them by less high-tech means.

Suppose you don't know someone's User ID. Maybe someone told you in passing that they sell regularly on eBay and you want to look up their current offerings. If you have an individual's e-mail address, you can click Find User ID on the Search: Find Items page. Enter the e-mail address and a security code, click Search, and eBay will return the User ID—provided, of course, that it's the same e-mail address the individual listed when creating the User ID on eBay. If it's not the right e-mail address, you'll have to ask the person for the User ID yourself.

TIP: *If your search for an eBay member on the Search: Find Items page turns out to be gunked up—in other words, you can't find what you want to know—see if the individual has an eBay Store. Stores include an About the Seller page that might provide more information. If the member is also a Trading Assistant (someone who buys and sells for others and is approved by eBay), you can find lots of information about the person. Go to the Trading Assistants home page (**http://contact.ebay.com/aw-cgi/ eBayISAPI.dll?GetTAHubPage**). If all else fails, you can Google them. (Try putting "quotation marks" around it to get the name just right.)*

Uncover Bargains

Searching eBay isn't just a way to do research. By learning how to search efficiently, you can find bargains that other bidders might not notice. The fewer the competitive bids, the greater chances of winning what you want. Let's look at two approaches for using search techniques to uncover bargains.

Look for Typographical Errors

Millions of people sell on eBay. Some are good spellers; some aren't. Some take the time to proofread their sales descriptions and auction titles, and some are in a hurry to put sales online. A few sellers hire assistants to create their sales descriptions—assistants who may not be well acquainted with the items they are describing and who easily might make errors.

One way to degunk the process of finding what you want on eBay is to look for typographical errors that don't turn up in searches. If you are looking for something relating to Betty Boop, for example, and you search for "Betty Boop," you won't find an item in the search results if its seller has called it "*Bettie*

Boop." You can only find such items by searching for the correct spelling of an item and some common misspellings, or by laboriously browsing through sales categories so you don't miss anything that's up for sale. Both strategies regularly turn up items that are misspelled and mislabeled or poorly photographed (or perhaps not photographed at all) and that only an experienced and dedicated collector will dig up.

> ### GunkBuster's Notebook: Tips from a Pro for Finding Bargains
>
> Pamela Glasell (eBay User ID: gramasattic) says she has been buying and selling on eBay "since the beginning." She conducts auctions regularly in addition to running a user's group called the Vintage Tablecloth Lover's Club (**www.vintagetableslothsclub.com**). She suggests looking for typos when doing a search: "Type in the different versions of the product's spelling," she advises. "Mine are 'Tablecloth' and 'Table Cloth.'" Glasell also suggests the following strategies when searching on eBay. "Have different User IDs for buying and selling, especially if you are 'known' for specializing in a certain product. If you can, give yourself a two-week 'window' for buying and selling. Buy for two weeks, and then sell for two weeks. Also be sure to do a completed search on the item to set a 'price range' when you sell."

Browse for Bad Sales Schedules

eBay sales are predictable. Many of them take advantage of the fact that the largest number of shoppers is available for bidding on the weekends, when they're not at work. The best time to end a sale, in fact, is Saturday or Sunday evening, when people are most likely to be home.

Not all sales end at such times, however. If you find a sale that ends at a time when many bidders aren't likely to be available at the end of the sale—such as Tuesday morning or Wednesday afternoon—your chances of winning the auction increase. Search for such auctions, and make a point to be available at the end of the sale so you can place a last-second bid.

TIP: The items listed on eBay's home page (www.ebay.com) aren't always bargains. Their sellers have paid big bucks to list them on one of the Internet's most frequently visited locations. But you might find some special deals on eBay's category opening pages. These are the pages that serve as home pages for individual categories. Click on the name of the category either on the home page or on the eBay site map to access a category opening page. Look for any special promotions under headings such as Deal of the Day.

Summing Up

Searching on eBay is easy, which is one reason why the site has become wildly popular but also very gunked up. As you continue to search the site, try sorting your search results. Look for sales that end soon; look for items whose sellers live in your immediate geographic area. Save your searches, and have eBay e-mail you when your favorite items come up for auction. The key is to make a commitment to control your searches and filter your search results rather than accepting what the site's search utility gives you initially. Otherwise, you'll really be wasting your time having to scan through all of the clutter you get. Don't use the search options with one hand tied behind your back, but take advantage of everything eBay gives you to work with. There are lots of tools available, as well as a few pointers included in this chapter, that will help you degunk your eBay searches.

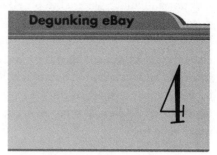

4

Bidding and Winning More Auctions

Degunking Checklist:

√ Learn easy tactics for increasing your winning percentage, such as synchronizing your clock with eBay and using multiple windows and monitors.

√ Place smarter bids by comparison shopping to learn the value of what's being sold.

√ Find out why auction fever is so dangerous.

√ Adjust your bidding strategy to match the type of auction that you're in.

√ Try different approaches to placing snipe bids, including using software and Web-based products.

√ Place proxy bids and nibble away at reserve prices.

√ Learn to recognize dishonest bidders, and find out what you can do about them.

I t's not difficult to place a bid on eBay, but it's definitely getting harder to win auctions. All too often, the process of bidding—and not just bidding, but bidding to win—gets gunked up. Bids don't get through to eBay in time for the end of the sale; you are beaten by last-minute "snipe" bids; your proxy bids are too low. Occasionally, dishonest eBay members conspire to gunk up the process by violating the rules. In this chapter, you'll get some inside tips for beating experienced eBayers at their own game and learn some strategies for winning more auctions.

Increase Your Winning Percentage

Degunking, eBay style, doesn't mean winning every single auction in which you place a bid. Sometimes, the bidding skyrockets beyond what you wanted to spend. Part of the degunking eBay process means staying within your budget and finding bargains when they appear. It also means improving your winning percentage: giving up on the items that get too pricey and buying only what you really need—while skipping the stuff that will only gunk up your house and garage.

Synchronize Your Clock with eBay

One of the most important ways that eBay auctions differ from traditional auctions is the time the auction ends. In most auction houses, the auctioneers control when the last gavel or hammer comes down, which signals that bidding is over. On eBay auctions, the clock signals the end of the sale. It pays to synchronize your clock with eBay's official time.

Finding eBay Time

eBay sales take place in the time zone where eBay's home office is located—in the Pacific Time zone in San Jose, California. By setting your computer clock to match eBay's, you can snipe (place a last-minute bid) down to the last second. Normally, you can't actually see the seconds pass on your computer clock (at least not on a Windows machine). If you want to track the time, adjust your clock by double-clicking the time as displayed in your system tray. When the Date and Time Properties dialog box appears (see Figure 4-1), you can move it to a corner of your screen to watch the seconds pass; you can keep an eye on the auction you're monitoring in another, adjacent browser window.

If you want to change the clock to eBay Time, click the Time Zone tab and choose Pacific Time from the drop-down list.

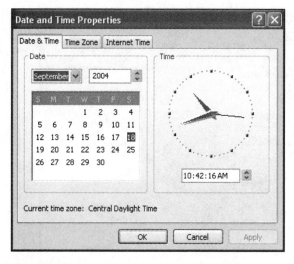

Figure 4-1
Use this dialog box to adjust your computer time and
watch seconds pass.

TIP: Look at any current eBay auction to find out if eBay is operating under Pacific Standard Time or Pacific Daylight Time: the abbreviation PDT or PST appears after the current time. PST runs from late October to late April (winter); PDT lasts from late April to late October (summer).

The current eBay Time appears on the auction description window. A more detailed explanation of eBay Time appears on the official eBay Time Web page (**http://cgi3.ebay.com/aw-cgi/eBayISAPI.dll?TimeShow**), shown in Figure 4-2.

Keep in mind that eBay Time varies depending on which version of eBay you're using. If you're in the U.S., Pacific Time is eBay Time. But if you're in another country where eBay has a site, such as Japan, the U.K., or Brazil, the official eBay Time is completely different. You'll find a page full of links to eBay Time around the world at **www.greenwichmeantime.com/ebay/ebay-time.htm**.

If you want to keep the hour to match your local time, that's fine; the important thing is to get the minute and second to match eBay Time so you can snipe with precision. Keep in mind that you should always allow a "cushion" to allow for technical problems. It doesn't do any good to place a snipe bid five seconds before a sale ends if your Internet connection is slow, your server suddenly slows down due to Internet traffic, or your computer clock is running slow.

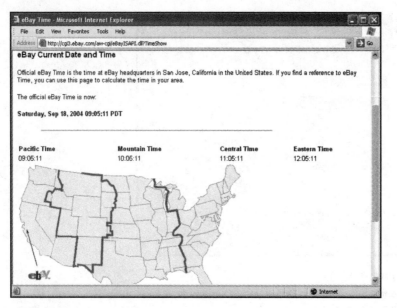

Figure 4-2

The official eBay Time page compares eBay's time zone to others in the U.S.

NOTE: Some eBay members post messages on the auction site's discussion forums claiming that eBay "adjusts" the official time to defeat automated sniping software, but there's no proof that this actually occurs. The point is to bid a minute or two (not seconds) before the sale is supposed to end.

Using Multiple Windows

Think of how many windows you might want to keep open when you are monitoring the bidding at the end of a sale. You might have the Date and Time Properties window open. You certainly want to keep the auction description window open. To place a snipe bid at an exact moment, you may want to keep a separate window open showing the Place Bid part of the auction description. In one window, you show the time and the current high bid; you keep refreshing this window to track the sale. In the other window, you display the Place Bid box and button so you can adjust and place your bid when you need to.

Using Multiple Monitors

Keeping all of those browser windows open in the same screen can make things crowded, especially if your monitor is 15 or 17 inches wide. Some longtime eBay users employ multiple monitors for bidding, shopping, and selling. In one screen they can monitor a sale; in other screens they can answer e-mail, place bids, or put new items up for sale. If you run a business on eBay (a practice described in Chapter 12), you should consider doing this. Remember that the cost of the computer equipment you buy is deductible as a business expense if you itemize your tax returns.

Know How Much Something Is Worth

Before you start bidding, you need to do some comparison shopping in order to know how much to bid. The whole idea behind buying on eBay is to save or make money. If you're buying, you want to buy something at less than the prevailing retail price. If you're selling, you want to make a profit. But if you're too eager and buy something for more than it would cost at a retail store or another Web site, you've defeated yourself. Being patient often helps you find a better price for an item. So does a little comparison shopping so you can set a bid limit.

Tools to Help You Comparison Shop

eBay itself is the best place to start; after all, it's one of the best sources of information about the value of items that sell in the real world. To search eBay's completed auctions, do a keyword search to see what's available right now and what the high bids are. To determine how much you might bid on one of the items, click Completed Items in the column on the left-hand side of the page, and then click the Show Items button. A list of recent completed sales appears.

TIP: *Scan the lists of What's Hot items in a particular category to determine if the type of item you want is especially collectible and likely to attract lots of bids. (If it is, you might want to click the Buy It Now option if it is available to avoid getting into a bidding war.)*

If it's collectibles you're looking for, the many price guides to different varieties of collectibles can help you determine what constitutes a reasonable bid. Use them to do your homework on what's hot and not. There are plenty of guides available at antique stores or bookstores that cover antique furniture, watches, jewelry, radios, Fiestaware, Hummel figurines, carnival glass, and many more.

An especially good tool for getting comparison prices on a variety of consumer goods is Google's comparison shopping service Froogle (**http:// froogle.google.com**), shown in Figure 4-3.

Search for an item using its name and model number or a set of keywords and Froogle returns prices and descriptions from a variety of commercial sites. Suppose, for instance, you're looking for a Sony VAIO K23 Notebook and you want to know whether to buy it on eBay or through another site. You also want to know how much to bid if you do decide to try for one that's being offered

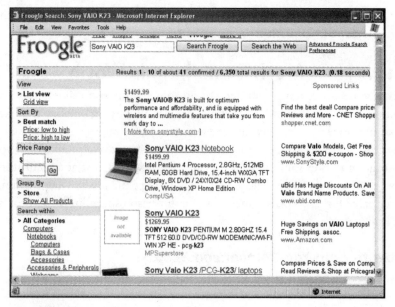

Figure 4-3
Froogle helps you compare current eBay prices with those on other Web sites.

at auction. First, you could do a completed items search on eBay to find that the following instances of this model have been sold:

√ Sept. 2: $1300 (41 bids)

√ Sept. 5: $1250 (6 bids)

√ Sept. 7: $1275 (40 bids)

√ Sept. 7: $1375 (38 bids)

√ Sept. 13: $1125 (4 bids)

√ Sept. 15: $999.99 (1 bid)

√ Sept. 17: $1498 (3 bids)

Then, you could do a search on Froogle to gather the following prices for comparison:

√ Sonystyle.com: $1499.99

√ CompUSA: $1499.99

√ MPSuperstore: $1269.95

As you can see, the people who bought the computers on eBay didn't always get the best possible price. The high number of bids on some sales indicates that a bidding war ensued, one in which getting the high bid at the end of the auction became more important than actually getting a bargain. By waiting a week or two, they could have bid on a computer that attracted few takers and that went for a comparative bargain. For new electronics and other consumer items, eBay isn't always the best option. By getting prices from other online marketplaces, you can determine whether or not to place a bid in the first place.

GunkBuster's Notebook: Beware Auction Fever

Don't get trapped in an auction fever. This is the most common way that people end up wasting money and paying more than what something's worth in their zeal to outbid everyone else. If you're running an eBay business, this type of behavior will devour your profits and may even create a money-losing operation. And you don't want that!

We all get wrapped up in auction fever from time to time. It can happen when you're looking to buy a house. Say you've just found your dream house in your dream neighborhood, and it's priced at $150,000, the limit of your budget. Your real estate agent says that this house is hot and won't last long. You dally and delay, and lo and behold, another buyer offers the seller's asking price. Your real estate agent then encourages you to outbid them and put in an offer of $160,000. And even though this is more than you can afford and more than the house is worth, you do it. Then the original buyer ups the ante to $165,000, and your agent says they won't go higher and you can probably get the house for $170,000. Should you bid?

The financial gurus call this "escalation of investment." We call it a gunked-up bidding process. Know the value of what you're bidding on, and don't get caught up in auction fever. Rather than wasting your money on an item that you lust after but will lose money on, spend your time looking for underpriced items for which there is a good potential for profit. And remember that, with millions of items going up for sale on eBay every day, even if you walk away from an auction that gets too pricey, you're likely to find a similar sale before too long.

Know the Competition

If you shop frequently for a particular type of collectible or other household item, take a look at the individuals who are bidding on it. After a while, you start to recognize the User IDs of members who bid and win on a regular basis. Once you know who the most active bidders are, you'll know whether you should avoid the sale (because the active members have outbid you in the past) or whether you should bid confidently because the current high bidder doesn't typically bid on this type of item. Click on the link for the number of bids (for example, the underlined link <u>10 bids</u>) to get a list of the current bidders.

Once you know who the high bidder is, you can take an additional investigatory step that can indicate whether or not you might get into a bidding war with someone. If the current high bidder is someone who has purchased four dozen pieces of the same type of item in recent weeks and paid hundreds of dollars for similar items, you might not want to bid against that person; at the very least, you might want to evaluate how much you really want the necklace and how much you are willing to spend for it. To research a bidder, you need to make note of that person's User ID. Then follow these steps:

1.   Click Search in the eBay navigation bar.

2.   Click Items By Bidder.

3.   Enter the User ID of the bidder you want to research.

4.   Check Include completed items (last 30 days) if you want to research past auctions to see if the bidder won or not.

5.   Adjust the number of search results you want by choosing a number from the drop-down list.

6.   Click Search.

Why go through the trouble of researching someone's bid activity? You can determine the person's bidding habits. Someone who bids and buys all the time is likely to be a professional dealer; you'll have a hard time outbidding them unless you are prepared to bid a high amount. For instance, suppose you are shopping for a Morgan silver dollar. You search for the User ID of either the current high bidder or a previous bidder, and you determine that they tend to place a bid early in the auction and then swoop in at the end with a snipe bid at the last second. That tells you that you had better get ready to snipe—and place a sizeable snipe bid—if you want that coin.

Tailor Your Auction Strategies to eBay Auction Types

You're probably familiar with all of eBay's basic sales formats already. Armed with current knowledge, you can tailor your bidding approach to the type of sale to maximize your chances of winning. Like a good poker player, you've got to take odds and probability into account. When your odds of winning are good, make a bet. When the odds are against you, fold 'em. In other words, stop betting and wait for the next hand—I mean sale—to come around.

What types of eBay sales give you the best odds of finding a buyer or high bidder? That depends on whether the item being offered is desirable and on who is bidding at a given time. If something being offered is rare and the bidders have deep pockets, your chances are low. Still, if you really want something, some sales types are better bets than others. Table 4-1 runs down the sales types and your likelihood of winning. Assume that the same everyday household item is being offered in each format.

Table 4-1   eBay Sales Types

Type of Sale	Likelihood of Winning	Comments
Standard auction	Good	You don't have to meet buyer's reserve to win.
Reserve auction	Fair	You have to compete against bidders and meet the reserve.
Fixed-price (Buy It Now or BIN) sale	Excellent	If you can afford the price, you can buy the item immediately.
Standard auction with BIN option	Fair	Click BIN button quickly; BIN option disappears when first bid is placed; this sale often attacked by "BIN killers."
Reserve auction with BIN option	Good	You can either click BIN button or place bids that meet reserve.
Multiple-item "Dutch" auction	Excellent	The more items offered, the better your odds of winning; *lowest* qualifying bid wins.

This examination suggests that if you can find something at a Dutch auction, you should place a bid on it. The problem with such auctions is that they are rarely used for hard-to-find collectibles but are commonly used to sell multiple identical household objects. Fixed BIN prices are great when you are sure you want to buy something immediately, but you don't always find a real bargain that way.

For bargain hunters, auctions are the thing. With a standard No Reserve, or NR, auction, you know somebody is going to win. But so does everybody else who sees the sale. No Reserve sales can quickly soar as bids are placed by all of your fellow bargain hunters until suddenly the item being sold is no longer a bargain. What can you do to win items at bargain prices? Some suggestions are presented in the sections that follow.

Sniping: Pros and Cons

Sniping is, without a doubt, the most popular and best-known way to win an auction on eBay. As you have probably already discovered, sniping is a practice that allows people to bid at the last second and win. If you have ever been a high bidder for something you really wanted and watched the clock run down only to be outbid in the last few seconds by someone else, you have been beaten by a snipe bid. Many eBay users argue that sniping is the most effective way to win auctions.

Any eBay bidder can snipe, as long as they are present at the auction's Web page at the moment when the sale ends. You wait until a minute or two before the sale ends, place a last-minute bid, and see what happens. But that's a pretty haphazard way of sniping. Sniping can be an art, and the ins and outs of fine-tuning your sniping to increase your chances of winning are described next.

Sniping Manually

The easiest way to snipe is to sit at your computer and watch the sale end. You continually hit your browser's Reload or Refresh button to determine how much time is left in the sale. When the time gets down to a minute or two, your heart pounding, you quickly enter a bid amount—the most you want to pay—and click the Place Bid button. You eagerly refresh the Web page until the sale is over. Hopefully, you are listed as the high bidder and you win.

There are lots of problems with this scenario:

√ In order to snipe manually, sitting at your computer and placing the bid with your very own hands, you need to be present when the auction ends. If you're running an eBay business, you probably don't have the time to do a lot of sniping yourself.

√ There's no guarantee you'll actually win. You might be outsniped by somebody who placed a higher snipe bid (or someone who placed a higher proxy bid long before the sale's final moments). This is a risky way of trying to get an item, especially if it's important to your business.

√ You only give yourself a single bid at the end of a sale. And if your computer crashes or your Internet connection fails at the critical moment, your bid won't go through at all.

For all these reasons, you should consider using a sniping service to place your last-second bids for you more quickly, more reliably, and with less stress.

Sniping Services

Sniping with your home computer depends on everything working right at the critical moment when the auction ends. It can backfire if something unexpected occurs—if your computer crashes, your electrical power fails, your Internet connection fails to work, eBay suffers a service outage, and so on. Even if you use sniping software, the software depends on your computer being up and running and connected to the Internet.

A sniping service is a company that, through its Web site, gives individual users like you access to software that automatically places snipe bids on sales. You specify the sale, you tell the software how much you want it to bid, and you specify when the bid should be placed. (If you use a free sniping service rather than a paying subscription service, you might be limited in how short a period you can specify, however.) Here's an example:

1. Go to the HarvEX/Turbo Sniper Web site (**www.xellsoft.com/ HarvEX.html**) and click the link <u>Download 14-Day Free Trial.</u>

2. Click Open to download the software to your computer and install it.

3. When the Welcome screen appears, click Continue. The Welcome screen closes and you move to the main program window.

4. Use the Search Form tab in the HarvEX window to search for an auction you want to snipe (see Figure 4-4). Enter the search terms in the Search box; then click the Start Search button.

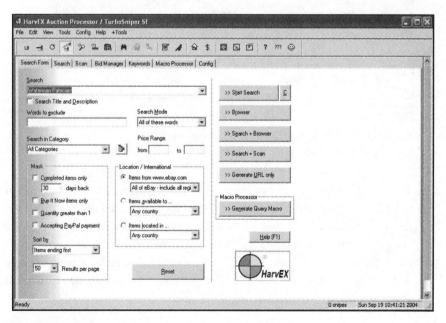

Figure 4-4

HarvEX lets you search eBay, create macros, and place snipe bids.

5. When the search results appear, click Browse to view the search results in a browser window.

6. Single-click the auction you want to bid on in the HarvEx Search tab (which displays the search results). Click the Place Bid button to create a snipe bid. The Add/Edit Bid window appears.

7. In the Add/Edit Bid window (shown in Figure 4-5), you specify your maximum bid and choose your Snipe Time Margin: the time before the auction ends when your bid will actually be placed. You might also want to add the shipping cost. You can specify when you want an alarm to be sounded on your computer just before the sale ends.

8. Click Bid Now! to start the bid progress. That doesn't mean the bid is instantly placed on eBay, however. Rather, you tell the HarvEX tool to check the sale just before it ends and place the bid for you.

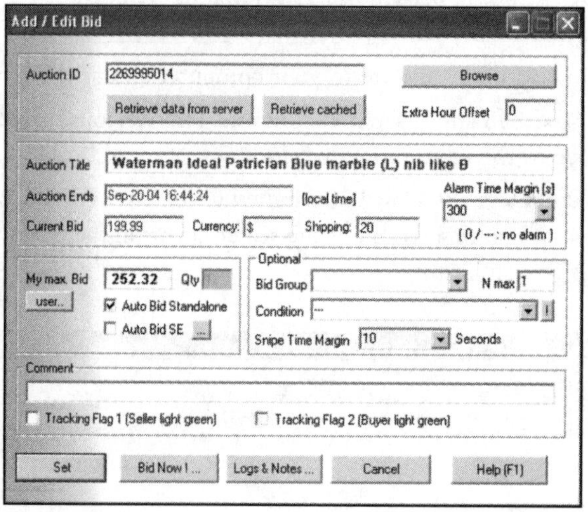

Figure 4-5

You can place a bid in a matter of 10 seconds before the sale ends using this sniping software.

You can use HarvEx for free for a 14-day trial period; after that period, if you want to continue using the software, you need to pay a $19.95 registration fee. It's important to note that HarvEX is sniping software that works on your computer and that depends on your computer and Internet connection. If a connection isn't present at the time you want the bid to be placed, the software dials up the Internet for you. But if your phone line is busy or not working, or your computer is turned off, you won't bid at all.

The other sniping option is to use Web-based software to place the bid. The software resides on the manufacturer's site and is placed using that company's software, not yours. You might have to download software, but the remote site does the actual bidding. Such services include Bidnapper (**www.bidnapper.com**); HammerTap (**www.hammertap.com/powertool**), and SnipeRight (**www.sniperight.com**).

Caution Sniping software that you access on the Web using your browser has one big downside: the software requires you to enter your eBay User ID and password. For example, the moment you connect to the SnipeRight home page (**www.sniperight.com**), you are immediately prompted to enter your eBay account information.

CAUTION: *Anytime anyone asks you for your User ID and password, be skeptical. You need to trust the sniping software's manufacturer not to misuse your information. If you don't feel you can trust the site, don't give your information.*

Handling Reserve Auctions

The words *No Reserve* are extra exciting for bidders. Without a reserve, it's certain someone is going to win. When a reserve is present, things get more complicated. Someone has to uncover what the reserve is by bidding at least that amount. If not, the seller is not obligated to sell the item. You've got a few options for turning the "Reserve not met" message into "Reserve met" so you can actually win the item (provided the reserve isn't higher than you want to bid).

Bidding against Yourself

I bet you never thought you'd have to bid against yourself in order to win an auction, but it happened to me. I was bidding on a fountain pen I really wanted. For some reason, and to my great surprise, no one else placed a bid. The current high bid—mine—was not enough to meet the reserve. But based on the desirability of the item, I was sure somebody would lift the bidding at some point. It didn't happen; the sale ended with my bid as the high one and the reserve not met. Did I win? Nope; you can only win a reserve auction if you meet the reserve. When I e-mailed the seller, making an offer to purchase the pen, I never received a response.

You can avoid this sort of situation by placing another bid if time is running out and the reserve has not been met. Once the reserve has been met, the seller is obligated to sell the item to you at your high bid price and you can use eBay's payment system to complete the transaction. If you don't increase your maximum bid and the sale ends without the reserve being met, there's no guarantee you'll actually get the item.

Sellers do want to make sales, and they want to avoid having to relist something. If the sale ends without the reserve having been met, you can e-mail the seller offering to purchase the item. The seller will specify a price, and you can then negotiate. Keep in mind that there's no way of knowing if the price the seller quotes you was actually the reserve—you have to take the seller's word for it. And there's another, potentially bigger drawback: If you reach an agreement privately, the transaction you complete now takes place outside of eBay's jurisdiction. That means you don't get eBay's Rules & Safety system and feedback system to help ensure that the seller follows through.

Proxy Bidding

Proxy bids are the safest and least stressful ways to bid on eBay. If a reserve price is present, a high proxy bid will uncover it. As you probably already know, the idea behind proxy bids is that you specify the highest amount you are willing to pay for something. eBay then places bids on your behalf in case other bidders place competing bids.

There are lots of ways you can handle proxy bids. Suppose a DVD player you want has a current high bid of $51 and the message "Reserve not met," which indicates that the seller's reserve is an unspecified amount higher than this. One kind of proxy bid you can place is the lowest possible amount. Since the bid increment is $1, you could place a $52 bid. That doesn't mean that you'll necessarily be the high bidder; the previous high bidder might well have placed a proxy bid of more than $52.

A better way of placing a proxy bid is by researching the item being sold to determine what it's really worth and placing the highest proxy bid you can. If you determine by research that the same DVD player can be purchased on other Web sites for $89, place a proxy bid of $88 on it. Then don't worry about the sale until it's over. If the reserve price is more than $89, you needn't worry; you know you can get the same item somewhere else for less.

Things get more complicated when rare and antique collectibles are offered and the exact value isn't well known. It may be that you can't find the item elsewhere, even after weeks of searching. If that's the case, you need to research past auctions for similar items as well as price guides. If the reserve price has not been met and you think the item might be worth $1,000, place a proxy bid of $1,001 on it and see what happens.

TIP: When you place a proxy bid, choose an odd number. There's a chance that, if you add a dollar or two or a cent or two to your bid, you'll beat out someone who placed almost the identical bid.

Nibbling

One way to discover the reserve price the seller has placed on an item is to place several small bids until the message "Reserve met" appear at the top of the auction description. Sometimes, sellers place reserves that are in predictable round dollar amounts, such as $50, $75, $100, or multiples of these, such as $250, $275, and so on. If the current high bid is $200 and the reserve has not yet been met, place a bid of $251 to see if the reserve is $250. If that's not the reserve, place a bid of $276. Keep "nibbling" in this way until your own bid limit is reached or the reserve is uncovered. Once the reserve is revealed, you can decide whether you want to keep bidding or not.

"Buy It Now" Killing

A special situation occurs when a seller offers an item with no reserve and with a Buy It Now option available. The Buy It Now (BIN) option is only available until the first bid is placed. Until a bid arrives, someone can snatch the item away immediately by paying the fixed price the seller has specified.

A special type of bidder—one who is hoping to find a bargain by bidding, and who doesn't want to pay the Buy It Now price—will place a small bid early in the sale to eliminate the BIN price. If the starting bid specified by the seller is $9.99, for instance, someone might well place a bid of $10 or $11. This forces the sale to go to the ending time the seller has specified. Such bidders are known as BIN Killers. Having removed the BIN option, the BIN Killer can return at the end of a sale to place a snipe bid that hopefully wins the auction. (By using sniping software, the BIN Killer can place the snipe bid at the start of the auction and not worry about the sale until the end.)

If you see something desirable offered at no reserve and with a BIN option, you can do one of two things: you can place a small BIN Killer bid, or you can click the Buy It Now button to end the sale immediately and win the item.

NOTE: *In rare instances, a high proxy bid placed during the sale can beat a snipe bid that comes at the end of the sale. The proxy bid has to be very high in order for this to work. For instance, if the current high bid is $150 and a snipe bid of $250 is placed seconds before the sale ends, the previous high bidder will win if their proxy bid was more than $250. If the previous bidder placed a proxy bid of $450 and the sniper bid $400 at the last minute, the sniper loses.*

Dutch Auction Strategies

Sometimes, you want to buy more than one item at the same time. You might need multiple samples of the same object for a party or for an awards ceremony. You can shop eBay for the items one at a time, but a far quicker and craftier way to buy them is through a Dutch auction.

NOTE: *The term **Dutch** auction originated with the tulip bulb markets in Holland, where many identical items needed to be sold for the highest amount. Its use is now colloquial, and eBay refers to such sales with the far less colorful title "multiple-item auction."*

Multiple-item auctions enable a seller to offer two or more identical items up for sale. When creating the sale, the seller specifies the minimum successful price as well as the number of items available. The goal at the end of the auction is to be among the highest bidders with the lowest successful price—in other words, you want to be holding the lowest bid that is still above the minimum price.

Dutch auctions are best explained by example: Suppose you have managed to find a box of a dozen original Corvette Sting-Ray Matchbox cars in their original boxes. Each item is exactly the same. Rather than creating 12 separate auction listings, you can place all 12 up for auction at the same time in a single multiple-item sale. You place a starting bid of $9.99 on each car. You receive 20 bids: one bid of $30, two bids of $28, three bids of $26, two of $23, three of $22, and one of $21. The remaining bidders place bids of $20 or less, but their bids don't count because only the highest 12 bids win (you have only 12 items, after all).

In this type of auction, the winners all pay the *lowest* successful bid. In this case, the winning bidders would end up paying $21, even though most of them bid more. The strategy, then, is to stay out of the "bubble" and be aware of timing. If 12 items are offered in a Dutch auction and 12 identical bids are received, for instance, then the bidders who placed their bid earlier will be the first chosen to receive the items. But if someone places a bid that is higher than the original 12, the higher bid will take precedence and knock one of the 12 out of the running. The higher the bid, the better the chance you have of winning.

To improve your chances of winning a Dutch auction, you need to avoid being the low bidder. When the auction nears its end, the low bidder is "on the bubble." Just what is the "bubble?" Table 4-2 provides an example for a Dutch auction in which 10 items are being auctioned.

Table 4-2 Multiple-Item Auction Example

Bidder	Number of Items Bid On	Bid
1	1	$22
2	2	$24
3	2	$25
4	3	$28
5	2	$31

In this example, the bidder who's at $22 is clearly on the bubble. The low bidder can easily be outbid by someone who places a last-minute bid that is higher, turning the previous low bidder into a loser. A safe bid by a new bidder would be $29 or $30. Make sure you bid enough to stay away from the "bubble," in other words.

Win with Live Auctions

If the waiting and uncertainty of most eBay auctions is too much for you, consider eBay Live Auctions (**www.ebayliveauctions.com**, shown in Figure 4-6).

Figure 4-6
If you can't find what you want in regular eBay sales, try Live Auctions.

Live Auctions is a far different world than the rest of eBay. On eBay Live Auctions, you don't have a Buy It Now option, but you don't have to wait a week to 10 days for a sale to end either. Sales are scheduled for a certain day and then held in real time on that day. Live Auctions sales are like the traditional sales held at traditional auction houses, with one big exception: rather than connecting by telephone, bidders participate online, via their computers, along with real bidders who are physically present in the auction house holding the sale. If you find conventional eBay sales too gunky, give Live Auctions a spin.

Becoming a Live Auction Player

Live auctions can take some getting used to, especially if you're used to placing a single bid on a standard or reserve auction. But the live auction system makes it easy for you to observe the action from the sidelines, as a spectator rather than a participant. To get started, you browse the catalog of items for sale on the Live Auctions site (**www.ebayliveauctions.com**). You can either browse through a catalog of merchandise being sold by a single dealer (see Figure 4-7) or search for something by entering keywords in the search box on the home page. Live Auctions sales are conducted by professional dealers rather than individual amateurs.

If you see something you want to bid on, you register to participate in the sale. Click Sign Up (a button that appears on every sales description) to register for the sale. Once you are registered, you can either place an absentee bid or return when the sale is held and place a bid. If the sale is going on currently, follow these steps:

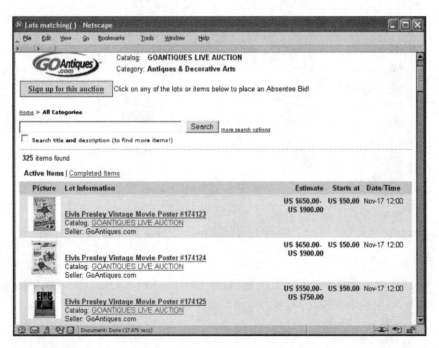

Figure 4-7
Browse through a catalog of items or do a search, then register to place a bid.

1. Click View Now. A separate browser window opens.
2. Wait for the viewing tool to appear. The Live Auctions site uses a Java applet to display items and refresh them when bids are received or to refresh the screen when each sale ends. It might take a minute or more for the applet to execute and begin displaying images. If it doesn't work, make sure your computer meets the minimum requirements for using live auctions.
3. Watch the sales speed by. In a sales lot that contains hundreds of separate items, each item is sold with amazing speed. In less than a minute, the sale might be over. Sometimes bids are received; in many cases, individual items go without attracting a single bid. When a bid is received, it's often for far less than the estimated value of the item—which makes it possible to find real bargains.
4. Place a bid. If the contents of the auction look interesting, click the button that says Sign Up to Bid Now.
5. Read the auction terms. Check the box that says you accept the terms, then click Continue.
6. Read the user agreement. When you are done, click Submit.

Once you see how quickly the live auctions appear on screen, it becomes clear that bidding during the actual auction can be impractical. After all, it might take an hour or more for the item you're actually interested in to roll by. Once it appears, you need to place that bid in a matter of seconds in order to register. (A high-speed DSL or cable modem connection to the Internet is pretty much a requirement here.)

You can place an absentee bid up to one hour before the live auction starts. When the auction starts, eBay calculates the absentee bids. If someone else places an absentee bid higher than yours, eBay places bids for you on a proxy basis until your maximum bid is reached, if necessary. When the live auction starts, the high absentee bid is shown as an Internet bid. Others participating in the live auction can then bid against your absentee bid—but if no one bids against your maximum bid, you win.

NOTE: *In order to participate in live auctions, your computer needs to have a central processing unit running at 350 MHz or higher, 64 MB of RAM, Windows 95 or later, and Internet Explorer 4.01 or Netscape Navigator 4.03 or later. You can use a 56K modem to connect to the Internet, but a cable modem or DSL connection is preferable.*

Often, sales end without any bids. Occasionally, someone who placed a proxy bid in advance turns out to be the winner. On other occasions, bidders in a real-world auction house such as Sotheby's compete against cyber-bidders like you for items. Even if you don't compete, it's exciting to watch the action, especially when bids climb high. It's even better when you see something you want and there are no bids or the current bids are within your price range.

Recognize and Avoid Dishonest Bidders

Some of the gunkier bidding problems on eBay have nothing to do with you. They are caused by dishonest bidders working alone or in collaboration. You can fight them by reporting them to eBay. You might not be able to win auctions they mess up, but you can learn to recognize such problems and avoid them in the future.

Bid Collaboration

In bid collaboration (also known as shill bidding), two or more people try to hike up the current high bid on an item to gain more money for the seller. Often, they are family members or close friends of the seller, and if the seller makes more money, they may get a cut.

In some instances, sellers have used secondary User IDs to artificially raise the level of bidding and/or the price of an item. Shill bidding is a risky practice. eBay will certainly throw you out if you are found to have done it yourself. You should also report any bidders you expect of placing shill bids to eBay.

Bid Shielding

Two people working together can influence the bidding on an auction in many ways. Usually, they try to make the bidding go up to higher levels than it would otherwise. But they aren't always trying to win the auction themselves; in fact, they might be trying to *lose* it.

NOTE: Bid shielding and other types of transaction interference are described by eBay at **http:// pages.ebay.com/help/confidence/programs-investigations.html**.

In bid shielding, two people conspire to bid on something. One bids a very low amount, such as $20. The other bids a very high amount, such as $500. The high bid is placed in the hope of scaring away other potential bidders; typically, the high bid is a far higher bid than anyone would reasonably place on the item. At the last moment, the high bid is retracted and the low bid wins. Since complaints will be received and the person placing the high bid will probably be suspended from bidding again, the User ID used in placing the high bid is probably a unique one that is probably used only for the purpose of placing the high bid.

Bid Siphoning

Bid siphoning involves illegal interference by an eBay seller. It takes place when someone e-mails the bidders in an auction, asking them to bid on or buy something else. Sometimes, the sender tries to steer you to something similar for a bargain price. Or, after you win an auction, someone makes an offer to purchase the item you just won.

Often, the siphoners urge you to complete the deal off eBay. This, by itself, should tell you that the approach is suspicious: the person making the approach may be using a hijacked eBay account and intends to defraud you of your money. You don't need to respond to any of these e-mails, but you shouldn't be threatening or abusive when you respond to them, either. Just suggest that the person try to sell you the item on a Buy It Now or auction basis so you can take advantage of eBay's auction safeguards.

Summing Up

You need to be a smart bidder to compete successfully with the many new and experienced members of eBay. This means you really need to take the time to degunk your bidding strategies as I have outlined in this chapter. Don't get stuck in a rut, shopping the same kinds of sales and bidding the same way all the time. You can vary the types of sales you try, and you can adjust the types of bidding practices to match the types of sales in which you participate.

Perhaps the most critical way to be a better and more successful bidder/shopper on eBay is to do your homework. Know the value of what you sell by looking it up, either on eBay or in the many price guides that are available both online and in book and antique stores. Determine the maximum reasonable amount you are willing to pay for any given item, and bid only up to that amount. When the bidding goes higher than your limit, "fold your cards" and wait for another item to go online rather than getting caught up in a costly bidding war.

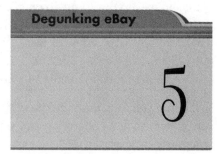

5

Degunking Your Communications

Degunking Checklist:

√ Communicate more effectively with buyers and sellers to improve your chances of winning bids and to build a good reputation.

√ Learn how to reduce unsolicited e-mail related to eBay.

√ Find archived eBay workshops to improve your knowledge base.

√ Turn to the Answer Center for help.

√ Search the discussion boards for answers to specific questions.

√ Contact eBay with complaints or questions.

√ Keep in touch with eBay auctions you're following.

√ Learn how to bid on and follow auctions with your cell phone or other wireless device.

Just about everything you do on eBay involves communication of one sort or other. It's easy to forget that you're dealing with real, live human beings when you post sales online or place a bid. Instead, you think you're only filling out a form and posting files on a server. eBay has lots of forms, and many servers filled with data, but the site works because of people.

The better you can communicate with the people you meet on eBay, the better your success will be at buying and selling. On eBay, you connect with other individuals on many levels. At the transaction level, you communicate through auction descriptions. You also communicate when you ask questions, work out shipping and payment arrangements, leave feedback, or post messages in the auction site's community forums. At every stage, you need to be clear and maintain a professional demeanor. Good communication involves anticipating what buyers and sellers need to know, and it involves quick and clear answers to questions. This chapter presents some tips for degunking the communication process with other eBay members so you can buy and sell more successfully.

Streamline Your E-Mail

Once I placed a bid in a sale and the sale ended without anything else happening. I didn't get an e-mail message saying I had been outbid or I had won. It wasn't until several days later that I realized my e-mail inbox was full and I couldn't receive *any* e-mail at that address. (Obviously, it wasn't my *primary* e-mail address or I would have checked it sooner.) As it happens, I didn't win the auction, but I shudder to think what could have happened if I had. The seller would try to reach me; the e-mail message would bounce back; the seller would think I had bid fraudulently; I would not only miss the chance to pay for the item I wanted, but I would get negative feedback on top of it.

E-mail management is an essential part of using eBay effectively. If you adjust your preferences so you don't get so many unwanted notices from eBay, you'll keep your inbox less crowded and save some time you might otherwise spend reading unwanted messages. If you learn where to look for information in eBay's voluminous community areas and where the best places are to turn for help and support, you'll develop an instant source of advice and support in case you run into problems with a transaction. In this chapter, you'll learn how to use eBay's many options for communicating with other buyers and sellers and with the auction site itself.

TIP: For sellers, one aspect of effective communication is knowing how to market to the kinds of individuals who are likely to bid on what you have to sell. Collectors have their own "lingo" that's specific to the objects they collect, and if you want to sell such collectibles, you need to know about silverplate versus sterling silver, for instance. If you are selling a video game, use language that is going to attract young people. If you are selling a set of incontinence pads, tailor your language to appeal to the older crowd. See Chapter 9 for more.

Reduce Junk E-Mail

Junk e-mail is an unfortunate part of just about everything you want to do on the Internet. It's part of eBay, too, but the problem is not as great as on a lot of other e-commerce Web sites. eBay's internal communication system keeps the unwanted traffic to a minimum. But occasionally you'll get e-mail you don't want, from either eBay or other sources.

Use Your E-Mail Address Sparingly

When I first signed up for an account with eBay in the mid-1990s, I used my e-mail address as my User ID. At first, I didn't run into any problems. But after a year or two, I began to receive a steady stream of spam. Soon, I was awash in as much spam as the visitors to the café in the original Monty Python comedy sketch that immortalized the famous "Spam spam spam…" song.

The problem, of course, is that e-mail marketers who flood the worldwide network with spam use special programs (web crawlers, or "spiders") that scour the Internet for e-mail addresses that are openly displayed in the body of Web pages. When an e-mail address was used as an identifier to bid on an auction or put up something for sale, that address was "harvested" and added to spam mailing lists. Those who used a real e-mail address as a User ID were eventually prohibited from doing so and told to choose something else. Since then, eBay prohibits the use of an e-mail address as a User ID. The same rule applies: Don't put your e-mail address in the body of an auction description or an About Me page you create.

Instead, include a statement like this:

```
E-mail me for more information.
```

The word *me* in the preceding statement is a *mailto* hyperlink: it links to an e-mail address. Clicking on the link causes the user's e-mail program to open with the e-mail address in the To: line.

TIP: One way to avoid spammers from harvesting your e-mail address is to create a graphics interchange format (GIF) image that consists of your e-mail address. The viewer sees the address, but because it is not body text within the Web page, a program that scans the page won't recognize it as such. Another option: register for

*services using a "disposable" e-mail address: one you can use and then cancel when it
is overrun with spam. And yet another option: sign up for a service that filters out
spam before it reaches your inbox, such as SpamCop (www.spamcop.com).*

Change Your E-Mail Preferences

If you never change your e-mail preferences and continually bid, buy, or sell on
eBay with the default settings, you'll receive the same set of e-mail messages
over and over: "Your bid has been received," "You have been outbid," or "Congratulations! You're the winner!" If you don't want to receive so many e-mail
messages from eBay, you don't have to. You can easily get rid of this clutter. Just
change your notification preferences by following these steps:

1. Click My eBay in the eBay toolbar and sign in with your User ID if
    prompted to do so. Your My eBay page appears.

2. In the My Account section of My eBay Views on the left-hand side of the
    page, click eBay Preferences. The eBay preferences appear in the main
    display area of My eBay (see Figure 5-1).

3. Click view/change next to Notification Preferences in the eBay Preferences
    section near the top of the page.

4. Log in with your User ID and password if you are prompted to do so.

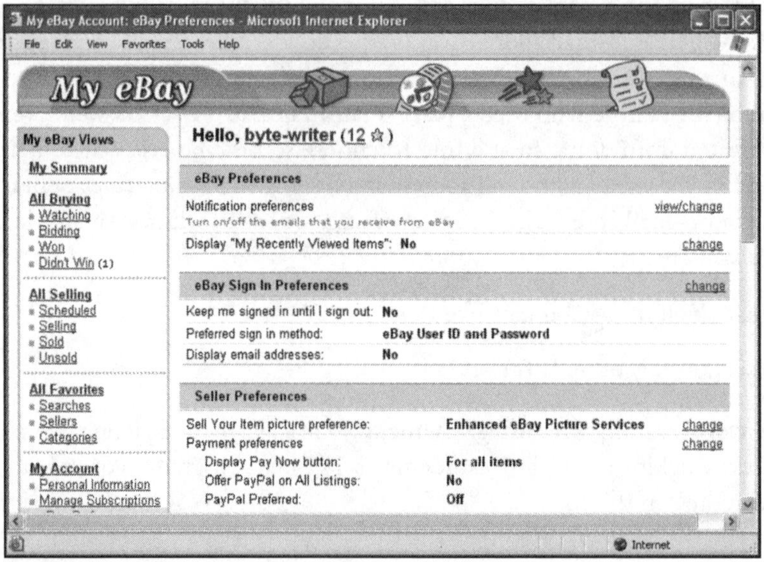

Figure 5-1
Change or cut back on the e-mails you receive using this area of your My
eBay page.

TIP: The need to log in, by the way, is another preference you can change; you can tell eBay to keep you logged in as long as you are on the site so you aren't continually prompted to enter your password when you perform functions such as this.

---

5.   Scroll down to the Transaction Emails area and review the different types of e-mail messages eBay can send you. If there are any types of e-mails you don't want to receive, uncheck the check box for that item.

6.   Click Save Changes to add the new settings to your My eBay page.

If you have been getting phone calls about special events like Free Listing Days or unsolicited e-mail from eBay about such events, scroll down to the Other Contacts section at the bottom of the preferences page. Uncheck eBay Telemarketing or eBay Direct Mail. Also make sure the eBay Email item in the preceding section, Legal and Other Emails, is unchecked.

By default, the other options are typically checked:

√   Bid notice: You are notified when eBay receives a bid you place.

√   Outbid notice: You are notified when you are outbid.

√   Daily status: If you have set up a watch list of items you want eBay to watch for, eBay sends you a list of any items whose sales will end within 36 hours.

√   Listing Confirmation: When you create a sales listing, you receive a notification e-mail.

√   End of auction notice: You receive e-mail messages from eBay when a listing ends and you are not the winner and when one of the sales you are conducting ends.

Most of these notifications are useful, but you don't always need to receive an e-mail message when you have placed a bid or when you have been outbid. If you revisit a sale on a regular basis, you can check the status of your bid for yourself.

Be Professional

One aspect of communicating effectively on eBay is simply remembering that you may be using the site for months or years at a time. The more courteous and professional you are with your comments toward other members, the better your feedback rating will be. Simply responding to people quickly and making sure you either send in a check for payment or ship something out for delivery as quickly as possible will earn you positive feedback. A higher feedback rating will increase your business as a seller and improve the way sellers respond to you when you want to buy from them.

Simply being polite and patient with people is only common sense. So why am I mentioning it? Because if you are in business on eBay as a seller, or if you are currently a buyer and are planning to go into business, your comments are important. They might stay out there for everyone to see in eBay's discussion forums and chat rooms for weeks or months at a time. (If you make a remark in one of eBay's workshops, your comments will be archived along with the rest of the workshop for a year or more.)

If you sell on eBay, you might have to change the way you normally behave with other people. If a buyer makes what you think is an unreasonable complaint or demands a refund for some reason, you might just have to give it out rather than start a fight. The key is to provide good customer service and maintain your positive feedback rating over the long haul. A couple of setbacks with customers might irritate you, but write them off and move on so you can keep the "big picture" in mind.

GunkBuster's Notebook: Quick Responses Pay Off

eBay seller Phyllis O'Reilly (User ID: philopaint) maintains a high level of customer service and is proud of all the thank-you notes she receives from her customers. She likes making money, but she also likes making personal connections on eBay. And she knows that the more effort she puts out to communicate with her customers, the better her business will be.

"I may receive thank-you notes for two reasons," she comments. "I always reply right away and also mail as soon as I'm paid. I seldom wait for personal checks to clear because I have never received a bad check yet. I respond to a winning bidder with the following letter instead of having eBay bill the person:

"Congratulations for being the winner of the bidding on my _____ . The shipping to_____ is $_____ for a total of $_____.

"I will accept PayPal, a money order, or personal check. I will cheerfully refund your money if you are not happy with the purchase.

"Payment may be sent to:

"Phyllis O'Reilly

"[address follows]

"Thank you.

"Phyllis

"Also, if I know something about the piece's history, I mention that too.

"I handle three to five pieces each week, and I find that unidentified pieces, especially pottery and glass and costume jewelry, are difficult to sell, so I try to identify them.

"I sold a school desk and a buyer came from Massachusetts to New Jersey because the desk had been manufactured by his grandfather. When I sold an item to a woman in Devon, England, I told her how much I liked it when I visited there and she sent me pictures. Another lady thanked me for china because she was having a large family reunion and wanted to surprise them by serving on china with the same pattern her grandmother used. I am amazed at how honest and friendly people are."

If You Don't See It, Ask for It

Part of good communication is about making sure you have all the information you need so you don't run into problems and confusion after you place a bid or after you win an auction or make a purchase.

Don't be afraid to ask for what you need. If you don't see enough photos in an auction description, ask for them. If you have questions about the condition of an item, about whether something can be shipped by UPS rather than the USPS, or whether the color you see on the auction page is really red or actually pink, you need to ask. Questions prevent disagreements, but they also tell you something about the responsiveness of a seller. If the seller gets back to you immediately with a full and courteous response, this indicates that the seller is probably one who can be trusted. If the seller takes days to respond and is offhand or uncooperative, you might want to think twice about dealing with them.

TIP: Another thing you can ask for is feedback. Feedback numbers count on eBay. Buyers and sellers who have positive feedback in the hundreds or even the thousands are trusted more than those with relatively low feedback rates. Most buyers and sellers need to be reminded to send in feedback. You shouldn't be reluctant to do this. If a week passes after the end of a transaction and the other party hasn't yet left feedback for you, ask them to do so.

Use eBay's Community Area

The eBay Community area is among the best resources on the auction site. The more you visit it and the more you exchange information with other buyers and sellers, the smarter you'll be. The fact that there's a wealth of information in the community area is one of its assets. But this can also make specific information hard to find.

Not only that, but some members of the community have been participating for years. Participants of longstanding forums like the eBay Café have developed their own language, their way of determining who's "cool" and knowledgeable and who's not. Certain members with User IDs like **bobal** and **Deadbeat** have a reputation for being knowledgeable and helpful—often, even more available and helpful than eBay's staff members. You can easily appear naïve if you make the wrong step. On the other hand, if you do things right, you can develop an ongoing means of getting questions answered and problems solved.

Find the eBay Workshop You Need

Workshops are interactive forums that are often held by experienced eBay sellers. They are among the best places to learn how to perform basic tasks on eBay. Best of all, you don't have to be present at your computer while the workshop is actually going on to benefit from them. That's because the workshop proceedings are archived—for a year, at least. One way to take your eBay experience to a new level is to attend workshops that address topics you need to learn about. If you can't attend a live workshop, call up the record of an archived session.

The problem is that it's not as easy to find eBay workshops as it used to be. Not so long ago, eBay archived every single workshop that has ever been held on the site. Earlier in 2004, eBay cut back on its publicly accessible archives; you could only find links to workshops that had been held earlier that year, 2004. The hundreds of useful workshops held in 2003, 2002, and previous years weren't accessible on the main Workshops page (**http://pages.ebay.com/community/workshopcalendar/current.html**). Many of the workshop topics are timeless: they don't go out of style, and taking digital photographs, opening an eBay Store, and other topics are always of value.

Luckily, eBay is not the only place that archives its old workshops. The voluminous servers over at Google hold records of them as well. It takes a little advanced searching to find workshops that are from previous years, but you *can* find them:

1. Go to the Google home page (**www.google.com**) and click Advanced Search, or go directly to the Advanced Search form at **www.google.com/ advanced_search?hl=en**.

2. In the Find Results boxes at the top of the form, enter the "eBay Workshop" in the box labeled "with all of the words."

3. In the box labeled "domain," enter "forums.ebay.com" and leave "Only" in the box just before the phrase "return results from the site or domain." (See Figure 5-2 for an example.)

4. Click Google Search.

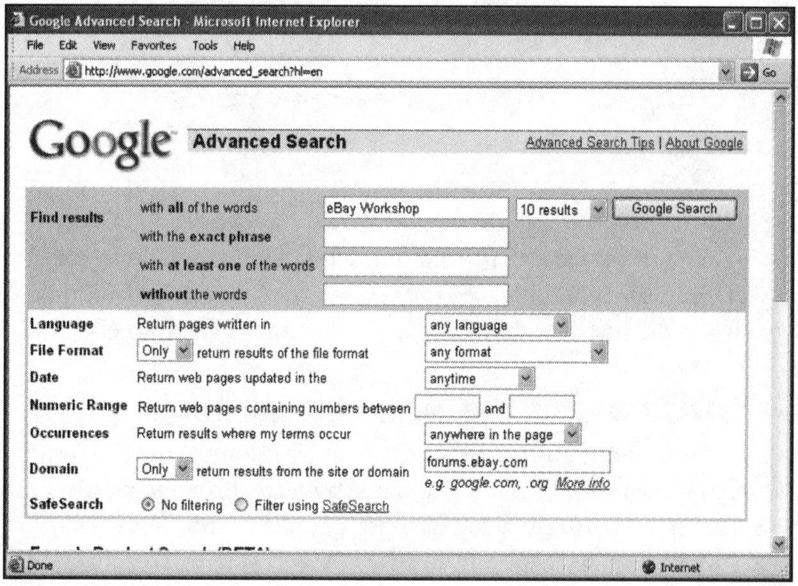

Figure 5-2
Search for older archived workshops using Google's Advanced Search page.

TIP: If you want to find workshops from a particular year, enter the date in this form: /02, /01, or /00. That's because each search result contains the date of the workshop in a form such as this: 03/22/01. You'll come up with a variety of workshops that contain the date in the day or month position, but you'll come up with a number of results from the year you want, too.

When the search results appear, you'll have to do some scrolling to find the older ones that aren't archived on eBay's site. Table 5-1 provides some examples of older workshops I came up with that seem as if they still have value, along with the link to each one (they are still archived on eBay, but you just can't find links to them for some reason).

Table 5-1 Older eBay Workshops

Workshop	Date	URL
Using eBay Toolbar	9/17/03	http://forums.ebay.com/db2/ thread.jsp?forum=93&thread=1222766 &modifed=20030917151538& ssPageName=CMDV:IC1171
eBay Shopping, Safely and Securely	10/14/03	http://forums.ebay.com/db2/ thread.jsp?forum=93&thread=1222781 &modifed=20031014154649& ssPageName=CMDV:IC1170
Wholesale Lots	1/16/03	http://forums.ebay.com/db2/ thread.jsp?forum=93&thread=32918 &modified=1042761995000
Seller Business Development	7/31/02	http://forums.ebay.com/db2/ thread.jsp?forum=93&thread=32877 &start=80&msRange=40

Get in the habit of looking through eBay's listings of upcoming workshops and making note of the ones that seem of interest. The ones held by expert members are especially good because they present real-world tips from people who actually use the site on a daily basis as clients rather than from eBay's own staff.

Get Answers in the Answer Center

When I think about posting messages on eBay, I think about discussion boards and well-known social venues like the eBay Café. I tend to overlook the Answer Center, and I think a lot of other people do, too. This is precisely the reason why you *should* use the Answer Center: you're more likely to get an answer there, and get an answer quickly, than in other locations that are crowded with activity. Not only that, but you can also potentially get answers from half a dozen or more different eBay users. That's due to the format of the Answer Center, which is organized differently than other parts of the eBay community.

Search for Answers on the Discussion Boards

The discussion boards are the best-known parts of the eBay community, and you should visit them when you have a question or are encountering a specific problem with a transaction. There's a simple way to get more out of them: take advantage of the search box that appears when you click the Search button. It can be found at the bottom of virtually every discussion board page (see Figure 5-3).

The search box lets you search all of the comments made on the board you are visiting, at least in the past seven days. You can search only one board at a time, so

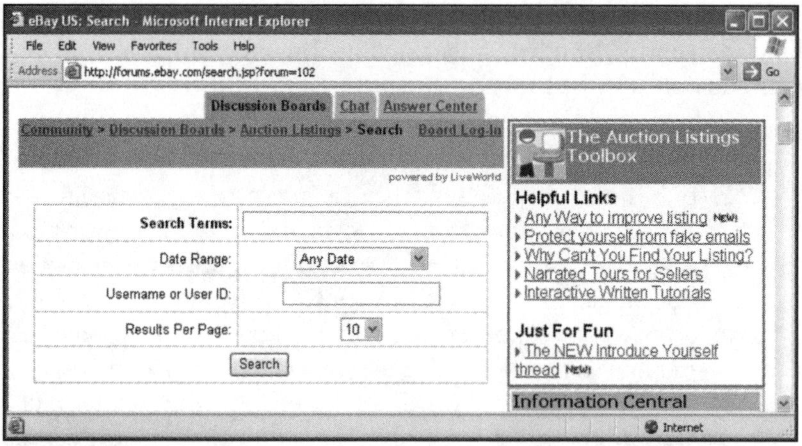

Figure 5-3
Before you post a question, do a search to see if it's already been answered.

it's important to scan the lists of boards on the Community: Discussion Boards page (**http://pages.ebay.com/community/boards/index.html**) to make sure you've picked the right forum and aren't overlooking a better one.

E-Mail the "Pinks"

Suppose you're really fed up and disgusted with something you see on eBay. (It happens.) You can't believe that eBay suddenly decided to remove the Search button from its navigation bar after having it in the same predictable place for many years, for example. Naturally, you think to yourself, "Is someone from eBay actually going to get back to me? Are they going to get back to me this week, or this month?" You wonder, "Is this really going to do any good?" Gradually, you talk yourself out of trying to contact eBay, and you remain unhappy.

Don't give up: try to contact eBay using one of the following approaches:

√ Click Live Help on the eBay home page. A chat window opens, and you can use it to type a message to someone at eBay.

√ Click Help in the navigation bar, then click Contact Us. A set of interactive boxes appears; choose your topic from the lists shown and click Continue. You'll be directed to either the Live Help chat window or a box that lets you submit a question to eBay.

√ If you see a message from one of the "pinks" (in other words, an eBay staffer, whose comments are highlighted in pink), either in a workshop or on one of the discussion boards or chat areas, e-mail the person.

The last option in the list should be pursued only if everything else fails. Approaching someone out of the blue in a discussion forum with a question that is obviously off topic may irritate them. You might be ignored, or you might be directed to one of the other contact options. But there's a chance you might get your question answered, too.

GunkBuster's Notebook: Be Honest or Get Caught!

My publisher relayed this story to me. Shortly after the first Degunking book came off press *(Degunking Windows)* and before the book was available for sale, a few copies appeared on eBay auctions. The publisher thought, "Wow, those eBay sellers work really fast." After looking into the matter, the publisher discovered that some enterprising fellows were engaging in the practice of selling books that were sent for review purposes only. (It's a standard practice in publishing to send out free review copies that should never be sold by booksellers.) The folks at the review site were making a tidy profit by selling books they would receive for free under the pretext that they would be reviewing them. Other publishers caught on to this and the business got a lot of bad press as a result. Stealing from people who work in the media is never a good idea.

Always keep in mind that eBay is a very public place with a very watchful user community, and if you do something you shouldn't be doing, you'll likely get caught by a number of people.

Search the eBay Radio Archives

eBay Radio is a regular Webcast that eBay holds each Tuesday from 11:00 A.M. to 1:00 P.M. Pacific Time. Occasionally, the Webcast includes good content, but to hear it, you need to wade through lots of audio gunk: small talk and lots of commercials.

Luckily, you can degunk eBay Radio by accessing its archive page, **www.wsradio.com/ebayarchive/ebayarchive.htm,** shown in Figure 5-4. It's especially easy to find something in the archives because they are organized either by date or by topic.

There are good interviews with buyers and sellers, as well as other experts, on shipping and wrapping, finding inventory to sell, and other useful topics. When you begin to play a broadcast, skip past the first two or three minutes, however; the interviews and features don't start until then.

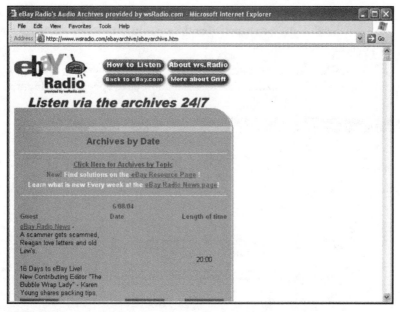

Figure 5-4
Skip past the fluff to find the content you want on eBay Radio.

Keep Yourself from Being Outbid

Using the right communication tools will help you win more auctions. Sometimes, simply being in the right place at the right time is the key to winning auctions on eBay. But you can't be expected to be in front of your computer all the time. If you are a seller, you need to be available to answer questions; you naturally want to check in on your sales to see if they have attracted any bids or buyers. When you shop on eBay, you want to know if you have been outbid or if you have won an auction, especially when you're on the road. These days, it's easier than ever to find access to the Internet, whether you're in a hotel, a public library, or a coffee shop. But it's even more convenient to check in with your cell phone or PDA, as described in the following sections.

Sign Up for Wireless Alerts

By default, eBay notifies you by e-mail when you have been outbid on an item. But you can't always be at your computer when a sale ends. Chances are, though, that even if you aren't at your computer, you have your cell phone with you. If the cell phone can send and receive e-mail messages, you can configure it to receive "outbid" messages from eBay:

1. Go to your My eBay page, and go to the Notification Preferences page as described earlier in this chapter (see the steps in the section "Change Your E-Mail Preferences").

2. Click <u>Add or change notification services</u> under the heading Notification Methods. The Notification Services Selection page appears (see Figure 5-5).

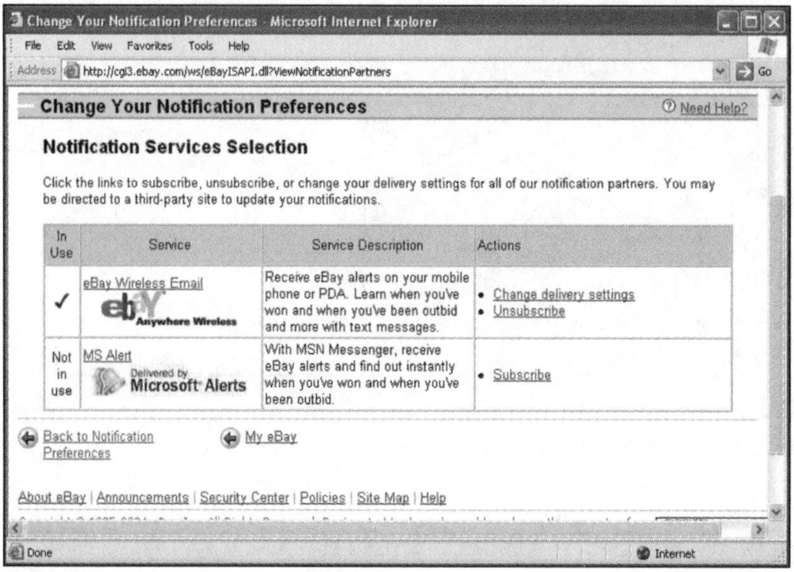

Figure 5-5
You can customize the way you want eBay to notify you on this page.

3. Click <u>eBay Wireless Email</u>, and sign in if prompted to do so.

4. When the eBay Wireless Email page appears, check the box next to Send wireless email alerts to the address below, and enter your wireless email address in the box provided.

5. Click Save Changes.

Make sure the e-mail address you enter is one you can access from your cell phone. You might need to configure your e-mail address with the help of your cell phone provider. There will probably be an additional charge for Internet and e-mail access via your cell phone, but most cell phone providers offer free text messaging these days.

Bid with Your Wireless Device

Suppose you get an e-mail message from eBay that tells you you've been out-bid and the auction you've been following will end in 10 minutes. What do you do? You whip out your cell phone or PDA and place a bid with your handheld device! You will need an account with a wireless provider to do this; you have to pay extra to access the Internet and get e-mail on your phone. (I pay an extra $7.95 per month to AT&T Wireless for this privilege.) You then have to purchase a phone that is capable of browsing the Web and sending and receiving e-mail. You can see some examples of how the eBay data looks on the Bonfire Media site (**http://bonfiremedia.com/ ebayserver/servlet/Controller?Command=ws_products_attws**), shown in Figure 5-6 (though the actual screens look far better on my cell phone).

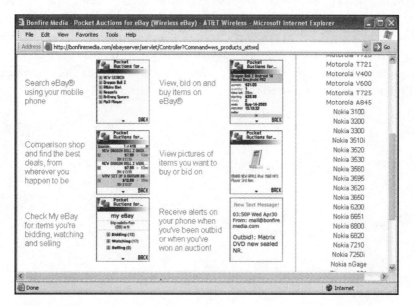

Figure 5-6
You can surf eBay and place bids from your wireless device.

When you see the small screens and read a description in a book like this, you don't really see how time consuming the actual process is. First, you need to connect to the Internet. On my phone, this can take a matter of a few seconds—or, it can be impossible, depending on your location. Then, you have to find eBay, and then, you have to either type the item number or do a search for it. If your phone doesn't have a slick keyboard like my Nokia, it can be very laborious. This is a much slower process than simply surfing the Web from your home computer. It can be done, and if you have no other way to get online and place a bid on eBay, you should do it. But give yourself plenty of time to actually locate the item you want and place the bid; be sure to give yourself more than a few minutes before the end of the auction.

Summing Up

eBay's basic communications system works well. By contacting other buyers and sellers using the internal message system rather than the public Internet, you do maintain your privacy. Once you establish contact with others, you can then switch to your "real" e-mail accounts for subsequent communications. But as with anything, you can use the set of tools the service gives you, or you can take them a step further so you can get ahead of the crowd. You'll improve the quality of your eBay experience by guarding your e-mail address, by responding quickly and clearly to questions, and by asking questions so you know exactly what to expect when you bid on or buy something. When you need specific answers, learn to take advantage of eBay's community venues, including the workshops and the Answer Center. And to improve your chances of winning, configure My eBay's preferences to receive wireless alerts so you can respond quickly if you need to.

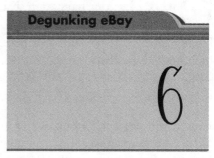

6

Improving Your Image on eBay

Degunking Checklist:

√ Boost your feedback rating so you can build a good reputation that will attract more business.

√ Respond to negative feedback comments that can hurt your reputation and discourage potential customers.

√ Create a free About Me page that supports your eBay buying and selling activities.

√ Construct a Web site that gives customers another way to do business with you.

√ Link your current eBay sales to your Web pages.

√ Advertise your sales to help potential buyers find them more easily.

√ Attain the prestigious eBay PowerSeller distinction and gain more bidders and buyers.

√ Supplement your eBay sales by becoming a Trading Assistant for other members.

On eBay, it's your reputation that counts. The stronger the level of trust that other members have in you, the more success you'll have in both buying and selling. For instance, there is a direct correlation between having a high positive feedback rating and generating a perception that you give outstanding customer service and write accurate descriptions. This, in turn, leads to your success in selling what you have to offer.

Even if you don't sell on eBay, you need to maintain a good feedback rating. You need a certain feedback number in order to post messages, open eBay Stores, and in some cases, place bids. Sellers who have been burned by untrustworthy buyers sometimes specify that they won't sell to buyers with feedback ratings of zero or less (in other words, a negative feedback rating). No matter what endeavors you are pursuing on eBay, your goal is to boost your reputation. That is what you will accomplish by following the degunking tips described in this chapter.

Boost Your Feedback Rating

The number that represents the amount of money you either save or make on eBay is important. But there is another number—the one that actually appears next to your User ID and that follows you everywhere you go on eBay —that has a direct impact on how well you do, and that is your feedback rating. If it hovers near zero or is negative, or if it is high but includes neutral or negative comments, potential customers may be skeptical of doing business with you. Luckily, there is a lot you can do to impact your feedback number. You'll improve your chances of success on eBay by taking steps to clean up your feedback and boost your rating.

NOTE: *Neutral feedback is technically neither positive nor negative. Someone might leave you neutral feedback if you are slow to respond to e-mails or take several weeks to ship out what they have purchased from you. But the bottom line is that neutral feedback is considered a negative by most eBay members.*

Clean Up That Gunky Negative Feedback

You might assume that changing your User ID on eBay, which you can do at any time, would be a good way to make a fresh start. In fact, your feedback comments follow you and appear next to your new User ID (unless you have chosen to hide the comments, as described next). This does not, however, mean that feedback is permanent and unerasable. You can actually "adjust" feedback in several ways:

√   You can respond to feedback comments that have been left about you.

√   You can dispute feedback and negotiate to have it removed.

√   You can conceal your feedback comments by making them "private."

It pays to become familiar with these and other feedback "adjustment" options that can be accessed from the Feedback Forum page (**http://pages.ebay.com/ services/forum/feedback.html**, shown in Figure 6-1). Don't leave negative or neutral comments sitting there in your feedback profile uncontested. It's not unusual for things go wrong in a transaction and for the other party to blame you, whether or not the difficulty was actually your fault. Respond with a clarification or turn to a mediator to iron out the problem. Your options are discussed in the sections that follow.

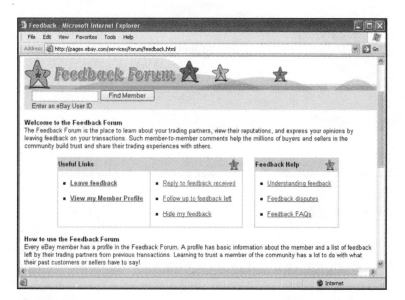

Figure 6-1
You can improve your eBay success rate by using the options in the Feedback Forum.

Responding to Feedback

You will have a more positive overall eBay experience if you treat your feedback comments like gold. Manage them, protect them, and "polish them up" when they get tarnished. Even a handful of negative comments can hurt your reputation. If you feel a response or clarification is needed to put comments someone has left about you in a more flattering context, follow these steps:

1.   Click My eBay in the eBay navigation bar.

2.   Sign in with your User ID and password if prompted to do so.

3. Click Feedback under the My Account heading on the left side of the page.

4. Click Go to Feedback Forum at the top of the page.

5. When the Feedback Forum page appears, click Reply to Feedback Left. A page appears with your feedback comments on it. The difference between this list and the list in My eBay is the link Reply that appears on the right next to each comment (see Figure 6-2).

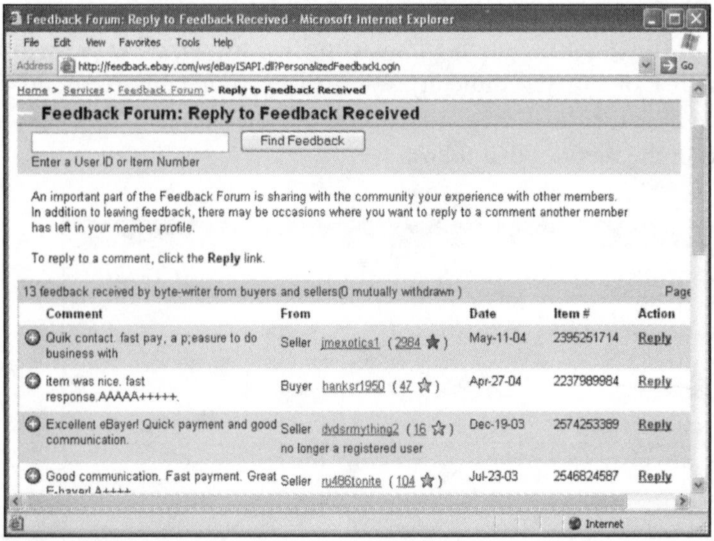

Figure 6-2
By replying to feedback, you clarify situations for members who may be deciding whether or not to do business with you in the future.

6. Click Reply next to one of the comments. When the Reply to Feedback Received page appears, enter your comment in the box provided (you have an 80-character limit).

7. Click Leave Reply.

Once you have replied, your response appears next to the original feedback. For example, someone complains that an item arrived late and you point out that the delivery person left it at the wrong address, even though the information on the label was correct. This response will appear on the Feedback Forum list.

Disputing Feedback

Sometimes, simply clarifying a feedback comment isn't enough. If someone attacks you unfairly in the Feedback Forum, you don't have to accept the blot on your record. For a moderate fee ($20) paid to a company called Square Trade, you can go into mediation in an attempt to get the comments "withdrawn" from the forum. This company, which conveys approval on commercial Web sites that conduct business in a reputable way, has partnered with eBay to provide feedback dispute resolution services. The process takes some work, but it can be worthwhile if you are trying to improve your percentage of positive comments.

NOTE: *For transactions that ended before February 9, 2004, SquareTrade has the ability to completely remove feedback from the Feedback Forum if the dispute resolution process finds that removal is justified, and if eBay concurs. For transactions that ended after that date, SquareTrade can only "withdraw" the feedback. Withdrawal means the feedback is not counted in your feedback rating, but the comments do remain on your Feedback Forum list.*

Here's how it works:

1. Go to the SquareTrade Web site (**www.squaretrade.com**).

2. Click the eBay icon under Dispute Resolution.

3. Click the button labeled "How to Remove/Withdraw Feedback."

4. When the next page appears (see Figure 6-3), click the File a Case link and follow the instructions on subsequent pages.

The SquareTrade system gives you access to professional mediators. They help you and the other party work out your disagreement (that is, if the other party responds). Then, if it's mutually agreeable, the comment can be withdrawn. If a

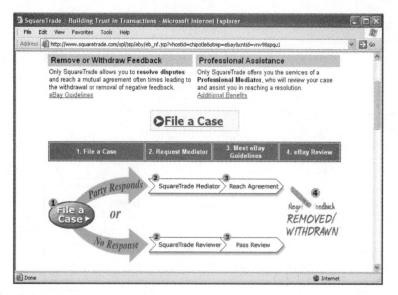

Figure 6-3
This online service mediates disputes between eBay members over feedback.

consensus can't be reached, the case is reviewed, which can still lead to your desired result of having the feedback withdrawn.

NOTE: *Any system has its abusers, and I've heard anecdotally that some eBay sellers count on buyers being lazy. They routinely cheat other members without worrying about receiving negative feedback because they are prepared to pay the $20 fee to go into mediation over those comments. They are hoping to get the comments removed by default because the people who were cheated don't want to bother with mediation or don't want to have anything to do with the offender. Don't let this happen to you: if you were really wronged but your feedback is disputed, take the time to go into mediation and explain your side of the story to SquareTrade.*

Making Your Feedback Private

The couple who for many years had the highest feedback rating on eBay, Jay and Marie Senese (User ID: onecentcds), now keep their feedback private. I'm not sure why: their feedback rating must be well over 100,000 at this point. But on their feedback profile page, shown in Figure 6-4, you don't see any individual comments.

I don't recommend making your feedback private. If anything, it'll make your eBay experience more gunky, not less. People will wonder what you have to hide.

I can think of only two reasons for doing this: you really do have some negative feedback you want to conceal, or you want to bid on eBay auctions and not have everyone be distracted by your extremely high feedback rating.

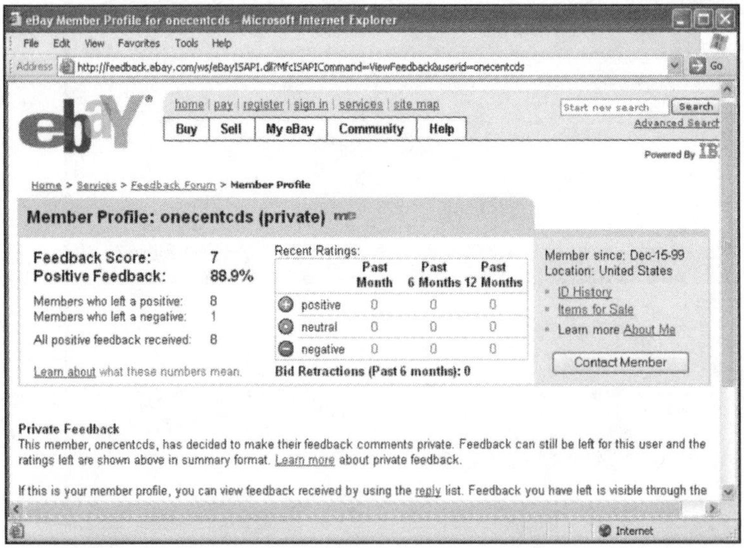

Figure 6-4
You can keep your feedback private until you clean up or respond to comments you don't like.

TIP: Comments you have left for other members are not written in stone. It's not unusual for something to happen after you submit your comments that will make you want to add details or clarify what you said earlier. Go to the Feedback Forum page, click Follow up on feedback left, sign in, and follow the steps shown on subsequent pages.

Fishing for More Positive Feedback

Think about it: When you scan a crowd of passersby on the street, you check out their physical attributes. When you are browsing eBay, you check out other people's feedback numbers. If you see someone with a feedback rating of 10, you react one way. If you see someone with a feedback rating of 1,210, you give that person a little more attention. And what if the member with the User ID **theblueox**, who has a feedback rating at this writing of 28,724, bids on one of your items or makes a comment on a discussion board?

The point is that feedback gets your attention. It's really good to keep your positive feedback above, say, 95 percent and to work toward the goal of eventually building up a feedback rating into the hundreds or even the thousands. Your prize will be that people will be eager to buy from you and that sellers will also feel good about doing business with you.

There are many actions you can take to build up positive feedback. Whether you are buying or selling, you should follow through by behaving professionally during all phases of a transaction. You respond to e-mails quickly; you pay quickly; you ship quickly; you pack carefully.

NOTE: In reality, eBay users who have User IDs with high feedback ratings usually employ a separate User ID for buying or message board posting so they can go incognito. If they bid on something, it's bound to attract attention and will probably drive up the bidding.

GunkBuster's Notebook: Automate Your Feedback

Once you have started a business on eBay, it gets more difficult to take the time to leave feedback. Suppose you have suddenly had a frenzy of activity and let 30 or 40 transactions pile up without leaving any comments. Can you spare a couple of hours to laboriously leave the same sorts of comments, one after another? If the answer is no, there's still a way you can avoid the ill will generated by neglecting to leave feedback.

As you might expect, software is available for automating the process of leaving or reviewing feedback. Amherst Robots offers a variety of programs (called, not surprisingly, *robots*) that automatically gather information or leave information of one sort or another on eBay.

NOTE: *Amherst Robots has a complicated way of charging for some of its services. Rather than simply receiving a bill for a dollar amount, you purchase a certain number of credits. You then apply the credit to the use of feedback or other software. Find out more about the credit system at http://bin.vrane.com/cart/items.htm.*

Build Credibility with Web Pages

In any business, public relations plays an important role. This also applies to business done on eBay. Whether you are buying or selling, having an image as a knowledgeable and reputable professional will help your sales. After you build up some positive feedback, another option is to create a Web page related to you or to your area of interest. eBay gives all of its members a convenient (and free) way to do this through its About Me feature. You can also go a step further and create your own Web site to promote yourself and your eBay activities.

Craft an About Me Page

eBay isn't just a marketplace. It's also a Web host: a service that gives individuals space on Web servers where they can publish content. Much of that content is in the form of auction descriptions. Other content consists of About Me Web pages. An About Me page can be a simple description of who you are, what you do, and what you collect or sell.

If you want to increase your sales on eBay, or the number of bargains you find at auction, you need to put your About Me space to good use. Even if you have already created a straightforward profile page, consider taking it to the next level by adding content that improves your image among your fellow buyers and sellers:

√   *Show off your knowledge.* If you have written anything in your field, won any awards, or have any especially rare items, tell people about them. If you have been collecting for 20 years, tell how you got started. If you have been on eBay since 1995, tell what it was like in the early days. Do anything you can to impress people with your knowledge of your field.

√   *Hand out free advice.* Write an article that explains something about the items you buy and sell. If you can assemble a set of frequently asked questions (FAQs), this will help people. A short essay about how to identify or find what you buy and sell would also help. By providing useful information, you aren't just being generous, you're also helping to boost your own image.

√   *Show off your work.* If you are a creative artist or if you manufacture items, show off photos on your About Me page. This also has the benefit of showing people how skillful you are.

√   *Include resource links.* On an About Me page, you can publish a hyperlink to a business Web page if you have one—something you can't do in the body of an auction description. If you have created a full-fledged business Web site, you can use your About Me page as a sort of gateway that directs people to it. You can also provide links to an eBay Store if you have one.

An About Me page that promotes your knowledge, your business policies, and your shipping instructions or that provides useful information will generate interest among potential customers and build trust with existing ones. It will attract inquiries and make people bid or buy from you with more confidence. Pamela Glassel's About Me page (**http://members.ebay.com/ws2/ eBayISAPI.dll?ViewUserPage&userid=gramasattic**) directs visitors to her Grama's Attic Linens store (**www.gramasattic.net/catalog.htm**)—which, in turn, refers visitors back to her eBay sales. It's a type of synergy you should emulate: make your auctions, your About Me page, your eBay Store if you have one, and your business Web site provide customers with multiple ways to purchase from you. You get more coverage and you can use each outlet to publicize the others and attract customers to your wares.

Create a Business Web Site

A business Web site is one of the most effective ways to boost business on eBay. Customers get a strong message that you are serious about doing business online if you go through the time and effort required to create a Web site. They will be even more impressed if your Web site has features such as a catalog full of items for sale, an interactive shopping cart, or a checkout area where customers can pay with a credit card.

Include a Sales Catalog

Many businesses are integrating their Web site sales with their eBay auctions. They might use their auctions to unload excess inventory or special bargain merchandise, while they continue to feature their first-rate products on their Web site. Or they might offer items such as antiques and collectibles on eBay while selling less unique products on the Web. To find an e-commerce host, look for a service that provides you with the ability to create an online store, including a sales catalog, a shopping cart, and a way to securely process credit card payments.

Yahoo! Small Business (**http://smallbusiness.yahoo.com/merchant**) has a $39.95 per month starter pack. It includes a Catalog Manager tool that helps you manage your product inventory, sort items into distinct categories, and add as many as 50 sales attributes for each item. You can also track your available inventory so you know how many items you have in stock at any time. The Yahoo! merchant called OpticsPlanet.com (**www.opticsplanet.com**) has merchandise arranged in a variety of categories, including binoculars and telescopes, as shown in Figure 6-5.

Figure 6-5
An e-commerce Web site with a sales catalog can complement your eBay sales.

If you look on eBay for the User ID opticsplanet, you discover that this same organization is a PowerSeller with a feedback rating of 990 and an eBay Store, shown in Figure 6-6. The About the Seller section of the store contains links that direct the prospective customer back to the e-commerce Web site, thus providing the customer with additional products to consider, as well as an additional way to purchase them.

Provide Personal Details

The more people feel that they know you as a person, the more likely they are to buy from you and return to you as a repeat customer. It's a paradox of doing business on the Web: Although you may never meet the people you do business with face to face, you still need to build personal trust. A business Web site gives you plenty of room to talk about yourself and your significant others. Here are some things you should be sure to mention:

Figure 6-6
An eBay Store can link customers to an e-commerce Web site that's
located off eBay.

√   Any clubs or professional associations you belong to and any certifications
    you have. I know of at least one eBay seller who obtained certification as a
    professional auctioneer so she could successfully sell on eBay and off.

√   Awards or honors you have received that relate to your sales on eBay.

√   Examples of notable things you have bought or sold.

√   Quotes from satisfied customers. This might apply if you are a Trading
    Assistant, someone who has been certified by eBay to handle auction sales
    for other members.

TIP: *Even if you don't include a lot of personal details on your Web site, you can publish
a mission statement, a one- or two-sentence summary of your business goals. It can
give people the big picture of your company and how your eBay sales fit into your
overall objectives. Letting people know that eBay is only one way you sell online is
certain to boost your reputation.*

Add Contact Information

eBay is protective of its members' privacy, and contact information such as
addresses or phone numbers is prohibited in auction descriptions.

When your goal is to generate all or part of your income on eBay, however, you
have to be as open as possible with your contact information. You need to give

potential customers as many ways to contact you as possible. The more types of information you put online (fax number, phone, e-mail, cell IM, and eBay User ID), the easier it will be for them to send inquiries and make purchases from you. Be sure to list all available contact options in your eBay Store and your e-commerce Web site.

Link Your eBay Sales to Your Site

You might think that even if you sell already on an e-commerce Web site, your eBay sales are a separate matter. Not so! You can drive more potential customers to your eBay sales by providing links to them on your Web site. You have several options for making the two sales venues work together, and they are described next.

Make a Hyperlink

The simplest way to link your eBay sales to one of your Web pages is to create a hyperlink. Whenever you want to retrieve a list of your current sales on eBay, start up your Web browser and make sure the Address box is displayed in the browser toolbar. Then, do a search by seller:

1. Click Advanced Search just beneath the search box on virtually any eBay page.

2. When the eBay Search: Find Items page appears, click the Items by Seller link on the left-hand side.

3. When the By Seller page appears, type your own eBay User ID in the Enter Seller's User ID box, then click Search.

4. When the list of your current sales appears, copy the URL shown in the Address bar. This is likely to be a ridiculously long URL, like this:

   ```
   http://search.ebay.com/_WOQQnojsprZyQQnojsprZyQQpfidZOQQ

   sassZyouruserIDQQsofindtypeZ15QQsofocusZbsQQsorecordsperpage

   Z50QQsorecordsperpageZ50QQsosortorderZ1QQsosortpropertyZ1QQss

   pagenameZhQ3ahQ3aadvsearchQ3aUS
   ```

5. Select the URL and copy it to your clipboard. Click anywhere in the Address bar one time to highlight the URL and press Ctrl+C to copy it. Or scroll across the entire URL (be sure to get the whole thing) to highlight it so you can then copy it.

6. Open the Web page on which you want the link to appear. Make sure you are looking at the source HTML code for the page. You'll need to view the page in a text editor, a Web page editor, or a Web editor provided by your Web hosting service.

7. Position the link at the spot in the Web page where you want it to appear. It's a good idea to add an introductory phrase that explains what visitors will find when they click on the link, such as "Be sure to check out my sales on eBay." Paste the URL you copied just beneath this phrase. Be sure to create a hypertext link with the HREF tag, like this:

```
<A HREF=" http://search.ebay.com/_WOQQnojsprZyQQnojsprZy…"> Be

sure to check out my sales on eBay </a>
```

8. Save your Web page with the new link, and publish it to the Internet along with the rest of your Web site.

It's true that each one of your eBay sales has its own URL. But it's far less work to paste a link to your By Seller search page on eBay than it is to add separate links to each of the sales. The By Seller search will turn up links to all of your current sales on eBay. The downside is when they click on the URL, visitors are taken away from your Web site and instead go to eBay's search page. After they investigate your sales, the burden is on the shoppers to make the effort to return to your Web site so they can check out other items you have for sale or find out more about your business. It's not always a good idea to send visitors away from your Web site. If you do, make sure you have provided enough attractive and useful content so that they'll want to come back again.

Use the Editor Kit and Merchant Kit

Adding static links to your eBay sales is time consuming and inefficient. Every time a sale ends, you have to delete the link, and every time a new item goes online, you have to create a new link. It's preferable to install some software made available by eBay, the Editor Kit and the Merchant Kit. Each package automatically pulls a set of links to your current eBay sales and displays them on your Web page whenever the page is viewed. The Editor Kit gives you a simple list of auction titles and is a good choice if you create auction descriptions only occasionally and don't sell through Half.com or an eBay Store. The Merchant Kit is for sellers who hold auctions as well as fixed-price sales.

To use either package, you need to first become a member of eBay's affiliate program, Commission Junction (**http://pages.ebay.com/affilate**). This program is free to join, and it enables you to earn a little extra money. You earn five cents anytime someone clicks one of your eBay Store links or other links and ends up placing a bid on eBay or five dollars if they click on one of your links and subsequently register on eBay.

Becoming a Commission Junction member also gives you access to the Editor Kit and Merchant Kit. To start using the Editor Kit on your site, follow these steps:

1. Go to the program's home page (**http://pages.ebay.com/api/ editorkit.html**).

2. Click Get Editor Kit Now, and sign in with your User ID and password.

3. Click I Agree after reading the license agreement for the program.

4. Fill out the form on the Create Your Editor Kit page, then click preview. The next page presents you with a block of JavaScript code you copy and add to the page where you want your eBay sales links to appear.

For the Merchant Kit, go to **http://pages.ebay.com/merchantkit.html** and follow a similar set of steps.

TIP: You don't have to use the Editor Kit or Merchant Kit to display your sales on your Web page. If you already use services provided by Auction Relay (www.auctionrelay.com) or Auctioncentric (www.auctioncentric.com), you can use their tools for displaying eBay auction listings on your site.

Strive for PowerSeller Status

One of the most coveted icons that can appear next to an eBay member's User ID is the PowerSeller icon: a symbol that the member is a seller who has established a consistently high level of service toward his or her customers. eBay seller Kim King has the PowerSeller icon next to her User ID, along with several others (see Figure 6.7). Together, they suggest to a prospective buyer that she is someone who has been on eBay for a while and is someone who can be trusted.

How can you be so sure that a PowerSeller won't try to take advantage of you in some way? It's simple: A PowerSeller isn't just someone who sells a lot. Rather, it's someone who *needs* to treat buyers well in order to maintain this coveted status. PowerSellers have to meet the following rigorous requirements, among others:

√ Sell at least $1000 in gross monthly sales for three months.

√ Maintain a feedback rating of at least 100.

√ Maintain a 98 percent positive feedback rating.

√ Be an eBay seller for the last 90 days.

√ Sell a minimum of four monthly listings, on average, for the past three months.

TIP: You can find out all about the requirements of becoming a PowerSeller, as well as the many benefits for sellers, at http://pages.ebay.com/services/buyandsell/ welcome.html.

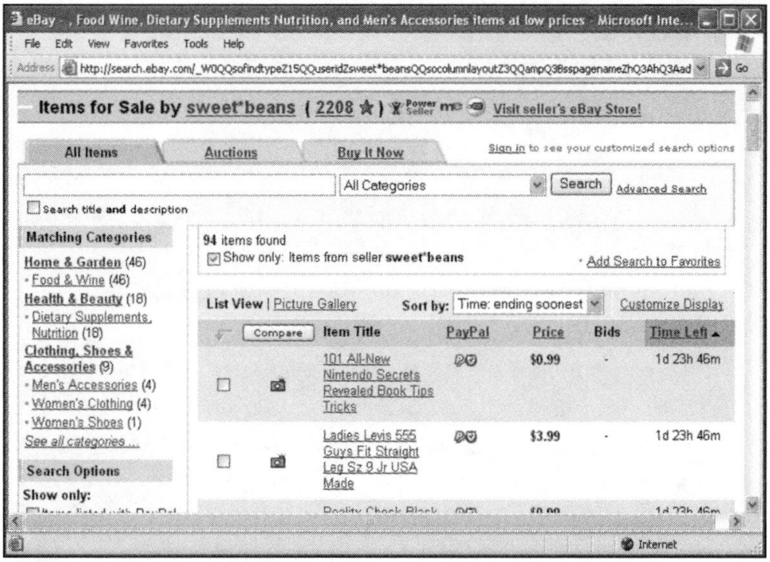

Figure 6-7
PowerSeller status is a reliable indicator that an eBay seller can be trusted.

There are some nice, tangible benefits to attaining PowerSeller status. You get merchandise with the eBay logo that you can give out to your customers as an extra perk. You are even eligible to apply for health insurance for yourself and your employees. And sellers who rank in the top four of the five tiers of PowerSeller status get priority customer service, as indicated by Table 6-1.

Table 6-1 Customer Support for PowerSellers

Tier	Gross Monthly Sales	E-mail Support	Toll-Free Phone	Access to an Account Manager
Bronze	$1000	Yes	No	No
Silver	$3000	Yes	Yes	No
Gold	$10,000	Yes	Yes	Yes
Platinum	$25,000	Yes	Yes	Yes
Titanium	$50,000	Yes	Yes	Yes

A PowerSeller isn't necessarily someone who has a huge feedback number; there are PowerSellers with feedbacks in the thousands and those with feedback ratings of a few hundred. The important thing is that PowerSellers sell often and maintain a very high feedback rating.

GunkBuster's Notebook: How to Become a PowerSeller

If you are a PowerSeller, you are certain to gain more attention from other buyers and sellers on eBay. If you want to really boost your sales, become a PowerSeller. It's not easy, and it takes a consistent level of work. How do you do it? Here are some suggestions:

√ Sell at least 100 things as quickly as you can.

√ Develop a system for responding to e-mail inquiries and shipping out your items quickly. If you need employees or assistants, hire them.

√ Work on a schedule. Sell on Sunday, e-mail on Monday, ship on Fridays, or something similar.

√ Use sales automation software (see Chapter 7 for suggestions).

You can't fill out a form or send eBay an e-mail request to become a PowerSeller. You need to meet the requirements and wait for eBay to invite you to enter the program. One of the most important things you need to do is come up with a system for finding inventory to sell consistently on the auction site. You can do this by striking up a relationship with a wholesale supplier of new merchandise such as figurines and ornaments that you can sell any time of year. But the most important thing is to respect the community values that eBay touts: treat people honestly and with respect, and respond in as timely a manner as you can.

Become a Trading Assistant

Another title that can make you look more knowledgeable to other eBay members is that of Trading Assistant (TA). A TA is someone who has been certified by eBay to sell for others on consignment. Lots of people have heard of eBay and have desirable household goods they could sell. But they don't want to go through the effort of taking photos, creating sales descriptions, and dealing with bidders or buyers. They want to "outsource" the work, and you can be the person they call upon.

NOTE: *You don't have to be a TA in order to sell for other people. Chances are good that, after you've been selling on eBay for a while, you'll be approached by friends and relatives who want you to sell things for them, too. You can be an "unofficial" eBay consignment seller and advertise by posting notices in your local supermarket or on message boards like the popular Craigslist (www.craigslist.org). In either case, you stand to make a few extra bucks and boost your feedback, too.*

If you become a Trading Assistant, you are listed in a directory with others who have been designated as consignment sellers on eBay (see Figure 6-8). The listings can be searched by geographic location or by area of specialty. The geographic location option is important: you'll want to be close in proximity to your customers so you can photograph their merchandise and take it to your home/office so you can ship it out.

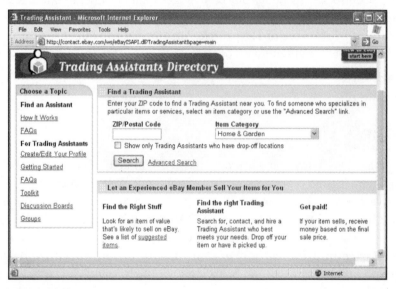

Figure 6-8
Prospective customers access this database of Trading Assistants for one in their area.

To become an eBay Trading Assistant, you need to meet several requirements:

√   You must have sold at least four items in the past 30 days.

√   You must have a feedback rating of at least 50.

√   You must maintain at least 97 percent positive feedback

As a Trading Assistant, your job isn't easy. In addition to your own sales activities on eBay, you need to inspect the items for sale, determine how much each one might sell for, prepare the auction description, take photos, handle the payment, prepare the item for shipping, and leave feedback. You also have to educate the people whose possessions you put up for sale. They might expect to receive a certain amount of money, in which case you have to explain to them how eBay works and make sure they know there's no guarantee of a specific sales amount.

If you meet the Trading Assistant requirements, you need to prepare a description of your eBay business or your buying and selling activities. You will need to explain your qualifications to sell a particular type of merchandise and spell out how much you're going to charge for your services. Different TAs charge different fees for sales; check the TAs who live in your own area to determine their fee schedule and charge something that seems competitive. Because eBay leaves it up to TAs to figure out their wages as independent contractors, you have to use your judgment. You might charge 20 to 30 percent of the final sales price or a flat listing fee of $10 per sale. Additionally, you might add on a fee to the buyer (a "buyer's premium") of 10 to 15 percent of the sales price. That way, some your fee is charged to the buyer and not all of it comes from the seller.

Summing Up

You'll be able to buy and sell more effectively on eBay if you can boost your reputation. A good reputation helps you stand out from the increasingly competitive crowd of experienced eBay users. In fact, so many of those users already have good reputations, PowerSeller icons, About Me pages, and other image enhancements that you have to create your own just to compete on a level playing field. It's relatively easy to establish a good reputation. Begin by buying a number of items and behaving responsibly when you complete each transaction. Leave feedback yourself, and urge the other party to do so for you. You can also build a reputation by creating Web pages, either on eBay itself or on other sites, that tell customers about you and possibly offer merchandise for sale. The PowerSeller icon and Trading Assistant designation are guaranteed to boost your reputation and encourage other members to work with you as well.

7

Degunking eBay Software and Services

Degunking Checklist:

√ Track and organize your sales activities with My eBay.

√ Have eBay "watch" sales so you don't miss a chance to place a bid.

√ Develop profitable relationships with reliable sellers.

√ Use the eBay toolbar to search the site and revisit favorite pages.

√ Watch a sale so you can place a last-minute bid.

√ Use Turbo Lister to prepare and format auction descriptions.

√ Manage auctions and schedule multiple sales with Seller's Assistant.

√ Automate e-mail responses and feedback with Selling Manager.

Y ou're reading this book because you want to "Do It eBay," as the auction site's television commercials proclaim. But by doing so, there's a chance that you've encountered some gunk in the software and services provided on eBay's home page.

Whether it's a matter of using all of the features on your my eBay page, installing eBay's browser toolbar, or using some of the software that automates selling on eBay, you're sure to ramp up your transactions by using eBay's software more effectively. You just need to avoid some of the gunk that comes with add-on software. You'll learn about all that and more in this chapter.

Organize My eBay

You don't always have to purchase or install software. There is software that you access on the Web for free and that you use with your Web browser. That also applies to a good deal of eBay software. It makes sense to start with tools that are available to you for free. The easiest to use is My eBay, a page that eBay sets up for each of its members automatically. Specific aspects of My eBay have been mentioned in preceding chapters, but here I will show you how to really organize this useful tool so you can get a more accurate and useful picture of what you are doing on the auction site at any time.

Create a Summary Page

The My eBay page is a useful gateway to many different kinds of information. Chances are you use only certain functions on a regular basis. The other ones just might get in your way and be a source of clutter. My own impulse, initially, was to click on one of the headings in the left-hand column of My eBay whenever I needed a specific type of information. But My eBay can be a good starting page for eBay itself, especially if you take advantage of the My Summary page, which is intended to present the information you need the most in one location. You can customize the My Summary page so your most frequently used data is gathered automatically and you don't have to click through several different pages to find it. This can be a real time-saver.

To customize your summary page, do the following:

1. Go to My eBay, click My Summary, and click Customize Summary.

2. When the Customize My Summary page shown in Figure 7-1 appears, review the choices in the Available Views box and click the right-pointing arrow to move them to the Views To Display box. You can also pare down the information presented in My Summary by selecting options in Views To Display and clicking the left-pointing arrow to move them to Available Views.

3. When you're done, click Save to save your changes.

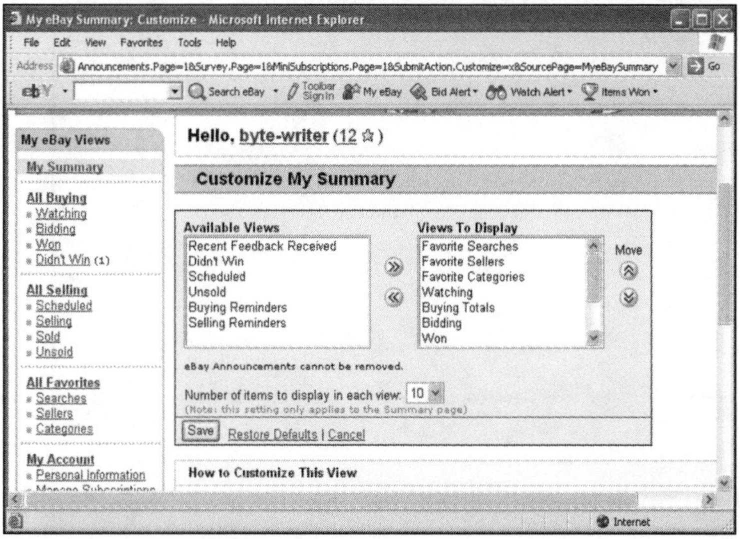

Figure 7-1
You can customize the My Summary page to serve as an opening page
for eBay.

Once you customize My Summary, consider making it your browser's startup page or adding it to your browser's Bookmarks/Favorites list so you can revisit it frequently.

You can customize My Summary so that it contains a snapshot of your buying or selling activities. As a buyer, you'll benefit by placing the Favorite Sellers, Favorite Categories, and Favorite Searches items in My Summary (see Figure 7-2). That way, you'll have every part of eBay that you view most often at your fingertips. As a seller, you might move Selling Reminders, Selling Totals, and Sold to the top of the My Summary page.

NOTE: *As the note on the Customize My Summary page points out, removing information from My Summary doesn't mean you can't find it again. You can always click one of the links under All Buying, All Selling, All Favorites, and My Account to find what you need.*

Receive an E-Mail Alert

How often has this happened to you? You look passionately for an item for a while, you fail to win it, and you take a break from eBay for a few weeks. When you return, you do a search for that item only to discover that it sold recently and for a much lower price than before. This won't happen to you if you designate a search for the item as one of your favorite searches and have eBay e-mail you when the item comes up for sale again. (It happens more often than

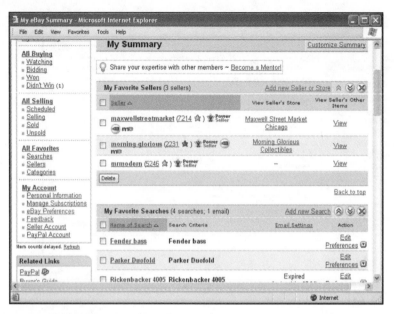

Figure 7-2

Place your most frequently used information in your My Summary page.

you might think; millions of items are put up for sale on eBay every day.) Formally designating an item as one you want as a "favorite" means that you add that item to the Favorite Searches area of My eBay. Then you tell eBay to e-mail you when an item matching your description is put up for sale. Start by searching for the item you want New. You can do this either by clicking Add new Search in the My Favorite Searches area of My eBay or by going directly to the Search: Find Items page. The process is different depending on which method you choose. The following steps apply to the Search: Find Items page:

1. Enter your search terms on the Search: Find Items page. When the search results page appears, click Add to Favorites.

2. When the Add to My Favorite Searches page appears (see Figure 7-3), leave Create a New Search selected, and enter a search name so you can distinguish this item from others in your Favorite Searches list.

3. Check the box next to Email me daily… and choose a time period (from every 7 days to every 12 months) from the drop-down list. The period you choose indicates how long you'll be receiving e-mails from eBay whenever an item you're interested in appears. If items that match your search appear daily, you'll receive e-mails every day; if you choose 7 days from the drop-down list, you'll get those e-mails for only a week.

4. Click Save Search to add the search to My eBay.

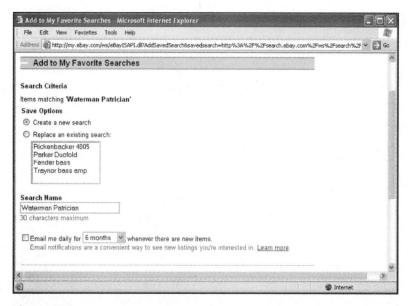

Figure 7-3
Use this form to designate a favorite search and tell eBay to send you
e-mails about new items.

You can also initiate the search from My eBay. Go to My eBay, and click Favorites under the heading Searches. Then follow these steps:

1. In the My Favorite Searches section of the page, click Add new Search.

2. When the Search: Find Items page appears, enter your search criteria and then click Search.

3. When the search results appear, follow the preceding set of steps.

NOTE: *You can receive e-mails for a maximum of three favorite searches on My eBay.*

Watch a Sale with My eBay

It's frustrating when you consider placing a bid on something, you decide to return near the end of the auction in order to place a last-second "snipe" bid, and you forget about the sale at the critical moment. You don't have to forget the end of the sale, however; eBay can watch the progress and send you a notice when the end of the sale nears. To watch a sale, follow these steps:

1. Find the item you want, either in a current or completed sale.

2. With the item description displayed, click the link <u>Watch this item</u> in the phrase "<u>Watch this item</u> in My eBay" near the top of the auction description. The auction page refreshes and the link changes to <u>This item is being watched in My eBay</u>.

3. Keep your e-mail application open and stay logged in so that any incoming messages trigger a notification sound or icon.

You can expect to receive a notification e-mail from eBay about five hours before the end of the sale. The notification message comes from the sender **watchauction@ebay.com** and has the subject line "eBay watched item ending soon!"

GunkBuster's Notebook: Using Your Calendar

Some people just love planning ahead, making lists, and recording data for future use. If you're one of those people, take advantage of an inconspicuous, easy-to-overlook link called Add to Calendar. This link appears beneath the ending date and time of the sale. (See Figure 7-4 for an example.) When you click this link, a small Add to Calendar window opens in the corner of your computer screen. If you have a calendar program such as Microsoft Outlook up and running (and if you're someone who's into planning ahead, you probably have it open all the time), click the Save and Close link within this window. This link is only visible if Outlook is available or if your browser supports calendaring. Otherwise, you'll see another Add to Calendar link; when you click it, the Add to Calendar window will simply close and nothing will happen.

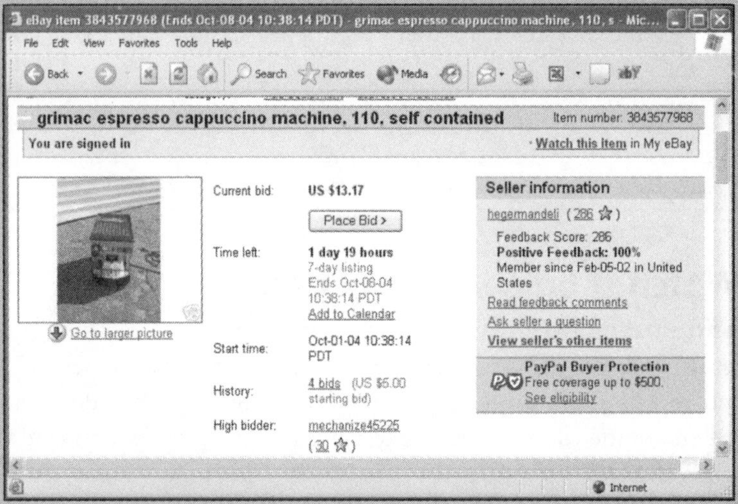

Figure 7-4

If you have the right calendar software, you can automatically add a sale's ending time to it.

TIP: *The calendaring feature mentioned in the preceding sidebar is supported by software such as Apple's iCal and Palm's Desktop. (You can, of course, also add the ending date and time of the sale to your palm device or other planning tool.) You can find out more about calendar reminders at http://pages.ebay.com/help/buy/ calendar.html.*

Stick with Favorite Sellers

It's the same in the virtual and the real world: when you find a store or seller you like, you return to that merchant in the future when you need something else. You'll save time and trouble—and possibly a few dollars—if you record contact information for your favorite sellers in My eBay's All Favorites page. Go to My eBay and click Favorites (unless you have added My Favorite Sellers to your My Summary page, as described earlier in this chapter). The Add new favorite seller or favorite Store page appears (see Figure 7-5). Enter the seller's User ID or eBay Store name and click Save Favorite.

Once you have identified favored sellers and revisit them on a regular basis, you stand a chance of obtaining special deals and an additional level of service. The rewards of an ongoing relationship are mutual: it means more business for sellers and more deals with reduced hassles for buyers.

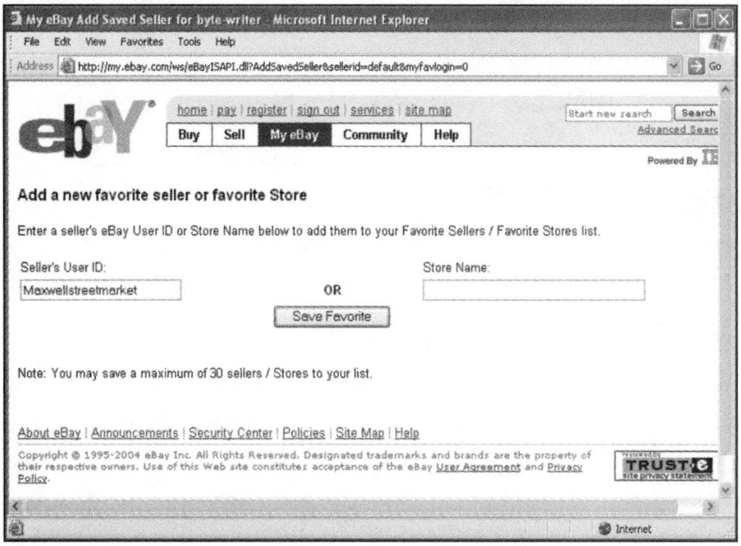

Figure 7-5
Save your favorite sellers so you can track their current sales and make repeat purchases.

Repeat customers often get benefits from sellers that first-time buyers don't get. Here is an example, taken from an auction description on eBay:

```
Personal checks are happily accepted but wait to clear unless you
have over One Hundred Positive Feedbacks or are a Repeat Customer.
```

In addition, some sellers encourage repeat business by offering discounts to return buyers. An example is shown in Figure 7-6: the seller, an electronics dealer, gives a credit toward future purchases to every winning bidder. All long-time, successful merchants know that return business is what keeps them going: purchases by returning customers are often more frequent and larger and, thus, more profitable. Anything you can do to develop a core group of loyal buyers who sustain you over the long haul will be beneficial to your business.

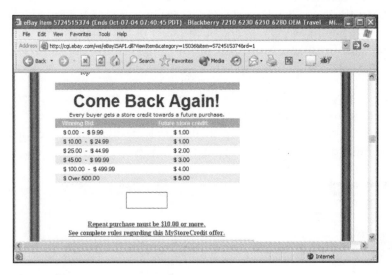

Figure 7-6
Like this eBay seller, you can encourage return buyers by offering discounts.

Degunk the eBay Toolbar

Google's got one. So does Yahoo! Now, eBay's got one, and it can save you time and send you alerts about sales that you're watching. eBay Toolbar can be added to your Web browser's existing set of toolbars to help speed up your use of eBay. eBay Toolbar provides a set of buttons that are added to your Web browser's toolbars that takes you directly to various locations on eBay's Web site. It gives you a way to search eBay from wherever you are on the Web and receive alert messages in your browser window. The alert function will help you stay on top of all your active auctions and is especially valuable if you're in an intense bidding session.

CAUTION: *There's one big restriction to keep in mind when you're thinking of installing eBay Toolbar: It only works with Windows operating systems, not the Macintosh or Linux. The toolbar works with Microsoft Internet Explorer 5.01 or later and Netscape Navigator 4.51 through 4.79. You can find out more about eBay Toolbar at http:// pages.ebay.com/ebay_toolbar.*

Install the Toolbar

It's easy enough to install the toolbar—as long as you don't use a Macintosh, have an earlier version of the toolbar already installed, or had the toolbar installed once and then uninstalled it. Don't forget to turn off any firewall programs you have running before starting the installation process. First you go to the eBay Toolbar page, then click Download, and then click OK when a security warning page appears. The toolbar downloads automatically. After your browser window refreshes automatically, eBay Toolbar appears along with your other browser toolbars just above the main display area (see Figure 7-7). A sign-in page prompts you to sign in with your User ID and password. Sign in, and you can start searching eBay from the toolbar.

Receive Bid Alerts with Your Browser

Suppose you've signed up to receive bid alerts on sales you're watching, as described in "Watch a Sale with My eBay" earlier in this chapter. Normally, the

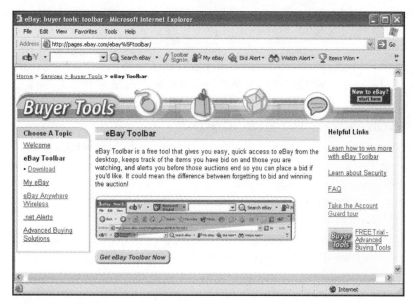

Figure 7-7

eBay Toolbar can save you some time entering URLs in your browser's Address box.

alert message comes to your e-mail inbox. This requires you to have your e-mail program running and your inbox ready to receive messages. If you're using eBay's Toolbar, you can track auctions you're watching: all of the "watched" sales you've added to My eBay are available in a drop-down menu list that appears when you click the Watch Alert button in the toolbar.

You can also configure the toolbar to present you with a list of auctions on which you've placed bids: once you have logged in to eBay, you can click Bid Alerts in order to view a list of such sales. If you have bid on an auction and have adjusted your My eBay preferences so that you receive Bid Alerts, you'll receive notifications 10, 15, 30, 60, or 75 minutes before the end of the auction. The alerts give you an opportunity to return to an auction if you want to place a last-minute bid. (If the list isn't quite up-to-date, choose the Refresh Bid List option, which appears on the Bid Alerts drop-down list along with the list of sales.)

Search with the Toolbar

As you learned in Chapter 3, searches are one of the most common functions performed on eBay, as well as one of the gunkiest. The toolbar makes searching go much quicker. First of all, the search box keeps a record of up to 25 of your most recent searches. Click the drop-down arrow next to the search box and choose one of the previous searches that appear in a drop-down list.

The other useful option is the button labeled "Search eBay." When you click it, an extensive list of search options appears. The options at the top of the submenu let you choose how you want to search eBay. The others provide you with categories and subcategories for searching. You choose an option, then enter a word or phrase in the toolbar's search box to actually conduct the search. You can also search within eBay Stores, by seller, and for Buy It Now items.

Bookmarks on the Toolbar

A *bookmark* is a saved record of a Web page that your browser keeps so you can get to that page more quickly in the future. The buttons on the eBay toolbar enable you to surf various parts of the eBay Web site, no matter what Web site your browser window happens to be displaying at the time. The following buttons are to the right of the search box:

√   Toolbar Sign In: This takes you to eBay's Sign In page, where you can enter your User ID and password. You need to sign in so you can receive Bid Alerts and Watch Alerts.

√   My eBay: This takes you to your My eBay page.

√   Bid Alert: This button opens a Bid Alerts menu, which displays all of the auctions that are still active and on which you have placed bids. Choose Refresh Bid List if the list is not up-to-date.

√   Watch Alert: This button provides you with a list of items you are "watching" in My eBay (when you "watch" a sale, eBay will alert you when a bid is received or when a sale is about to end).

NOTE: Some users report technical difficulties (specifically, JavaScript runtime errors) when attempting to install eBay's Toolbar. Problems frequently occur if you once had an early version of the toolbar installed, then uninstalled it, and then tried to install it again. The only solution is to contact eBay support staff directly. I was sent a software utility that erased references to the toolbar from the Windows Registry and that enabled the toolbar to be installed.

Account Guard

The Account Guard button on the eBay Toolbar helps you protect your eBay account information. Account Guard warns you when you are on a potentially fraudulent (spoof) Web site. It also lets you report such sites to eBay. The feature identifies when you are on an actual eBay or PayPal site. (It might look like you are on eBay, but it's sometimes difficult to tell if the site is really a well-designed fake.)

Optimize eBay Software and Services

If you sell on eBay, you know that it takes some time to upload photos, type up a description, preview the listing, add some formatting to gain some visual interest, and get the sale online. If you have to put, say, 10 sales online in succession, things get tedious very quickly. For sellers who work in volume (and even for those who sell only occasionally), eBay provides a variety of software programs to streamline the listing and selling processes. They can go a long way toward degunking the process of preparing auction descriptions.

TIP: Links to all of the software and services listed in this section can be found on the eBay Downloads page (http://pages.ebay.com/download/index.html).

Turbo Lister

Turbo Lister speeds up the process of listing sales on eBay. The big advantage of Turbo Lister is that it's free. It not only automates the process of creating descriptions but also helps you add design elements to your listings. In case you need to relist a sale (because it didn't attract any bids or because your reserve price wasn't reached), you can retrieve it easily because Turbo Lister saves and stores descriptions.

Turbo Lister includes many other degunking features: The program comes with preinstalled auction templates like the one shown in Figure 7-8. The templates

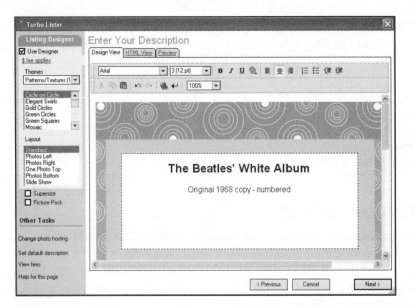

Figure 7-8

Turbo Lister lets you apply predesigned templates to add graphic interest to descriptions.

let you add typefaces and colorful graphics to descriptions. If you use a template, you are charged a small fee in addition to a description's other listing fees. It also includes a bulk listing tool, which comes in handy if you want to get a group of sales online simultaneously. (If they go online at the same time, they can end at the same time.)

Turbo Lister may be free in terms of purchase price, but not in terms of system requirements. It runs only on Windows 98 or later operating systems (not the Macintosh). It requires at least 64 MB of RAM and 20 MB of free disk space. And you have to use Microsoft Internet Explorer 5.01 or later.

To get started, download Turbo Lister from its home page (**http://pages.ebay.com/ turbo_lister/**). First, you download a small setup application that looks through your file system for any necessary files that have already been installed. The program is then automatically installed. You double-click the icon for Turbo Lister on your desktop and you can start creating listings immediately.

Seller's Assistant

If you are interested in managing ongoing auction sales and preparing sales descriptions, Seller's Assistant is a convenient choice. Seller's Assistant is a sales management tool that eBay provides for a monthly fee. Like Turbo Lister, Seller's

Assistant enables you to create sales descriptions. It also contains templates for adding design elements to those descriptions. But it also lets you upload sales listings in bulk—you can upload as many as 20 sales at once.

Seller's Assistant comes in two versions: the regular version, which eBay makes available to users for a fee of $9.99 per month, and Seller's Assistant Pro, which costs $24.99 per month. The Pro version also provides you with features that let you prepare sales reports for tax purposes, print mailing labels, and relist multiple items. Seller's Assistant, like Turbo Lister, is software that you download and install on your computer. The regular version requires you to download 17.3 MB of files, while Pro's file to download is 20.5 MB in size. In other words, Seller's Assistant does require an investment in disk space and processing speed. If you want an auction management tool that you don't have to install and that is available as an online service, try eBay's Selling Manager.

TIP: You can try out both Seller's Assistant and Seller's Assistant Pro free for 30 days before you decide to keep the software. Find out more at http://pages.ebay.com/ sellers_assistant/index.html.

Selling Manager

Selling Manager is a versatile tool for managing auctions. This online service is only intended for *managing* auctions, however. It doesn't let you design or upload auction listings; for that reason, many sellers use a combination of both Turbo Lister and Selling Manager. The big advantage of Selling Manager is that because it's an online service, you can access it with a Windows, Macintosh, or Linux computer. For sellers who carry out dozens of transactions each month, Selling Manager gives them the ability of creating e-mail templates, as well as the ability to store feedback comments and choose which one of the stored comments they want to send to a buyer.

Selling Manager is less expensive than Seller's Assistant, too: you can try the program free for 30 days, then pay $4.99 per month to keep it. Some sellers take advantage of eBay's special rate of $9.99 per month for using Seller's Assistant Basic to create listings and Selling Manager to manage listings. Find out more about Selling Manager at **http://pages.ebay.com/selling_manager**.

Summing Up

The greater the number of transactions you are able to conduct in a period of time, the higher your profit margin. My eBay, the free Web page full of data that eBay provides to each member, can help you track auctions so you can place bids in case you fall behind. You can have eBay send you an alert message when an item that you've been waiting for comes up for sale. Special sales software from eBay, such as Turbo Lister, Seller's Assistant, and Selling Manager, can help you degunk sales descriptions and upload photos and text to eBay efficiently and quickly—more quickly than you could if you manually prepared and uploaded them one at a time. Anyone can buy and sell on eBay, but there's a difference between doing everything yourself manually and taking advantage of software tools that help you come up with a system for success.

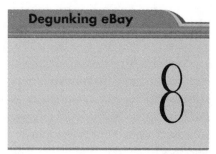

8

Sprucing Up Your Auction Descriptions

Degunking Checklist:

√ Avoid meaningless clutter in your auction descriptions.

√ Create a sales template so that you can make your sales descriptions more consistent.

√ Find ways to get more sales listings online.

√ Improve the quality and quantity of auction photos.

√ Write auction headings that attract attention.

√ Make full use of the Sell Your Item form.

√ Clean up the payment process for your customers.

Y ou can't control who's going to see your auction listings, and you can't control how much money a prospective bidder or buyer is willing to spend. But if you want to become a better seller and make more profits, you'll need to learn how to degunk your auction listings and create more compelling ones. One way to do so is to improve how your sales items are described and presented. If your descriptions are well written and encourage viewers to bid, you'll get more business. When you add more photos and improve the quality of those images, you'll see a direct impact on your sales figures. This chapter describes some strategies for degunking your eBay sales descriptions to ensure that you'll attract more bids and purchases. Once you learn how to degunk your listings, you can move on to learning how to improve your selling strategies in Chapter 9.

Degunk Your Auction Descriptions

Millions of items go up for sale on eBay every day. Shoppers spend hours viewing photos and reading descriptions of those items. The fact is that most buyers are positively influenced by descriptions that are well crafted and turned off by sloppy and amateurish descriptions. By getting the gunk out of your descriptions, you'll make it easier for shoppers to decide whether they want to buy your merchandise or not. You probably know just what sorts of gunk I'm talking about because you've undoubtedly seen examples in the course of your own searching and shopping on eBay:

√ Titles that contain meaningless terms like L@@K

√ Descriptions that are too short and vague

√ Descriptions in which the name of the item is misspelled or the model name and number is wrong

√ Descriptions that use words or phrases that we are all really tired of seeing, such as "one of a kind," "limited offer," "other exclusive deal," and "big savings"

√ Descriptions that greatly overexaggerate the features or condition of a product

√ Shipping instructions that don't spell out costs clearly

√ Photos that are dark and blurry or that don't show the item from several different angles

√ Photos that have wildly inaccurate colors

√ Photos that show a different product than the one the seller is actually selling

Taking the gunk out of your sales listings will leave you with descriptions that grab someone's attention and compel them to consider placing a bid. Once the gunk is gone, you can work on adding some keywords and terms that attract attention. You can then automate your sales so you can build up your volume and improve your eBay business's bottom line.

CAUTION: *You may be proud to be American, but don't advertise your patriotic or religious sentiments to the point where you can't read the description or the page looks busy. Graphic embellishments like eagles and flags and crosses and bunnies and hearts will add unnecessary gunk to your auction listings and turn off potential buyers.*

Avoid Overformatted Descriptions

The first step in degunking your current sales descriptions is to review them and remove any unnecessary elements. I use the word *elements* because I'm talking about more than words and images. An overformatted description is one that uses too much distracting detail that can take the shopper's attention away from the item being sold. Here are some elements to avoid:

√ Backgrounds that make a description difficult to read

√ Too many colors in your headings and auction description text

√ Colors that are difficult to look at

√ Text that might offend someone

√ Background sounds

√ Animations

√ Too many type styles

√ Odd typefaces that are hard to read

√ Graphics that take too long to load

In other words, the same things that make Web pages unattractive and hard to parse make auction descriptions appear all gunked up.

Don't try to do too much when you prepare an auction description. Distill the most important aspect or quality of the item into a single sentence. Then position that sentence strategically at the very beginning of the description so that it grabs your viewers' attention.

How do you avoid posting a gunked-up listing? Review your auction descriptions before they go online. It's all too easy to scan a description quickly and push the button that creates the listing. Next time you list something on eBay, look at the description and remove any distracting fluff. Try this exercise: review the description of an antique men's hat shown in Figure 8-1 and make note of anything that can be removed.

Figure 8-1

Descriptions should contain facts relating to only the item you want to sell.

When you review this description, you should notice unnecessary details and elements that don't work as well as they should:

√   The heading "Cool Man's Hat!" isn't very descriptive. Specifically, the word *cool* should be changed to something more specific about this article of clothing, such as its date, its manufacturer, or its style.

√   The introductory paragraph, "Another exclusive deal…," is in a bad place. It's a good idea to market your business, if you have one, in your eBay descriptions. But shoppers want to read something about the merchandise right at the top of the text. Move this paragraph to the very bottom of the description, even after the terms of sale.

√   Speaking of a phrase like "Another exclusive deal …," my advice is that if you want to make statements like this, try to say something a little unique to help better position your business or your products. Auction pages are full of phrases like "Special Offer," "One-of-a-Kind …," "Not Available in Stores," and so on. eBay buyers get tired of seeing phrases like this and they just tune them out. They also lose respect when having to deal with sellers who make such empty and meaningless claims.

√   The story about finding the hat in a barn is good but too long—and most important, it's not specific to the hat in question. A story about seeing the hat on a shelf or uncovering the box from under a pile of debris would be better.

√   Exclamation marks are overused!!! Only use them once in a while and when absolutely necessary.

What's a better way to describe this item? Suppose you want to sell a men's fedora hat from the 1950s. Rather than thinking about novelties that will amuse shoppers and impress them, look at the hat (or any other object you want to sell) and ask yourself the following questions:

√   What makes this particular item special?

√   What sets it apart from other hats just like it?

√   What one or two qualities might induce bidders to place a bid on this hat rather than other, similar ones?

In this case, the fact that the hat is old is of interest, and the fact that it is a fedora sets it apart from other hats. The condition of the hat or whether it comes with a box is also of interest, as is the size or any other specific quality. Details that involve numbers, brand names, model names, or sizes give shoppers the information they need to make decisions. This information also sets your item apart from similar ones in the marketplace. Do your best to begin your description with this type of identifying information.

GunkBuster's Notebook: Think Small and Focused

In many ways, setting up an auction page to sell an item is a lot like designing a Web site. And if you look at how Web sites have evolved over the past five years or so, the trend now is to design sites that are small and focused. In the early days of the Web, designers went crazy and tried to make their sites as large as possible. They also got caught up in the practice of using the latest gimmicks, like animated graphics and flashing text. Who really needs this stuff?

The reality is that people just don't have time to wade through numerous pages of text, graphics, animations, and all of the other gunk that just gets in the way. As Web sites like eBay get larger and larger, people will have less time to see everything that they might be interested in. By presenting your own information in a focused manner, you'll be helping to reduce the overall problem of clutter. Your customers will also appreciate the fact that you don't want to waste their time and that you are focused on getting them just what they need.

A good approach is to try to design each auction listing so that it is as short and as narrowly focused as possible. Think about trying to include just the elements that are needed. What does a customer really need to know in order to make a buying decision? It's simple: size, brand names, model names and numbers, colors, and condition. Condition, above all, is the single quality shoppers are concerned with, especially when it comes to items like clothing, antiques, and household goods. Provide three or four clear photos, state the facts, describe the condition honestly, and move on to the next sales listing without wasting space on unnecessary details.

If you are interested in learning more about the art of designing and communicating effectively by using less, get a copy of the book *Small Websites, Great Results*, published by Paraglyph Press. This book shows you how to market your small business on the Web, do more with less, and develop good techniques to really get your message tight and focused.

Set Up a Sales Template to Make Your Descriptions More Consistent

A surefire way to speed up the process of improving your sales descriptions, making them more consistent, and getting more of them online with less effort is to create a standard sales template. A *template* is an electronic document that comes with standard elements already entered into it. The standard elements can be used more than once; the author or publisher of the document can customize content in the template without having to re-create or retype the elements that were previously entered.

Several different kinds of content are typically reused by sellers:

√   General, introductory information about the seller

√   Shipping instructions

√   Return policies

√   A statement about what makes the seller's offerings unique or distinctive

Two PowerSellers who have received attention for their efforts (including a mention in *Newsweek* magazine) are Suzanne Ziesche and Shannon Miller of Venus Rising Limited (User ID: venusrisinglimited). Suzanne and Shannon have a lot to say about their high-end bedding products, including sheets and pillowcases. Here are some examples of the kinds of elements they repeat from sale to sale (and at any time, they typically have 50 or more sales in progresson eBay):

The Only Gold Fine Linen Specialist PowerSeller on eBay! (Visit Our Store Now to Experience What the Press is Raving About! (link to eBay store follows)

VENUS RISING LIMITED IS UNPARALLELED, THE _ONLY_ GOLD FINE LINEN SPECIALIST POWERSELLER ON EBAY ~ We specialize in fine bedding linens and luxury items and invite you to see for yourself how few PowerSellers exist within this Specialty area. We are, in fact, the _ONLY Gold PowerSeller_ specializing in this area—with the best products available worldwide. Venus Rising Limited offers the most exquisite, largest array of Specialty Bed and Bath linens available. Achieving and maintaining our honored Gold Powerseller status is no small feat, requiring the same continued dedication and commitment to our customers as when we first began. With the highest quality products offered, quick shipment and excellent communication throughout the experience, Venus Rising Limited maintains a loyal and repeat customer base with new customers every day.

There are also plenty of links to the business's eBay Store, as shown in Figure 8-2.

You have two options for creating your own templates:

√   You can manually assemble the text in a word processing file that you save on your hard disk.

√   You can use eBay's Inserts feature to create text that is stored by eBay and that you can reuse in your descriptions.

The first option is potentially more work for you, but it gives you more flexibility. The template you create manually can be used not only with the Sell Your Item form but also with other tools for creating auction descriptions, such as Turbo Lister (see Chapter 7). The second option is convenient if you only use Sell Your Item to create your listings. Instructions for both options are described in the sections that follow.

Create Your Own Template

If you know how to create a simple word processing document and cut and paste text, you can easily assemble your own auction sales template. Just follow these steps:

1.   Open your word processing program of choice.

2.   Type the text you want to have repeated from auction to auction. You might

    type the following:

Figure 8-2
You can include links to your eBay Store or general information in your sales template.

> Auction Bargains Ltd.
>
> [paste item description here]
>
> We ship by USPS Priority Mail only. PayPal, cashier's checks, personal checks, and money orders accepted.

3. Save the file on your computer. Save the file as a plain text (.txt) document so the contents are easier to cut and paste.

4. Select all of your template text and press Ctrl+C to copy it to your computer clipboard.

5. Open the Sell Your Item form on eBay or a program you use to prepare auction listings.

6. Select a category for your sale and then move to the Describe Your Item page. Under the Item Description heading, you can view the form that enables you to enter your auction description. Click anywhere within the main body of this form and press Ctrl+V to paste your template content.

7. Type the parts of your description that are specific to the item you want to sell. (Replace the placeholder phrase "paste your description here" with the new text.)

8. Post images and complete the rest of your description.

With a template, you can potentially enter 75 percent or more of your description in a matter of seconds. You might only have to type a heading and a few sentences of text that applies to the item at hand because the rest of the template is reusable material.

Create eBay Inserts

Realizing that many of its longtime sellers have already created their own sales templates with material that they need to reuse from item to item, eBay has added a feature called inserts to the Sell Your Item form. Inserts gives you another way to create and reuse text without having to repetitively type it. Open the Sell Your Item form, choose a category for your auction, and move to the Describe Your Item page. Under the Item Description heading, you can view the form that enables you to enter your auction description. Click the arrow next to the Inserts drop-down menu and choose Create an Insert (see Figure 8-3).

When the Create an Insert window pops up, type a name for your insert so you can remember it easily the next time you want to create a sales listing. Then

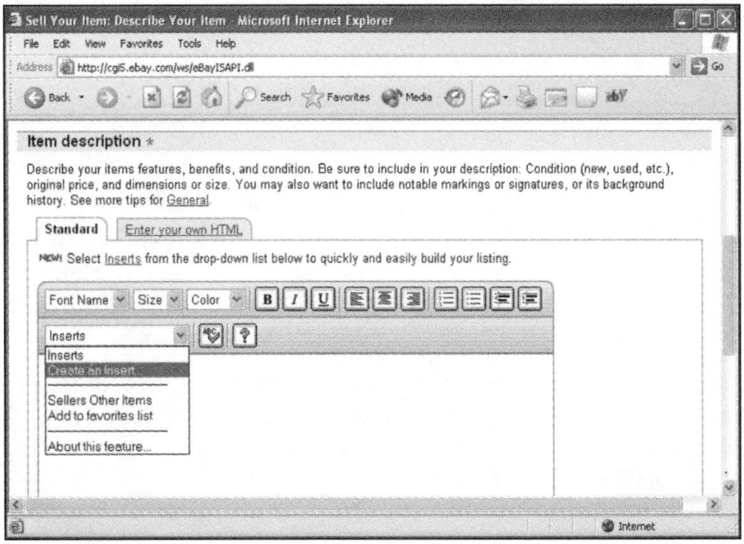

Figure 8-3
You can create reusable bits of text called inserts using this part of the Sell Your Item form.

type or paste the insert itself in the Enter your text or HTML box (see Figure
8-4). As the name implies, you can add HTML formatting to an insert. Then
click Save to save the insert on eBay's Web site. The next time you create an
auction listing, you can access the inserts you previously saved by choosing
them from the Inserts menu.

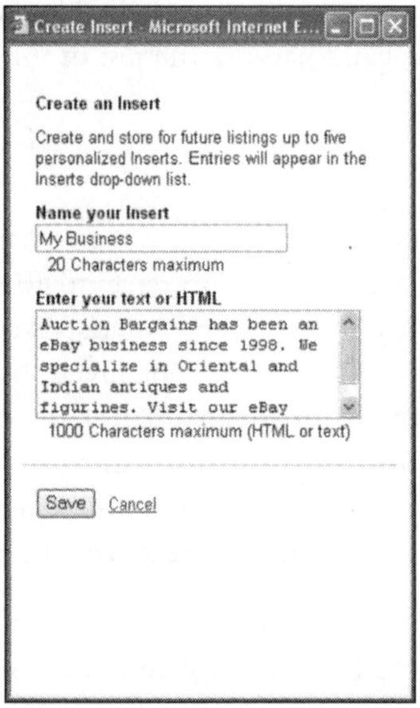

Figure 8-4
Name and type your insert here,
and eBay stores it on its servers
so you can access it later.

Your reusable items or inserts don't have to consist solely of text. You can also
include a logo or graphic image. Just make sure the image advertises your business, like the Sands-o-time logo shown in Figure 8-5. Be sure to avoid an
attempt at making a political or social statement by including American flags or
religious symbols in your sales descriptions. If it's not related to selling the item,
it's just gunk.

TIP: *You don't have to type your reusable inserts by hand on the Sell Your Item form.
You can cut and paste them from a word processing document, as described in the
preceding section. This enables you to keep a copy on your own computer and take
advantage of your word processor's spell-check function, too.*

Figure 8-5
You can make logos part of your eBay auction templates, too.

Automate Your Sales Listings

Until a vending machine has been invented that can spit out auction descriptions when you insert the proper amount of change, the process of automating eBay sales descriptions will always involve time and effort and software. To come up with a system by which they can be produced as quickly as possible, you should pursue one or more of the following options:

√ Draw up a sales schedule. Devote a block of time one or two days each week to the process of taking photos and typing up sales descriptions and then publishing them on eBay. Setting aside a solid block of several hours will help you get more done rather than spreading the process over a period of several days.

√ Install software, such as Turbo Lister or Seller's Assistant (see Chapter 7), that helps you publish multiple sales at preselected times.

√ Hire someone to help you. A relative or a student (or better yet, a family member who is also a student) will have time to spend getting sales online. You can take the photos and jot down some notes about each sales item, and your assistant can do the rest.

√ Sell similar items. If you sell items that are by the same manufacturer, you don't need to type a lot of fresh and unique information about each one. Suppose you find a wholesale supplier who sells you a lot of Christmas figurines, and you want to resell 20 or 30 of them at a time on eBay. You can create a sales template that describes the manufacturer and provides specs about the size and color of the figurines in general. You only need to provide a sentence or two about each item, as well as a photo or two.

All of these options are ways of treating eBay more like a business than a hobby. In any business, you have to stick to a schedule, and if you find the right assistants to help you, you'll speed up the sales process and increase the volume of things you sell on eBay.

Write Auction Copy That Sells

When you read an auction description, what really holds your attention? Although images play an important role, it's the headings that initially grab your interest and the text that helps you decide whether or not you want to bid. The way you describe your items makes a difference in the amount of attention they get. One of the best and simplest ways to sell more effectively on eBay is to make the most of your descriptions, as suggested in the sections that follow.

Create Gunk-Free Headings

It's obvious why headings are important: they are what you see when you browse a set of listings. The heading and accompanying photo should give you enough detail to decide if you are interested in something and to distinguish it from the nearly identical items that are inevitably grouped with it on eBay.

Too much information in an auction heading is confusing. Too little information doesn't encourage anyone to ask a question or place a bid. A gunk-free heading includes just enough details to prompt visitors to investigate further and just enough information to set your item apart from other, similar ones. Do the following:

√ **Choose a word.** Pick a single word—the perfect word that describes your item. If an item is especially rare or has a desirable feature (it's a true diamond ring rather than a cubic zirconia one, for example), say so.

√ **Go by the numbers.** The dedicated collectors who tend to bid enthusiastically on eBay want to know if you are selling a 1959 rather than a 1958 model or model 101a rather than 101b. Including the model numbers and brand names makes items easier to find and encourages shoppers to place bids. Double-check your numbers to make sure they are accurate.

√ **Avoid fluff.** I already explained fluff such as keyboard characters like @@@ and !!!! After shoppers have seen lots of auction titles that contain such characters, they are less likely to be impressed by them.

√   **Trim the verbiage.** Limit your title to 6 to 8 words, if possible. (It *has* to be fewer than 46 characters or it won't fit.) When you're done, read through your heading and cut out anything that's not necessary—anything that's gunk, in other words.

Take a look at the real eBay search results shown in Figure 8-6 and see if you can identify which ones are "gunky" and which are gunk free.

Figure 8-6
Model numbers, brand names, and dates make items more attractive.

Who would want to buy an old wooden tennis racket? Someone who collects them, not someone who wants to play tennis. Admittedly, there may be many reasons why certain wooden rackets attract bids. I've noticed that the sales that have bids usually include a brand name, date, or model number in the title. They don't waste time with words like *rare* or *L@@K* that don't add any value. The more specific the title and description, the more likely an item is to attract bids.

Include Evocative Details

You don't want to take a tight-lipped approach when writing descriptions. Instead of simply giving out the barest set of facts in the shortest period of time, take the time to say everything you possibly can about what you have to sell. Can't think of anything to say? Just ask yourself the following questions:

√ How would I use this item?

√ Why do I think it's desirable or cool?

√ Where did it come from? Who made it? How old is it?

√ Why is it better or more desirable than similar items on eBay?

√ How could someone use this object? What might they do with it? Where could they put it?

√ What kind of *pleasure* would having the item give to a buyer? What kinds of feelings or emotions could it produce in its owner?

√ Is there any tactile or sensory interest that your item can evoke? How does it feel, smell, taste, or look? If so, be sure to mention these in your auction description.

If you only add a few of these details, you'll stand out from many of the other sales on eBay. Lots of sales listings are only one or two sentences in length. Which of the following listings would you take the time to read and examine closely?

```
Two Old Lighters

Ronson, ASC table lighters, silver, old, working condition.



Two antique table lighters in working condition: a Ronson crown
model and an ASC, both faultless, with original flints and wheels.
```

It doesn't take more than a minute to type the additional details in the second example. If you aren't sure exactly what an item does or how much it is worth, ask auction sellers in the discussion groups. Knowledgeable collectors and dealers will be happy to tell you about it. (I'll show you how you can use better research techniques in Chapter 9 to learn more about the products you plan on selling.) Imagine that you don't have any images to include with your listing and your item has to depend solely on the quality of your description. You'll make it as detailed as possible and make sure you've included all the item's important qualities in your description. Even if your photos show the very same things you've written, potential buyers will be reassured that you're telling the truth.

CAUTION: *Don't start your description with negative or apologetic statements. This will turn buyers off. Focus on what's positive and desirable about what you have to sell and why someone might like to purchase it.*

Describe the Outcome

One way to turn a run-of-the-mill description into one that induces bids is to describe what could or should happen after someone buys what you are offering: the product will look great in a display case, it will look great if you wear it to a party on Saturday night, or it will look terrific in your driveway. This is an effective way of getting bidders to envision how they will use or enjoy what you are offering.

Do you have to resort to this sort of salesmanship? No. But this additional public relationship effort is a tried-and-true sales technique that has been proven to move merchandise. Since moving merchandise is your ultimate goal, add a few such phrases to your own auctions and see if your sales results improve.

Tell a Story

Everyone likes a good story. A good story draws you in, gets you involved, and holds your interest. Auction descriptions have precisely the same goals. If you can, tell a story about what you have to sell. If you are selling a one-of-a-kind collectors' item that you acquired from a huge barn sale in the country, all you have to do is tell how you came across it. If you are offering a fairly new appliance, it's harder to tell a story about it. If you have literary ability, this is the time to get imaginative. I have a friend who makes up stories about even the most mundane things. "Marilyn Monroe would have loved this red brassiere," she might write. "This Betty Boop cookie jar was once a favorite goal of many a hungry youngster coming home from school in the afternoon."

The point of telling a story is not to entertain prospective buyers but to get them to envision how they might use, wear, or handle the thing you have to sell. It's always helpful to get prospective bidders to dream about a particular item.

Suppose you find an instruction manual for an old Packard automobile. Such manuals are of value all by themselves, especially if they are in good condition. The simple thing would be to write the following:

```
1958 Packard Clipper owner's manual, 6" x 9", excellent condition.
```

There's nothing wrong with this. But if you use your imagination, you can come up with something more interesting. Consider something like this:

```
My father bought our Packard when I was a little boy. It was one of
our first cars. He bought it used, and he spent weeks fixing it up
so it would run. I remember how big and luxurious it was; you could
practically camp out and make a home in the back seat. The rich
two-tone green color and abundant chrome were things you don't see
anymore. The Packard is long gone, but you can relive those days of
great American cars with this owner's manual in near-perfect
condition.
```

Think about how your item might have been used or who might use it in the future. If you can get your buyers to do the same, you'll increase the chances that they'll place a bid. (Find out more about engaging the imaginations of your customers in Chapter 9.).

Balance Facts with Lively Adjectives

It's important to include facts and figures with your auction descriptions. But too many sales listings contain only a sentence or two of description and nothing more. A few descriptive terms can make a listing more lively and engaging. Advertisers know this: they sprinkle words like *New! Free! Speedy!* and the like around their own advertisements. Consider the following just-the-facts listing:

```
1959 Edsel Tourmaster wagon, exc. cond., 87,000 orig. mi.
```

The same item seems much more interesting when you spice it up with a few choice adjectives and some more detail, like this:

```
A classic bit of 1950s design extravagance, this pristine 1959 Edsel
Tourmaster wagon is a real period piece, the kind of car your father
or grandfather would have loved to own. The best thing is that it's
in fantastic condition, with only 87,000 miles. Shiny faultless
chrome trim, original curved glass around the back. All original
components make this a true collector's item that would do just as
well in a museum of design as in your garage—provided you have a
garage big enough to fit it!
```

You probably see that the second description depends on humor and carefully chosen words to make its point. Remember that you're not writing a classified ad for a newspaper, where you might pay by the word; you have plenty of room on a Web page, whether it's a Web page that presents an auction on eBay or a Web page that describes your business or your personal side. Don't be afraid to add words that can work to your advantage.

Which words should you add? On eBay, certain words that are especially effective show up frequently in auction descriptions:

√ Original

√ NR (No Reserve)

√ New

√ MIB (Mint in Box)

√ Rare

These sorts of terms speak for themselves. You don't need CAPITAL LETTERS or other extra punctuation to generate interest. Only capitalize the most important terms so your auction listing is easier to read.

CAUTION: You'll get in trouble if you try to add some keywords to your sales description that have nothing to do with your item but that are an obvious attempt to draw more attention to it. This is called keyword spamming, and it's prohibited by eBay. For instance, if you are selling a run-of-the-mill Acme watch and your auction heading reads "Gold Plated Men's Watch Acme Rolex" or "Gold Plated Men's Watch Acme Not Rolex," you'll attract everyone who is searching for a Rolex watch and an Acme watch, but the Rolex searchers will be left feeling misled.

Improve Your Photos

Photos are among the most important parts of an auction description, and possibly the most important. The obvious types of photo-related "gunk" are photos that are too big and load too slowly (or not in their entirety), photos that are too dark and blurry, or an insufficient number of photos. Most of these problems can be resolved by acquiring two things:

√ A high-quality digital camera

√ A good set of lights

If you don't have a camera and are looking for the best device for taking photos of your merchandise, I highly recommend a digital camera. The quality is going up continually, and the price of the better cameras is going down. The better cameras aren't necessarily the least expensive ones, of course. To take photos for eBay or other Web sites, you don't need a camera that has a 5- or 6-megapixel capacity. Get a 2- or 3-megapixel camera with a built-in macro lens for close-ups and you'll be more than happy with the results.

When it comes to good lighting, you have to look for lights that provide more realistic and even light than the light provided by normal incandescent bulbs used in household lamps. Get two halogen work lights and mount them on stands. Point them from different angles at the object you want to photograph. Place the object on a table with a solid background, and remove any photos or distracting images from the wall behind the object. (You might drape a blanket or other covering on the wall behind the table.)

TIP: Consider going outdoors for your eBay photos. Plenty of sellers end up including parts of their driveways or backyards in the backgrounds of their auction photos. The important thing is not what's behind the auction item but the quality of the light overhead. Pick a nice sunny day with the sun overhead—or better yet, a bright but overcast day with more even light and no shadows.

Include Multiple Photos

You should try to include two or more photos with a typical auction description. But the truth is that it's almost impossible to include too many photos. As long as you're willing to pay a fee for each one, or if you have an image hosting service that allows you to publish many photos for a nominal fee, you can easily include more than two or three. I've seen auction descriptions that include six, eight, or even more photos of an item from every possible angle. The more expensive the item, the more photos you need. It's easy to see the value in posting six or more photos of a car in order to show it from many different angles, both inside and out.

I can't guarantee that including four, five, six, or more photos of an auction item is going to produce more bids, but you'll certainly attract more attention for what you have to sell.

Find a Photo Host

When you include lots of photos, you have to be concerned with two things: the size of your photos and the way they are arranged on the page. The way your photos are arranged depends partly on the software programs you use and partly on your photo host, the service that hosts your photos. If you use eBay as your host, you can use eBay Picture Services to host your photos (for each sale, the first image is free, and additional images cost $.15 each) and Listing Designer to arrange your photos and give a visual flair. If you post 100 photos a week with 25 sales, then 75 of those photos cost $.15 each. If you extend that over 50 weeks per year, you might end up paying over $500 per year to eBay to host your images.

Like many high-volume eBay sellers, you'll probably be better off if you use a third-party service to host your photos and access the service's software for posting sales online. Services like Marketworks (**www.marketworks.com**) are popular with many PowerSellers. For a $29.95 monthly minimum fee, you get access to auction design templates, software for preparing sales listings and putting them online, and 100 MB of space for storing auction images. More space is available for higher monthly fees, but if you consider that an auction image should be no more than, say, 50 K in file size, that gives you room for 2000 images. Only the biggest PowerSellers might need more. With that much space, you can easily sell 50 items per week and include 5 or more images of each one.

The eBay PowerSeller sweet★beans regularly includes multiple photos even of mundane items such as a group of Cliff's Notes study guides and women's boots. The Marketworks auction software this seller uses allows her to arrange

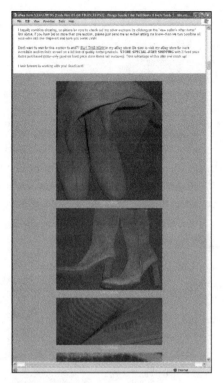

Figure 8-7
Picking the right host can help you
include more photos with your sales.

the photos in a single column in the center of the Web page (see Figure 8-7).
Don't use eBay Picture Services by default; you should shop around and make
sure you are getting the best deal you can find as far as image hosting.

---

*TIP: If you're looking to publish more photos along with your auction descriptions and
you have been deterred by hosting fees, look into Deazoom.com (www.deadzoom.com),
which charges only $5 per month for 10 MB of image hosting space. If you're on a
really tight budget, you can get 1 MB for free from Auction-Images (http://auction-
images.com).*

Clean Up the Payment Process

Making it easy for buyers to pay you and being clear about your sales terms are
two more tried-and-true ways to degunk your descriptions. As you probably
know, buyers are understandably anxious when it comes to handing over hard-
earned money to someone they've never met and will probably never meet

face-to-face. You will make the payment process more difficult than it needs to be if you do any of the following:

√   You don't allow any kind of credit card payment.

√   You allow only a payment service that's nonstandard (in other words, something other than eBay's own Pay Pal payment service).

√   Your payment terms devote more space to warnings and restrictions than they do to options your buyers *can* follow.

To avoid these problems, you should provide more than one payment option, spell out your terms clearly, and trust the payment *processes* you have chosen (even if you don't trust your buyers completely).

Sign Up with a Payment Service

PayPal, eBay's own payment service, is the most obvious alternative when it comes to payment options. PayPal is either loved or hated by eBay members. Those who hate it complain that it does not adequately pursue incidents of fraud. Those who love it (or at least are satisfied with it) feel that it gives buyers a convenient and safe way to pay for auctions with credit cards and it gives sellers a way to accept credit cards without going through the trouble of signing up for merchant accounts with financial institutions.

As a seller, you can streamline payment for those buyers who don't trust PayPal by providing other options. It might mean signing up with an alternative payment service like BidPay (**www.bidpay.com**). It might also mean accepting cashier's checks, money orders, and personal checks—or even cash, if a buyer insists on paying that way. (It's happened to me.)

NOTE: *BidPay, which has also been known as Western Union Auction Payments, enables shoppers to pay for auctions by obtaining Western Union money orders. The service is free for sellers, but buyers have to pay a service fee. Buyers can obtain money orders with a credit card or a check. Find out more on the site's FAQ page (www.bidpay.com/faqIndex.asp).*

Spell Out Your Sales Terms

When it comes to paying for items purchased on eBay, buyers simply want to know where to send their payment and what forms of payment are accepted. By being specific and responsive when the end of the sale comes, you can help buyers through this final stage of the transaction. By spelling out your sales terms clearly and succinctly, you will reassure them that you are a pro at selling on eBay and will deliver their merchandise promptly.

NOTE: *If you are planning to be out of town during or at the end of a sale, be sure to put a note to that effect in your auction description. This is especially important if you are offering something with a Buy It Now (BIN) option. Someone who purchases an item for the BIN price you have specified expects to communicate with you immediately. They're often in a hurry to receive what they've just purchased. If you've gone out of town, not expecting your sale to end while when you are gone, this might create anxiety with your customer. Anything you can do to alleviate this buyer's fears will save you trouble down the road.*

Be Clear on What You *Won't* Accept

If you are opposed to accepting a certain form of payment, such as PayPal, say so clearly in your auction description. All too often, sellers add warnings and requirements only after they have had a dispute with a buyer or encountered a failed transaction. Be proactive and try to anticipate trouble:

√   Tell people how much time they have to pay. Seven to 10 days is a common requirement. You might add that, after this time, you will relist the item and might leave negative feedback, including filing a Non-Paying Bidder (NPB) report with eBay.

√   If you prefer PayPal, you can specify this on the Sell Your Item form.

√   If you won't accept payment from certain countries or from buyers outside your own country, spell that out clearly.

√   If you have been burned by buyers who have low feedback and don't pay up, you might add a phrase such as "Do not bid if you have feedback of *[fill in the desired number]* or less."

√   If you accept checks (and you should, in my opinion), advise buyers that you'll wait for 7 to 10 days after payment is received before you ship. That should give you more than enough time to make sure the check has cleared.

The number of restrictions you place in the payment section of your description is up to you. Many sellers take a hard-line approach and go on for several paragraphs about how they won't sell to Malaysia or the Philippines, won't accept bids from those with feedback ratings of 10 or less, won't accept PayPal, and so on. Others simply list the common payment options (PayPal, checks, and money orders) and leave it at that. You should list any restrictions to prevent problems, and be sure to sign up with at least PayPal and BidPay to give your customers the options they need.

Summing Up

When it comes to selling effectively on eBay, the actual description is among the most important of the elements you can control. By adding the right terms, taking out unnecessary words and symbols, posting multiple photos, and streamlining payment options, you make transactions proceed more smoothly for your customers and for you. Be sure to proofread your listings before they go online, spell out what forms of payment you will or won't accept, and take lots of good photos. These basic approaches will help make sure that you sell more and you get more attention for what you sell. While this chapter covered the basics of creating sales listings on eBay, the next chapter examines some advanced strategies for selling more effectively, either at auction or fixed-price sales.

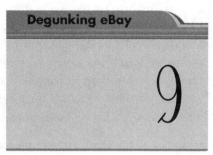

Strengthening Your Selling Strategies

Degunking Checklist:

√ Choose the best items to sell and ship to buyers.

√ Come up with a shipping plan before you sell.

√ Research the merchandise you want to offer.

√ Provide details that engage buyers' imaginations.

√ Improve your presentation by cleaning and talking up your items.

√ Choose keywords that help buyers find your sales.

√ Make sure your store or site is listed on Google.

√ Cross-promote multiple items you have for sale.

Now that you've learned how to spruce up your sales listings, it's time to take the next degunking step and learn ways to improve your selling strategies overall. The big challenge to consider is, How can you stand out from the thousands of other sellers who are doing the same thing? How can you increase the odds that someone will actually buy what *you* have to offer and that you'll get what you want for it? How can you improve your selling techniques so that you have a business edge over the competition?

Luckily for you, there's an extensive track record you can draw upon when you're trying to clean up and improve your sales performance. You don't have to reinvent the wheel and do something outlandish that no one else has attempted before. You just have to take the time to examine your current practices and follow some common-sense procedures to improve upon what you are currently doing. Plan ahead, and think like a businessperson rather than an amateur holding an online garage sale, and your overall results are sure to improve. The approaches detailed in this chapter will show you how to think more strategically.

Select the Right Things to Sell

I have a friend who has the overwhelming job of cleaning out her father's many years worth of possessions, all left in her basement after he passed away. I volunteered to show her how eBay can help her clean out all this gunk. So if you're in a similar situation, or if you just have a closetful of things, the sections that follow will lead you through the process of picking the right things to sell. It's important to not just waste your time and money by simply taking the "gunshot" approach and trying to sell everything that you can get your hands on. Even though it is relatively easy to try to sell any items that you might come across, a little planning and strategic selling techniques can go a long way. Besides, eBay is already cluttered with too many alarm clocks and TV sets. By putting a little effort into what you offer to your customers (just as every business should), you'll be in a much better position to build a sustainable income for yourself.

Plan Ahead with Shipping and Packing

Be selective and pick half a dozen to a dozen items that seem desirable because they are old and collectible, come in their original packaging, have recognizable brand names, or are unique or even rare in some way. In helping my friend recently, we came up with the following list:

√ A large cast-iron kitchen stove from the 1930s

√ An original Popeil Veg-O-Matic, in the box, with instruction booklet

√ A wooden Ace tennis racket made by Wright and Ditson

√ Ten coasters labeled "Schlitz: The Beer That Made Milwaukee Famous"

√ Two old cigarette lighters, one with the brand name ASR and one by Ronson

√ An ashtray, looking old and dirty and apparently made of pewter or tin, labeled "The Nat'l Emblem & Specialty Co., Toledo, Ohio"

This seems like a good start. But some items are more practical than others, especially when it comes to selling them on eBay. It might seem illogical, but before you even prepare your description, ask yourself, Am I prepared to pack this thing up and take it to the shipper? I've seen the old stove my friend mentioned; it's a period piece from the 1930s or '40s, and it's certainly worth money. But if someone buys it, how are you going to get it to them?

When it comes to a heavy item like a stove, the only practical option is to state clearly in your auction description that the high bidder or buyer must pick the stove up personally. This restricts the sale to bidders who live in your immediate geographic area. There is the advantage of being able to meet the buyer and receive payment in person. But many sellers would argue that receiving a credit card payment in advance through PayPal or BidPay is far safer than being handed a check by someone who picks up an object in person; if the check bounces, you can't get the object back.

To help you fine-tune what you should sell based on packing and shipping constraints, I've developed a three-step program for you to follow: start small, pick a shipper, and secure shipping supplies.

Step 1: Start Small

Pick objects that you can pack and ship easily, and save the bigger stuff for later. (Your local antique store can send employees to pick up your object at the same time they pay you for it.) The Veg-O-Matic in the preceding list (shown in Figure 9-1) is perfect—it's small, it's not terribly heavy, and it fits neatly in its own box, which can be placed within a larger box. Insulating material such as Bubble Wrap or newspaper can then be placed between the two boxes.

The "think about shipping up front" rule applies to just about anything you sell on eBay. Decide how you're going to pack and ship, and have a plan for doing so, even before you put anything up for sale.

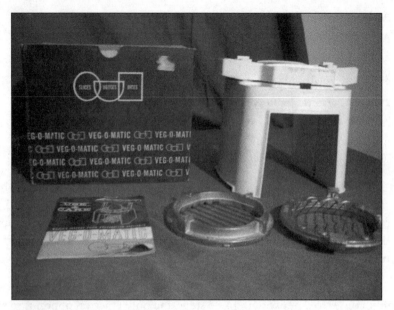

Figure 9-1
Relatively small, easily packaged items are perfect for eBay.

Suppose you sell something at a Buy It Now price several days before the sale was scheduled to end. Are you ready to send the item out to the buyer who pays for it with PayPal within a few minutes? You'd better be: delaying by several days can earn you neutral or negative feedback, something you don't want if you are trying to get better at selling items. (If your feedback rating is only 10 and one feedback comment is negative, it gives you a relatively low 90 percent positive feedback rating, for instance.)

Step 2: Pick a Shipper

Take a trip to your local post office and get the lay of the land: Pick up some free Priority Mail envelopes and ask for some Priority Mail boxes. Talk to the employees and ask if they have any tips for eBay sellers, such as good times to drop off merchandise. A personal visit gives you the chance to judge whether or not these employees are people you want to work with on a regular basis.

Next, visit your local UPS/Mail Boxes Etc. or Kinko's/FedEx office and talk to employees about their resources and tips for eBay sellers. Although the U.S. Postal Service will be your cheapest shipper, you may need better customer service, and these companies may offer the service levels that you require.

Step 3: Secure Shipping Supplies

Once you've settled (at least tentatively) on a shipper, invest in a scale so you can calculate postage. Once you have a rough idea of the shipping costs, you can specify them in your auction listings. Make sure you obtain a scale that can hold the heaviest item you're likely to sell. The logical place to purchase such items is on eBay itself: the 35-lb. digital scale shown in Figure 9-2 could be purchased at a Buy It Now price of $14.95.

Figure 9-2
Purchase a digital scale so you can calculate postage for your customers.

Obtain packing materials: secure tape, Bubble Wrap, newspaper, and boxes. A good source for such items is eBay itself. (See Chapter 10 for more about shipping.)

TIP: *There is a third option for unloading heavy or bulky merchandise: hand it over to someone else who will get rid of it for you on eBay. Not far from my house, there's a storefront opened by two women who work as consignment sellers on eBay. I could take the stove to them (or at least some digital photos of the stove) and see if they would be able to sell it. But if they aren't able to unload it, do I really want to take it back? I'd probably end up dropping it off at an antique store or resale shop and getting little, if any, money for it. eBay isn't the best place to sell every single thing, and bulky items like household appliances are on the list. (So are things like guns and liquor that eBay prohibits; learn more about the current list at http://pages.ebay.com/help/policies/items-ov.html.)*

Do Your Homework and Know What You've Got

Stories abound of eBay sellers who have put things up for sale and been astonished by how high the bidding has gone on their merchandise. On the other hand, some sellers severely overestimate the value of their products because they don't do their homework upfront and realize that there are a zillion other sellers on eBay who are trying to auction the same thing.

There are sources you can use, such as eBay's newsletter, the Chatter (**http://pages.ebay.com/community/chatter/index.html**), to track sales activities. This newsletter, for example, regularly publishes success stories like the beer can that was found underneath a home that sold for more than $19,000 and the fishing lure that sold for more than $20,000. These surprises are exceptions to the rule, however. The vast majority of sales on eBay involve mundane items that don't fetch thousands of dollars. You're better off doing some homework and knowing whether you have something of great value, something of virtually no value, or something that has an interesting history. Armed with this background information, you can adjust your sales in different ways:

√   If something is really valuable and you want to recoup what you paid for it (or make sure you get a certain amount for it), put a reserve price on it.

√   If something is really valuable and you're sure you're going to get bids on it, offer it at no reserve, which tends to attract more bids.

√   If something is of little value, you may want to group it with other, similar items or offer it at no reserve.

No matter what the value is, your sale will attract more interest if you can tell buyers something about the item—where it came from, who manufactured it, how old it is, and so on.

Research, Research, Research

When it comes to strategies, you can't do much better than an army general's strategy. Any general will do two things: draw up a battle plan and find out as much as possible about the enemy's numbers and location. Don't go into eBay sales in a huge hurry, simply posting sales online with only a sentence or two of description. First of all, do searches of both current and completed sales for similar items so you can determine the following:

√   How many products like the ones you plan to sell are being offered?

√   How many different sellers are selling them?

√   Are the products being sold by experienced PowerSellers?

√   How much are the products selling for?

√   Are other sellers using features such as reserve prices? If so, how high are the reserve prices?

√   Have the other auctions that have been offered successful?

√   Do the other auctions have better (or more) photos than yours?

√   Do the other sales have details in the descriptions that you don't have?

This type of research does take a little time because you need to track other auctions for a certain amount of time. But if you do your research homework, you'll be less likely to make mistakes. You'll also learn how to degunk your own selling techniques.

TIP: Often, other sellers who have products like the ones you plan to sell are knowledgeable and can provide details about them, although you can't know for certain if the person is really an expert or really telling the truth.

Research outside of eBay

You should also look around the Internet for details on collectors' sites or sites where enthusiasts of particular topics, events, or collectibles talk in great detail about what they love. The price guides found in the major bookstores or in larger antique stores also provide information about dates and models that are especially desirable.

Collectors are terrific sources of information about rare and valuable items. You discover that watches with Masonic symbols instead of numbers are desirable; bottles with the handle on the left side are rare; certain brands of guitars always fetch lots of bids. Collectors are usually more than happy to talk about what they love, too; don't be reluctant to approach them with questions.

TIP: Virtually all collectors frequent eBay these days. You can find them in the category-specific discussion boards and the Answer Center. Look for the board that's closest in topic to the item you hope to sell.

GunkBuster's Notebook: Researching Some Items

Consider the items being put up for sale by my friend with the basement full of debris. I did some research on eBay and gathered the following information about her merchandise:

√ *The tennis racket:* It's an old wooden tennis racket marked Ace and with the following maker's mark on the handle: "Wright & Ditson Championship." Also stamped on the handle was "9 S33." I discovered on the Woodtennis.com site (**www.woodtennis.com**) that the company had been founded by George Wright and Henry A. Ditson in 1871. I scanned some current listings on eBay and discovered that the length of a racket is often cited, as well as whether the original strings are intact. If I'm lucky, I might get $20 or so for the racket.

√ *The ashtray:* This thing is truly unattractive, but you can never use outward appearance as a way of determining whether an object will attract bids. It is imprinted with the Loyal Order of the Moose (L.O.O.M.) emblem and the letters *PAP,* which appears to be significant because this detail is listed in other eBay descriptions. Several eBay auction listings referring to a facility called Mooseheart indicate that the heart designs and moose logo mean this ashtray is associated with it too.

√ *The lighters:* I found from searching on eBay that the two lighters are called "table lighters." I found that there are three important criteria: the type of lighter, the condition, and whether the lighter actually works. The ASR lighter sold for $5.50 on a completed auction.

√ *The Schlitz coasters:* I didn't find anything very encouraging here. Such coasters are frequently put up for sale on eBay, and they don't often attract bids. Sometimes they are offered in an original sealed container (which I didn't have). Other times, they are dated (mine aren't).

√ *The Veg-O-Matic:* I was surprised to find that these aren't terribly rare, and it isn't unusual to find them in the original box or with the original instruction booklet.

These details are important because filling your descriptions with relevant background information about your merchandise doesn't just make the merchandise more interesting, it also makes you seem more knowledgeable. If you appear to know what you're talking about, you will seem more trustworthy. A feeling of trust and reliability can result in more (or higher) bids.

Research Completed Auctions

Besides uncovering details about your merchandise so you can sell it, it's a good idea to research completed sales to see how much your item is likely to fetch (or if it might attract bids at all). That way, you can decide whether or not to put a reserve price on it. I looked up completed auction data for the aforementioned items on eBay and on Andale, and the results are shown in Table 9-1.

Table 9-1   Items Being Researched for Sale

Item	eBay Completed Item	Andale Completed Item
Wright & Ditson tennis racket	Exact match sold for $18.00, only one bid.	Completed sales range from $9.99 to $22.
Ronson Mayfair table lighter	Sold for $16.50 with 7 bids (no reserve), but only $4.95 in another $4.95 NR auction.	Completed sales range from $4.99 to $27.95.
Schlitz coaster	One coaster sold for $3.	Average sales price $2.60.
Veg-O-Matic	Many have sold in the original box; prices range from $7.99 to $25.	The $7.99 auction had no photo. Average sale price $14.95.

Researching completed auctions is definitely worth the time and effort. It's not only fun, but it gives you insight into what makes some items more desirable than others and which descriptive words might have more impact than others. You might notice, as I did, that the word *vintage* is used in auctions of older objects. Some items sell better if they are from a particular time frame and if the condition is especially good (if the original felt is on the bottom of a cigarette lighter, for instance).

Sell at the Right Time of Year

Often, it pays to hold on to merchandise until the time is right to sell it. I sometimes have no problem finding winter clothing at the local resale shop at the end of the season, in March or April. But no one wants them then. If I hold on to them until October or November, I'm likely to have much better luck, however.

It's called "buying out of season," and it's something resellers have done for years. You take advantage of end-of-the-season sales, when retail and wholesale stores alike are emptying out the last of their seasonal inventory. You'll find bathing suits at deeply reduced prices in September; you hold on to them until the following spring when you can sell them. Do the same on eBay: Draw up a calendar, and organize your merchandise by season. Have a box or shelf designated for summer items, one for winter, and so on.

Engage the Bidder's Imagination

In Chapter 8, I mentioned the importance of telling your item's "story." If you can consistently engage the imaginations of eBay shoppers and get them to envision how they might use an item, you're more likely to convert those shoppers into buyers.

Play Up Rare Collectibles

If you have a scarce antique or a type of collectible that's currently in demand, you probably don't have to do a lot of selling in order to attract bidders and buyers. On the other hand, some collectibles are a dime a dozen on eBay. Often, the very items you've spent years hoping to see just once turn up at auction on a weekly basis. Suppose you have an old china doll you want to list. She bears tags from the manufacturer but lacks the original box because she is from the 1920s and she was Grandma's doll. You might think such items are scarce on eBay. However, you search through current auctions and, lo and behold, someone else has a similar doll up for sale. Both your doll and your competitor's are in more or less equal condition.

You are excited to notice that the doll already up for sale has a high bid of $400. Not only that, but the sale has one day to go: it's in day six of a seven-day auction. The level of activity indicates that the demand is hot for this doll because most bidders jump in at the end of the sale.

You know you can sell your own doll. At the very least, the second-highest bidder from the previous sale will be eager to bid on yours. How can you take advantage of the situation? Time is on your side, so you should make the most of it: set up your auction so that the sale starts on the last day of the competing sale—preferably, a couple of hours before the other auction closes. This strategy accomplishes two goals:

√   Those unfortunate bidders who were unable to win the other auction can bid on yours. They are likely to start looking for another one immediately after they lose, in fact.

√   eBay bidders who were outbid at the last minute receive a notice from eBay that will actually steer them to your sale. The note reads, in effect, "Sorry you didn't win, but here are other items up that you might be interested in." If you take care to make your description or your auction title close enough to the sale that just ended, your doll sale will be mentioned.

The "piggybacking" approach also works well if you have an item that isn't quite as good in terms of condition as one currently for sale. Suppose your doll has a cracked leg. Offer it a littler lower minimum. People who really want something and lost out on it will tend to go after a substitute. They have seen how high the bidding got in the other auction so they know it is a rare item and will take what they can get.

GunkBuster's Notebook: Attracting Collectors

Anyone who has shopped or sold on eBay for even a little while can tell you who the most rabid, crazy, enthusiastic bidders are. They're the collectors: the people who have shelves and closets full of the very objects you want to sell. They probably know more about what you have to offer than you do. If you're lucky, they have even dreamed about having an object like yours for years and they'll bid higher than you ever imagined to get it. If you're lucky enough to have an object that desirable, you don't have to do all that much. It practically sells itself. And, if a collector needs more information, they will ask you for the pertinent details.

Suppose you aren't sure if you have a rare or valuable object to sell. Or suppose you're pretty sure what you have is run-of-the-mill but you want collectors to bid on it anyway. One way to attract the attention of knowledgeable collectors is to speak to them in their own lingo. Learn the right terms to add to a sales listing. Practically every type of old or unusual item has them. A tennis racket might have *gut* strings, for instance. A cigarette lighter might be a *handheld* or a *table* lighter. A pocket watch might be a *railroad watch,* and it might be in a *hunter's case.*

How do you find such terms? Do the kind of research described in this chapter. Look up something in a collector's guide or on the Web so you know the right terms to apply to a description. At the very least, your descriptions will be more interesting and informative for those who aren't experienced collectors. In a best-case scenario, your descriptions should contain the "magic words" that enthusiastic collectors have been looking for.

How to Sell "Problem" Merchandise

If you have an antique to sell that's in its original packaging and has never been opened, pat yourself on the back. It's far more likely that your precious collectible is tarnished, dirty, or filthy. On top of that, it might be totally unattractive. Here's an example: Figure 9-3 depicts my friend's ashtray and two lighters as they were when they were originally dug out of her basement.

Figure 9-3
Before you put something up for sale, make sure you clean it up
and see if it works.

Clean Up Unattractive Objects

Presentation makes a difference in just about everything you have to sell. This
probably seems painfully obvious and simplistic, but the first step in creating a
good presentation for otherwise undistinguished items is to grab a rag and a
cleaner and get the gunk off. Just look at a few photos of old or antique items
on eBay. Most of the time, the items are clean and polished up; your merchandise simply needs to compete with it.

*CAUTION: Take care when choosing a cleanser or soap for your merchandise. Don't
choose something so strong that you take the paint or polish off. And, as the apprais-
ers on **Antiques Roadshow** say all the time when they're commenting on old furniture,
a refinished object is usually worth less than one with the original paint or finish. Just
give wooden furniture a light dusting; don't take the paint off or change the finish in
any way.*

Give New Life to Unappealing Items

You dig out a ceramic frog flower pot from the bottom of a forgotten shelf in
the basement. Your arm automatically moves to the trash can. But wait. Rather
than clutter up the trash with something that might earn you a few dollars, take
a different approach. Clean that item up and sell it on eBay.

The idea that the dirty, worn household items you find unappealing might find a new home with someone who loves them is itself an innovative strategy. Rather than automatically throwing something out, cleaning it up and describing it in a way that is sales and marketing savvy can help you make a few more sales and build up your feedback rating. For example, consider the ashtray my friend had to sell. Depending on how they are shaped and what shape they are in, ashtrays can be truly unattractive. What can you say about such objects to offset their appearance? Have an open mind. Realize that there's a collector for everything. Do your research. And learn from knowledgeable collectors who know how to handle oddball items. In this case, I surfed through some of the 2500-plus ashtray descriptions on eBay one day and came up with the following examples:

√ "Fabulous example of a primitive handcrafted ashtray with a fish in the center, one blue and one green cigarette rest, and background painted rusty brown. From the Gateway Lodge, Radium Hot Springs BC… The highway was built through the canyon in 1923, first as a one lane dirt road, to bring tourists to the newly discovered hot springs. The Gateway offered early lodgings. The ashtray has a few munches and bites out of it, but that it has survived at all is quite miraculous."

√ "This is an original parlour ashtray from the 1950's (I think). The ashtray has lots of character and would not look out of place in any modern living space. The piece is in excellent condition except for few very, very, very small marks on the wooden part of the base. I have tried to take a picture of it but it really is barely noticeable. The pictures do not do this ashtray justice. I assure you the chrome is absolutely flawless."

√ "Have you ever felt an instantaneous connection with something, that just makes you **FEEL THAT CLICK,** right there? And when you do, I bet that you feel **SO WARM AND WONDERFUL, DEEP INSIDE YOU…** Now I **WONDER** how you **WONDER** how when you've found that perfect thing and **FEEL ALL THE DELIGHT Areormatic Ceremonial Tobacco BRINGS?** What will you **GIVE TO** those you **LOVE?**"

NOTE: *The third example is actually given in verse and is much longer than the excerpt shown here. The interesting description is marred substantially by an audio clip describing Native American pottery that plays while you view the auction description, however.*

The bizarre ashtray shown in Figure 9-4 is enlivened by some logos and artwork that identify its seller. The logo is part of this seller's sales template (see Chapter 8); it appears in the same spot in each of the seller's auction listings.

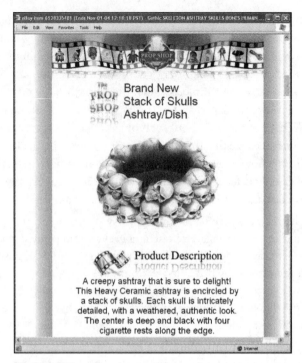

Figure 9-4
A colorful logo and some choice words can make even
the strangest items more appealing.

Make Your Sales More Visible

Every day, millions of sales are held on eBay. How do potential bidders or buyers
find exactly the sales items they want? One of eBay's strengths is that, if you have
something really notable and exceptional for sale, the dedicated collectors or
others who are familiar with the type of item will find it. When the bidding goes
up to more than $5,000, the sale gets included in a special page on the eBay site
called Big Ticket Items (**http://pages.ebay.com/buy/bigticket/**), shown in
Figure 9-5.

If you're a buyer, this is the place to find some of the most interesting sales on
eBay. For sellers, the problem is that there's no guarantee that their item will be
listed on the Big Ticket Items page. You can't list the item specifically in this
category, in other words. But you can get more attention for your sales by
taking some extra steps, as described in the sections that follow.

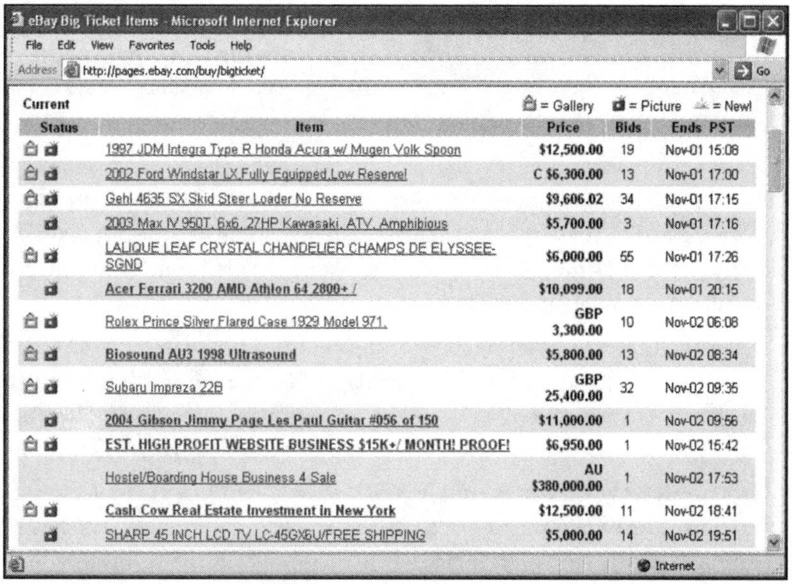

eBay Big Ticket Items - Microsoft Internet Explorer

File   Edit   View   Favorites   Tools   Help

Address http://pages.ebay.com/buy/bigticket/   Go

Current				
		🔖 = Gallery 🎞 = Picture = New!		
Status	**Item**	**Price**	**Bids**	**Ends PST**
🔖 🎞	1997 JDM Integra Type R Honda Acura w/ Mugen Volk Spoon	$12,500.00	19	Nov-01 15:08
🔖 🎞	2002 Ford Windstar LX Fully Equipped,Low Reserve!	C $6,300.00	13	Nov-01 17:00
🔖 🎞	Gehl 4635 SX Skid Steer Loader No Reserve	$9,606.02	34	Nov-01 17:15
🎞	2003 Max IV 950T, 6x6, 27HP Kawasaki, ATV, Amphibious	$5,700.00	3	Nov-01 17:16
🔖 🎞	LALIQUE LEAF CRYSTAL CHANDELIER CHAMPS DE ELYSSEE-SGND	$6,000.00	55	Nov-01 17:26
🎞	Acer Ferrari 3200 AMD Athlon 64 2800+ /	$10,099.00	18	Nov-01 20:15
🔖 🎞	Rolex Prince Silver Flared Case 1929 Model 971.	GBP 3,300.00	10	Nov-02 06:08
🔖 🎞	Biosound AU3 1998 Ultrasound	$5,800.00	13	Nov-02 06:34
🔖 🎞	Subaru Impreza 22B	GBP 25,400.00	32	Nov-02 09:35
🎞	2004 Gibson Jimmy Page Les Paul Guitar #056 of 150	$11,000.00	1	Nov-02 09:56
🔖 🎞	EST. HIGH PROFIT WEBSITE BUSINESS $15K+/ MONTH! PROOF!	$6,950.00	1	Nov-02 15:42
	Hostel/Boarding House Business 4 Sale	AU $380,000.00	1	Nov-02 17:53
🔖 🎞	Cash Cow Real Estate Investment in New York	$12,500.00	11	Nov-02 18:41
🎞	SHARP 45 INCH LCD TV LC-45GX6U/FREE SHIPPING	$5,000.00	14	Nov-02 19:51

Internet

Figure 9-5

If you can get a high-priced item on this page, you're sure to get more attention for it.

Add the Right Keywords

To conduct a search on eBay, you need to enter one or more keywords. The better the match between the keywords in your description and the keywords that shoppers tend to enter, the more frequently your description will turn up in a set of search results. eBay maintains a list of popular keywords at **http://buy.ebay.com**. You can research the terms you want to enter and see if they are on the list—or change your description to make sure it contains at least a few of the most frequently used keywords.

But there's a problem: eBay doesn't make it easy to find keywords by subject. Locating the right keywords is a time-consuming, hit-and-miss proposition. Suppose you want to write a description about an ashtray. If the keyword lists were organized in a user-friendly way, you could enter the term "ashtray" and find a group of keywords related to it. Instead, the keywords are listed in alphabetical order. You have to access them by following these steps:

1.   Write your description. Create a sales listing that contains four to six possible keywords. Make sure the words are relevant to the object you are selling. For example, if you're describing an antique tennis racket, you might write a description that looks something like this:

> This wooden tennis racket from the 1920s, made by Wright &
> Ditson, has all of its original gut string. It looks like it
> could hit a tennis ball in a championship match. It would also
> look good in a sporting goods collection or a set of tennis
> memorabilia.

2. Scan your description and do a search to see if your keywords are among eBay's popular keywords. In the preceding example, "tennis," "racket," "tennis racket," "gut," "tennis ball," "sporting goods," and "tennis memorabilia" are all possible searches.

3. Adjust your keywords if needed. Scan the list of popular keywords on the eBay Keywords page. "Tennis" is included. "Racket" is not listed by itself. However, "tennis racket" is included as a popular search term. Therefore, the strategy is to incorporate the phrase "tennis racket" in your sales listing.

4. Do a search for your most important keyword—in this example, "tennis." Look for the search terms listed under the heading Popular Searches in the search results page. Try to include one or more of those terms in your description. In this example, the term "table tennis" is included. It would be a stretch to include the following sentence in your auction description, but it will get your description more visits:

    Shown on the display table is this tennis racket…

    The point is that a search for "table tennis" will turn up your description.

5. Click the See more common keywords link under the Popular Searches heading (see Figure 9-6). Try to work more keywords into your description.

Figure 9-6
Pay attention to keywords and phrases that are commonly used by buyers doing searches.

Take Advantage of Google

Google may be the only search engine that matters, and that makes it an important advertising venue for anyone who runs a business, either on eBay or off. The preceding section described one resource on eBay (keywords) that can tell you what shoppers are interested in and what they search for most often. Chapter 11 mentions others, including Hot Lists. Google has the same kinds of resources, and you can use them to determine what kinds of items to sell on eBay: they're items that tie in to the interests shown on the Google Zeitgeist page (**www.google.com/press/zeitgeist.html**, shown in Figure 9-7).

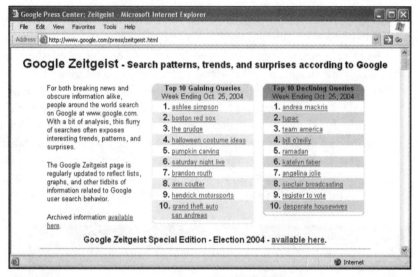

Figure 9-7

When you're searching for things to sell, use current trends and interests like these to guide you.

Admittedly, some of the items in the Top 10 query boxes at the top of the Zeitgeist page are seasonal. Search through all of the lists presented on the Zeitgeist page and make note of names and topics that occur several times; make note of these on a list and use them when you search for merchandise to sell on eBay.

Google is a particularly useful resource for sellers who have an eBay Store or a Web site through which they sell items. If you can get your store or site included at or near the top of Google's search results, your sales are likely to benefit. How do you take full advantage of Google? Follow these steps:

1. Create an eBay Store or a Web site. If you have one, you have a URL to which Google can make links.

2. Make sure your eBay Store or Web site is included in Google's index. Do a search for your site on Google. Does it appear? If not, go to **www.google.com/ addurl.html**. Add the URL of your site or store in the form provided. If you have an eBay Store, the URL will be in the following form:

   ```
   http://stores.ebay.com/[your-store-name]
   ```

3. In the Comments box, type a brief description of your Web site—a description you would like to see when your site turns up in a list of search descriptions.

4. Click Add URL, and check back in a few weeks to see if your site or store has been added.

5. Once your chosen URL is in Google's database, you can make your site one of those that shows up in the right-hand column of a set of search results beneath the Sponsored Links heading. Your site might also appear right along the top of the search results (see Figure 9-8). Such advertisements are surprisingly affordable. You typically pay an activation fee of about $5 when you first sign up for the program. Then, you decide how much you want to pay for an ad. You only pay when someone clicks on the ad. You can choose to pay $.05 per click or as much as $50 per click. The more you pay, the more likely your ad is to appear in the search results.

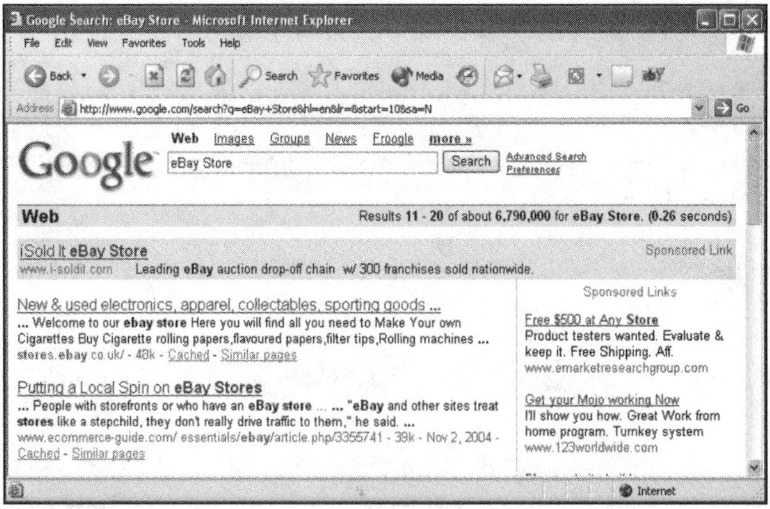

Figure 9-8
You can advertise your eBay Store or Web site on Google.

The AdWords advertising program is definitely worth a try. It's up to you, though, to specify the keywords and keyword phrases that you want Google to use as a "trigger" to display your ad. It's also up to you to specify how many viewers you want to reach: you can tell Google you want the ad to turn up only to viewers who live in your immediate geographic area; you might do this if you want visitors to come to your brick-and-mortar store. You might also want the ad to appear in the widest possible area—to overseas users as well as those in your own country. You'll have to pay more for such coverage; find out more at **https://adwords.google.com/support/bin/answer.py?answer=6385**.

Cross-Promote Your Merchandise

You've probably seen eBay sales that have an additional set of sales listed at the very bottom of the description, underneath the following heading: "See More Great Items From This Seller" (see Figure 9-9 for an example).

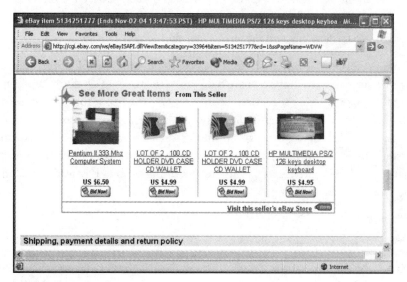

Figure 9-9
Cross-promotions are created for your items automatically by eBay if you activate this feature.

Sellers configure this feature using My eBay. If they have multiple items for sale, it allows them to advertise several items on a single listing. eBay sellers like this feature for several reasons:

√   It tells buyers about similar items that come from the same seller.

√   It gives buyers the chance to buy more than one item from sellers they know and like.

√   It gives buyers an easy way to buy more items so they can be shipped at the same time, which can cut shipping costs.

Cross-promotions make sense if you are currently selling a group of items that complement one another. If you have a computer for sale, for instance, you naturally want to tell buyers that you also have the keyboard, monitor, mouse, and other accessories that go along with the device. To use cross-promotions, you need to tell eBay that you want to include them with your sales listings. Follow these steps:

1.   Go to My eBay and log in.

2.   Click the link <u>eBay Preferences</u> under the My Account heading.

3.   In the Seller Preferences section, in the Participate in eBay Cross-Promotions row, click <u>change</u>.

4.   Sign in again with your User ID and password.

5.   When the Manage Your Cross-Promotions page appears, click the radio button next to "Cross-promote my items."

6.   Click Save Settings, and sign in *again* if prompted to do so.

Cross-promotions, by themselves, are a way to degunk a set of items you put up for sale: instead of each item being sold in isolation, some or all of the items are listed on one another's auction listing pages. Cross-promotions can also be made to work more efficiently. Suppose you are selling six items: a computer, a keyboard, a disk drive, a set of computer speakers, a set of golf clubs, and a poster. Suppose you preview your description of the computer and you find that the following items are automatically displayed by eBay at the bottom of the sales description page:

```
See More Great Items From This Seller

Keyboard | Golf clubs | Poster | Disk Drive
```

Obviously, this cross-promotion effort will work better if you advertise the other two computer items you have for sale, not the golf clubs and the poster. If you want to change the items displayed as cross-promotions, click the <u>Change your cross-promoted items</u> link. Click <u>Change to manual selection</u>, and then click the Change Item button that appears beneath each of the cross-promotion items displayed by default. When a list of your items for sale appears, click the Add button. (You can find a more detailed set of instructions at **http:// pages.ebay.com/help/sell/cp-change.html**).

Summing Up

Some rare and desirable items practically sell themselves on eBay. But these kinds of items are few and far between. In order to develop a steady stream of sales, you need to be able to sell merchandise that's not especially rare or unusual. By rescuing items you might otherwise throw out and learning from the way experienced collectors handle merchandise that many might find strange or mundane, you increase the number of bids your sales receive. Degunk your selling strategies by cutting out items that are difficult to ship, purchasing shipping supplies inexpensively on eBay itself, doing research on your merchandise, presenting your items in their best light, and marketing your sales. Taking a few minutes before you post a sales description will improve your sales rate and promote your image as a knowledgeable and careful seller.

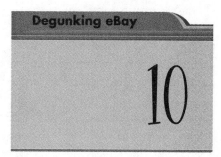

Degunking Your Shipping and Customer Service

Degunking Checklist:

√   Learn how to streamline your shipping process.

√   Establish realistic shipping schedules and costs with your customers.

√   Find out why special gifts and personal notes are important aspects of customer service.

√   Use the right tools (such as the Internet) to streamline the packing process.

√   Streamline your shipping with the "Big Three" delivery services, and pick the services that are appropriate for you.

√   Protect yourself with delivery confirmation and insurance.

√   Learn how to handle bulky, hard-to-ship merchandise.

The hard truth is that all of the degunking you've done around the house, on your PC, and on eBay itself can be undone by a gunked-up shipping process. It's easy to overlook packing and shipping when you are trying to streamline your sales activities on eBay. But this is precisely the point when consumers on eBay get the most nervous. Having paid for their merchandise, they can only wait for you to live up to your part of the bargain. After a few days, they start looking for the FedEx, UPS, or United States Postal Service delivery person to arrive at their door. Don't leave them waiting in the dark. Be clear about timetables and costs when shipping and pack your merchandise carefully, as described in the sections that follow. If you degunk your shipping and customer service process, you'll be sure to end up with satisfied customers and positive feedback.

Keep Your Shipping Process Gunk Free

You never really appreciate the importance of shipping until you have to do it yourself. As a buyer, you send a payment, and a week or so later (or maybe sooner, if you're using Priority or Express Mail), the package arrives and you tear it open eagerly. As you throw the layers and layers or newspaper and Bubble Wrap to one side, you wonder to yourself, "Why did this person put so much cushioning in there?" When the item emerges from its packaging unscathed, you are happy and you toss all the packing materials and don't give it another thought. Not until you yourself start shipping, that is.

Shipping Fundamentals

When you make some sales and have to start shipping out stuff, new sources of gunk appear:

√   Boxes. You need to buy them, and you end up purchasing bunches of them at the local office supply store, only to find that they are too large and too expensive.

√   Shipping charges. If you fail to add a shipping charge to your sales description, buyers are likely to complain when you tell them about this additional expense at checkout time. If you specify a flat rate, buyers could complain that the shipping charge is too high. If you estimate a shipping charge to a neighboring state and your buyer lives across the country, you could end up losing money on this transaction.

√   Insulating material. You begin to live amid piles of insulation material, and you shuffle across the floor, kicking stray packing peanuts as you go.

√   Getting to the shipper. You have to wait in line; you have to deal with unfriendly clerks; you have to make three separate trips each week, instead of just one, because all of your sales end at different times. You stagger up to the post office door carrying a tower of boxes; they spill and you worry whether anything was broken.

√   Problems with the shipper. Packages can get lost or damaged in transit; you need to protect yourself by giving your customers tracking numbers and paying extra for insurance in case trouble occurs.

√   Communication mix-ups. If your return policy isn't clearly stated, or if your shipping method isn't clearly understood by the buyer, you could end up with a very unhappy customer and, worse, poor feedback.

Packing and shipping can easily become the least pleasant and most tedious part of conducting transactions on eBay. But as long as you follow the common-sense practices described in this chapter, you'll be able to keep the packing and shipping phase gunk free. It's like baking: Things go much more smoothly if you buy your ingredients beforehand and follow the recipe to the letter. If you have your ingredients arranged on the counter before you start baking a cake, you are far less likely to make a mistake. If you set aside a room in your house for shipping materials and packing, you are likely to have a smoother time when it comes to actually getting things out the door. If you establish a relationship or account with a local shipper, you can confidently rely on certain shipping rates and delivery times.

Communicating Promptly with Customers

When you have e-mail messages or other communications sitting in your inbox waiting for a reply, they tend to pile up in your consciousness, too. On eBay, a delay of just a few days can make buyers anxious that you're never going to respond to their high bid. (I'm speaking from personal experience. Once, after three days of no response, I got a seller's street address and phone number through eBay's Find Members form and was on the verge of phoning him when he called to say he had been out of town.)

The way to deal with customer communications after the sale is made is to be systematic about it. You should develop a set of form letters that require you to customize only certain parts in the middle; as long as you have the beginning or the end ready as a template, you'll save time in composing a response. Your stock response might look like this:

Dear [Customer]

Thank you very much for your inquiry. I do get a number of e-mail inquiries every day, so it's sometimes difficult to get back with an instant response.

In regard to your question about [eBay sales number and name of item],

[fill in response here].

Thanks again for your inquiry and I hope to do business with you. Be sure to check my eBay Store [add URL] for more items that might strike your fancy.

Sincerely,

[Your name]

An important aspect of correspondence is not just what you say but how you say it. Degunking doesn't mean stripping down your e-mail messages to the bare minimum. It means preparing appropriate boilerplate messages beforehand and filling in the blanks as needed so they accomplish your business goals: keeping the customer informed, reassuring customers, and (ultimately) generating more business. Your tone should be friendly, yet businesslike.

A number of other standard types of communication can be handled more quickly with a form letter. Here are some examples:

√   The initial response to a buyer. This can be brief but should definitely be friendly: "I am happy to discover that you are the high bidder/buyer on my item [item number and name]. If you want to pay by check, here's where to send payment...."

√   The payment reminder letter. Don't immediately assume that the buyer is trying to cheat you. There may be a legitimate reason why someone is slow to pay. Be professional. "I haven't heard from you and it's been a week since the sale ended. I would appreciate it if you would let me know as soon as possible what your situation is and send payment by [fill in a definite date]."

√   The second payment reminder letter. If your first letter goes out and you haven't heard from the buyer for a week to 10 days from the time the sale ended, you need to be firm and state what's going to happen. But don't threaten; be professional at all times. Say something along these lines: "I sent a letter to you on [date] with no response. If I don't receive payment by [set a date], I will relist the item and file an Unpaid Item dispute with eBay, after which eBay will contact you."

√ The "shipment is on the way" letter. No matter how many things they've purchased online, buyers always feel better knowing the item is in the mail. This letter doesn't have to be long. Just tell the buyer "I have received your payment and wanted to let you know that your package was sent out by [shipper's name] today. You can track the package at [shipper's Web site URL]."

√ The request for feedback letter. In many cases, you'll have to remind buyers to send you positive feedback so you can boost your rating. Start out by saying, "Thank you for your purchase; I hope we can do business again in the future—and please don't forget to leave feedback...."

Sometimes, you can simply fill in the buyer's name and the item number and leave the rest of the letter as is; other times, you might want to customize the body of the letter to correspond to the situation. In either case, having words you can rearrange will jump-start the communication process so you don't have to type your letter from scratch every time.

TIP: If you're going to be out of town, be sure to mention it as part of your auction description: "I'm going to be out of town for two days right around the end of the sale; I will get back to the high bidder as soon as possible." While this isn't a great situation, because it means you'll be unavailable for last-minute questions, it also encourages people to get in touch with you earlier in the sale rather than later.

Sticking to a Schedule

When you turn recurring activities into rituals, you'll feel more in control of your eBay business. Establish a "shipping day," when your primary activity involves applying labels, putting things in boxes, and getting those boxes out to your appointed shipper. Make a note of all the materials you use in a day; after you have visited the shipper, you can head to your nearest office supply store and replenish what you've used (or go to the office supply store's Web site and order online). If you can purchase supplies in bulk, you will save money.

GunkBuster's Notebook: Use the Right Shipping Tools

Any carpenter or contractor can tell you the importance of using the right tool for the job. When it comes to shipping and packing, the process will go much more smoothly if you invest in the right tools at the outset.

One of the most important tools, when it comes to shipping, is a postal scale to calculate shipping costs accurately. Other useful tools are extra wide packing tape, boxes that are sturdy and clean (not necessarily new, however), dispensers for packing peanuts so they fall quickly into a box and don't get on the floor, and Bubble Wrap that comes in rolls so you can wrap it easily around your merchandise. You might also invest in a single-edged cutting tool, in addition to a good pair of scissors. Personalized labels that bear your business's name and eBay Store URL are an extra touch that will have a positive impact on your buyers.

Because you want to ramp up your eBay business, you will want to be treated as a professional. You are in this as a business, and you want your customers to regard you as having certain standards. If you use flimsy tape or old dirty boxes for shipping, it's just not going to make you look very good in the eyes of your customers.

A well-packaged box that is delivered on time and at the prearranged price is a sign that you're a professional. This will reassure your customers that you are someone worth doing business with.

Add an Extra Gift

Consider the following scenario: You embark on an extensive cleaning and sorting project around the house (as described in Chapter 11). You come up with some Christmas ornaments, holiday cards, and miscellaneous items that aren't of great value and probably not very collectible. Do you (a) throw them out, (b) save them for holiday time, or (c) offer them for sale on eBay in one lot?

The answer, of course, is (d) none of the above. You give them away as extra goodwill gifts along with the merchandise you send to buyers. If you can include a "freebie" along with your shipped items, you'll not only put a smile on your customers' faces, you'll increase the chances that they'll return to make more bids or purchases on your sales.

There aren't any rules about including a gift. You don't have to do it. It's just one of many things I've learned from PowerSellers over the years.

Include a Personal Note

eBay sales are a very personal business. Putting a thank-you note in your package along with your merchandise is an important customer relations tool. That doesn't mean you have to compose a personal letter with every sale. Come up with stock phrases that you can use over and over again. That way, if you have a repeat customer, you know what you're going to say; with a first-time customer, you might say something different. If someone required special treatment, you would say something different. If the sale occurs around the holidays, you might make note of the time of year ("Season's Greetings" or "Happy New Year," for instance). The whole point here, as in other aspects of the shipping process, is to not have to reinvent the wheel and do things from scratch every single time. You get credit for having the personal touch; at the same time, you're saving time and energy by taking an assembly line approach to repetitive work. Repetition also makes it less likely that you'll make a mistake.

Pack with Care

As an eBay seller, you will need to streamline processes so you can spend time getting sales online and building income. Packing is a prime target for eliminating unnecessary processes and reducing expenses. The sections that follow suggest ways to pack in a more businesslike manner so you can save time and money on this phase of your eBay transactions.

Find Free Packing Supplies

When it comes to finding shipping supplies, start close to home. Actually, you should start *at home*. Look for shipping and packing supplies around your own house. Do you have piles of old newspaper sitting around, waiting for the recycle bin? Do your neighbors? Newspaper is perfect as insulating material. Do you have a room full of empty boxes in the basement, each filled with packing peanuts? You've got instant eBay shipping material.

TIP: *There's nothing wrong with cleaning up your neighborhood (or more accurately, your neighborhood's trash disposal area) in your quest for free boxes and insulating material. Scrounge around your alley just before trash pickup day. If you see any clean boxes or other packing material that's strong and can be reused, grab it. You're recycling, so it's good for you and for the environment too.*

Double-Packing

One of the worst things that can happen to you, as a seller or a buyer, is to have merchandise get broken in transit. If you take out insurance before you ship, you can have your customer file a claim with the shipper, but they probably won't be happy at failing to receive what they purchased.

The best way to avoid damage is to double-pack your especially fragile items. Put your item in a box and insulate it with packing peanuts or bubble wrap. Then, take a larger box and place the first box inside it. Insulate the space between the two containers with more material. Yes, it will cost a few cents more to ship the larger package. Yes, it's a waste of material to use two boxes. But it's a far greater waste to have to pay out a refund or make someone file an insurance claim due to damage from inadequate packing.

Insulation

Gunk doesn't always involve clutter. It can involve dents, cracks, or other damage to merchandise you ship out. You don't want to have all of your hard work undone by getting a complaint from a buyer who discovers that something has been dented or damaged because it bumped around during transit. The fact is that you can't include too much insulating material in your packages.

> ### GunkBuster's Notebook: Pack Items Appropriately
>
> While it's important to use plenty of insulating materials when you pack, don't use the wrong packing materials either. All too often, sellers stuff a box with expensive materials that aren't necessary, which is a waste of money. It also increases the weight of the package, which makes it more expensive to ship. Such expenses can make the difference between making or losing money on the deal.
>
> You might think that extra shipping expenses aren't important because the buyer ends up paying for them anyway. True, but buyers aren't dumb. Many of them have purchased lots of items on eBay. They can tell the difference between something that's been overpacked and something that's been prepared correctly. If two or three items are offered on eBay at the same time, the shipping cost can be the deciding factor that determines which one will get the most bids. If your item has a starting bid of $.99 but a shipping cost of $10.00, you'll probably lose out over an item that has a starting bid of $9.99 and a shipping cost of $5.00. Bidders will quickly equalize the high bids and make the difference in starting cost irrelevant.

Ship with Care

Degunking your shipping process is largely a matter of planning ahead. Decide who your shipper is, and make an agreement with that shipper beforehand. Get an account set up; when you sign up for an account, you usually receive some shipping labels and envelopes along with your account number.

Also, get to know your delivery person. It's useful to have the same person or two, and encourage them to be in the habit of checking with you when they pass by your home to see if you have any shipments ready to go out.

TIP: Thank the people who deliver for you, and always be pleasant and professional. You'll see the benefits. They'll go out of their way to help you when you come in because they know you'll be a pleasure to deal with.

Speed Up Your Postage Path with the USPS

What's gunky about postage, other than the glue affixed to the back of your typical postage stamp? Plenty. Postage is potentially one of the gunkiest aspects of shipping. Why else would you haul everything to the post office and wait in line? You've done your packing; having to wait for someone to weigh your package, ask you how you want to ship, and apply various stickers for insurance and delivery confirmation is a time-consuming process when 6, 8, 10, or more packages are involved.

By speeding up any one of these aspects of determining postage costs, you'll streamline the overall process of shipping:

√ Weigh your packages at home.

√ Print out postage and labels from your computer and apply them yourself.

√ Call the post office and have a delivery person pick up your packages right from your door so you don't have to travel at all.

This is no pipe dream: it's a process you can do right now, thanks to the Internet and the United States Postal Service. I'm a big fan of the USPS because its rates are usually half those of private delivery services, it offers the same delivery confirmation and express shipping options, and it is extremely reliable. In many parts of the country, the USPS is also establishing a program where it will pick up Express Mail or Priority Mail packages from your location if you call in advance (find out more about this program at **www.usps.com/mailerscompanion/ mar2004/mc0304art1.htm**). eBay has a new shipping center page (**http:// pages.ebay.com/usps/home.html**) that leads you through the process of ordering shipping supplies or postage from the USPS too.

The USPS offers postage online. Just follow these steps:

1. Go to the USPS home page (**www.usps.com**).

2. Under the heading Buy Stamps & Shop, click The Postal Store if you need to buy stamps or click PC Postage if you want to print postage from your computer. (The rest of these steps explain the process of printing postage from your computer.)

3. When the PC Postage Products & Services page appears, click one of the online service providers shown. For this example, click Endicia (**www.endicia.com**), which is used by some of the PowerSellers interviewed for this book, including Kimberly King and Melissa Sands.

4. When the Endicia home page shown in Figure 10-1 appears, click Sign Up under the Free Trial heading so you can sign up for a free account with the service.

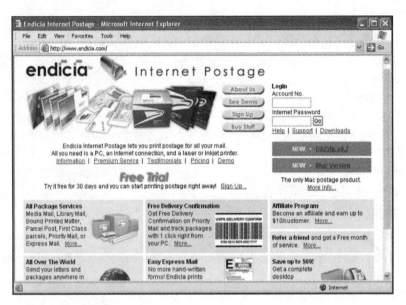

Figure 10-1
Many eBay sellers use postage services like this to avoid trips to the shipper's physical office.

5. Click Start and fill out the Endicia sign-up form. Follow the five steps presented in subsequent screens to complete the sign-up process.

As part of the sign-up process, you need to choose a billing plan. When you're just starting out, chances are you'll select the standard $9.95 per month service plan. You'll also need to provide a credit card number; be aware that after the 30-day trial period ends, your card will automatically be charged on a monthly basis unless you cancel your Endicia service.

If you're like me, you're probably wondering why you should pay $10 per month just to obtain postage you could get from the post office. You're mainly paying for your time, which is valuable; by not having to travel to the post office and wait in line to get your postage, you can work more efficiently. Endicia also provides you with delivery confirmation for free if you ship via

Priority Mail and only $.13 if you use other rates. You can also print out shipping labels from your computer and track packages online.

TIP: *Endicia isn't the only postage service around. You can also obtain postage online from Stamps.com (www.stamps.com) and Pitney Bowes (www.pitneybowes.com).*

Get Freebies with Priority Mail

Standard First-Class Mail sounds nice, but there's a problem with it: you have to buy or reuse envelopes and apply your own mailing labels or write the address by hand, which isn't terribly professional. First-Class Mail is actually a lot of work for you, the seller. Priority Mail is more expensive but far less gunky. That's because the Postal Service gives away free shipping materials—boxes, labels, and packing tape—that are adorned with the Priority Mail logo. You can pick up the materials from your local post office or have them shipped to you via the USPS Postal Store. Just to go **www.usps.com** and search for "Priority Mail," and you get results such as the ones shown in Figure 10-2.

While it's true that Priority Mail is more expensive than Media Mail or First-Class Mail, it's still a cost-effective solution. For packages under 10 pounds and to most locations, Priority Mail rates are usually only $1 or $2 higher than

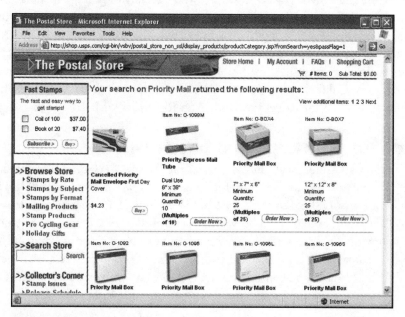

Figure 10-2

High-quality Priority Mail boxes and other shipping supplies are available from the United States Postal Service for free.

Parcel Post rates. For the nominal extra cost, you also get a relatively quick estimated delivery time of two to three days, which customers will almost certainly appreciate.

TIP: You can also obtain Priority Mail supplies by calling the post office at 1-800-610-8734.

Save Big Bucks with Media Mail

Many of the most popular items on eBay are also the most practical to ship: books, records, CDs, and DVDs are proven bid-getters on eBay. They're also easy to ship, especially when you use the US Postal Service's Media Mail rate. Media Mail is a special classification of mail for books, CDs, video tapes, and other items. Be sure to check the guidelines at your local post office for what constitutes Media Mail. Employees at the USPS are authorized to open your packages (I've seen it happen) to make sure that what you're shipping falls within the category, so don't try to save a few bucks on merchandise that doesn't qualify for a Media Mail rate.

It doesn't make sense to sell a CD or DVD for a dollar or two, or even an old LP for $5 or less, only to turn around and charge your customer to ship that item for $6 by Priority Mail. At that rate, you won't get any bids in the first place, and you certainly won't make any money on the transaction. Media Mail is a dirt-cheap rate that serves as a practical alternative. You can calculate Media Mail and other types of postage rates using the USPS Domestic Calculator (**http://postcalc.usps.gov/**). A small one-pound package being sent from Chicago to Berkeley, California, would cost about $1.42 at the Media Mail rate, compared with $3.75 for Parcel Post and $3.85 for Priority Mail, for instance.

Call for a Pickup from Big Brown

If you run a business that already uses United Parcel Service (UPS) for shipping, it makes sense to use it for fulfilling your eBay orders too. UPS isn't as inexpensive as USPS, but it offers one big advantage: its network of delivery people in those trademarked brown uniforms and driving those brown trucks. Its staff people will pick up as many boxes at your home base as you have. You do have to pay a pickup fee, but if you have lots of boxes, the fee is well worth it. With a UPS account, you can use the Web site (**www.ups.com**) to print out labels, calculate shipping costs, and order packing materials, too.

NOTE: *The charge for pickup depends on your location. When I calculated shipping costs using the UPS online calculator (wwwapps.ups.com/calTimeCost?loc=en_US), I came up with a charge of $6.60 to ship a one-pound package from Chicago to Berkeley if I dropped the package off at a UPS shipping location. But the charge rose to $9.95 when I specified pickup at my house—a 30 percent increase.*

Putting the Express in FedEx

The gunky way to pack and ship, if your shipper of choice is FedEx, is to run to your local FedEx box with your merchandise in hand, hurrying to meet the shipment deadline, and filling out your shipping label outside in the cold while the driver waits impatiently.

You don't need to do anything of the sort. Follow these steps to put the "Express" back into the process of working with FedEx:

1. Get an account number. Go to **www.fedex.com/signup/OADRSplash.jsp**. It's free to sign up for an account and if you choose the Online Express Shipping option, you get a 10 percent discount.

NOTE: *One of the advantages of having an account is that you are billed by FedEx on a monthly basis. You get nice printed statements that you can use when it's time to count your deductions at tax time.*

2. Get lots of packing materials in advance. You can either pick them up at a location that handles FedEx shipments (such as Kinko's) or order them on the FedEx Web site. Pile up all the labels, envelopes, and boxes you can so you can do the packing at home.
3. Use FedEx Ship Manager to calculate shipping costs and print out labels for your shipment (see Figure 10-3).
4. Call for a pickup. When you have a FedEx account number, you can call in advance and have the delivery person come right to your door.

FedEx isn't the least expensive alternative around, but time is money, and if you can take advantage of FedEx to help you save time, your advance planning will pay off in the long run. And for important, valuable, or time-sensitive shipments, FedEx is probably the most reliable way to ship.

Delivery Confirmation

If you have one shipment that gets lost, the resulting negative feedback can overshadow many other positive feedback comments and ruin your feedback rating. One way to prevent arguments and problems when something gets lost in transit is delivery confirmation: a statement by the shipper informing you that the package reached its intended destination. Delivery confirmation is

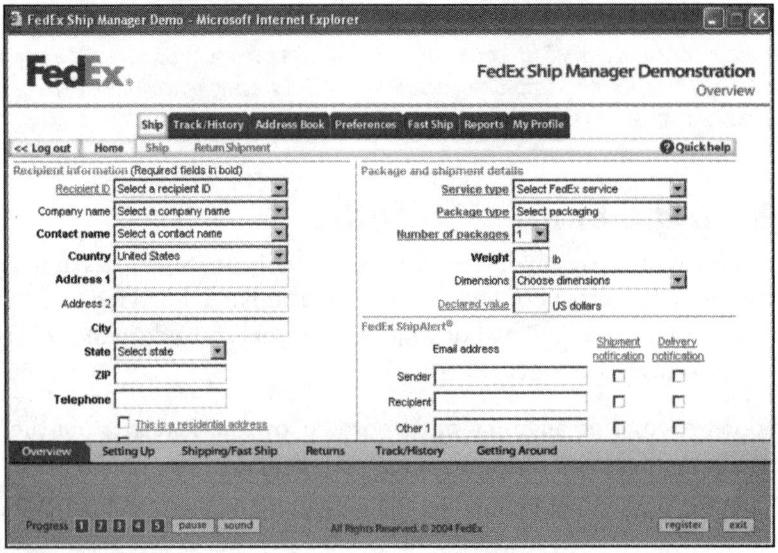

Figure 10-3

This FedEx online service helps account holders print labels and store frequently used addresses.

useful primarily because it tells you whether the package was delivered or not in case the buyer falsely claims it never arrived (which can happen). Delivery confirmation is also important because PayPal requires a delivery confirmation tracking number in cases of claims of non-delivery.

UPS and FedEx include delivery confirmation in their standard delivery services. If you use the USPS's Priority Mail service, electronic delivery confirmation is free too. For other USPS services, such as Parcel Post, electronic delivery confirmation is $.13 per item—an insignificant charge when you think about the peace of mind such proof of delivery can provide.

Insurance

One of the most unpleasant situations that can befall a seller is to have the buyer report that an item arrived damaged despite all your efforts to pack it carefully. If you don't obtain insurance for that item, you'll have to work out some sort of settlement with the buyer—perhaps a total refund or a discount on the sales price. If you obtain insurance, the buyer only has to file a claim with the shipper. It can take a while to receive reimbursement, but the shipper is then supposed to pay for the damage.

If you use UPS or FedEx, you have an advantage: insurance is relatively inexpensive (\$.35 per \$100.00 of insurance from UPS or \$.50 per \$100.00 from FedEx). But if you use USPS, insurance has to be purchased in addition to postage. And it can be costly:

√ For coverage of \$50.00 or less, the cost is \$1.30.

√ For coverage of \$50.01 to \$100.00, the cost is \$2.20.

√ For coverage of \$100.01 to \$200.00, the cost is \$3.20.

NOTE: *For a complete list of rates on insurance, delivery confirmation, and other services, go to the Domestic Mail Manual Contents page (**http://pe.usps.gov/text/dmm/r000toc.htm**) and click Services.*

To avoid gunking up your profits by overpaying for insurance, sign up with a company that provides insurance as an alternative to the Big Three carriers. Universal Parcel Insurance Coverage (U-PIC) charges \$.17 per \$100.00 of coverage if you ship with UPS or FedEx and \$.50 per \$100.00 if you use the USPS and have delivery confirmation. Find out more at **www.u-pic.com**.

Handling Large Items

When you're just starting out on eBay, you should stay away from selling items that are physically heavy and difficult to ship, like household appliances. But when you're degunking your own home, sometimes you don't have a choice: you have to get rid of that big stove in the basement, that big couch in the living room, or that wreck sitting in your driveway.

The simplest alternative, when it comes to selling big, bulky items, is to require the buyer to pick the item up in person: state this clearly in your auction description and in your terms of sale. If the buyer really wants what you have, they will find a way to pick it up or will hire someone to do so.

TIP: *If you are selling cars on eBay, you can use the services of Dependable Auto Shippers (http://pages.motors.ebay.com/services/das-shipping.html), which has an agreement to provide services to eBay customers. You can get an instant online quote by filling out the form shown in Figure 10-4.*

Summing Up

This chapter introduced you to the process of streamlining and optimizing one of the most important and easily overlooked aspects of conducting a transaction on eBay: packing and shipping merchandise. Advance planning and the right tools are a big part of the solution; so is choosing a shipper and setting up

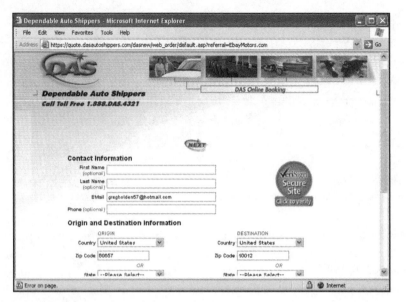

Figure 10-4

If you sell an auto on eBay, you can contract with an auto shipper to send
it to your buyer.

an account. Once you have an account, you can obtain shipping materials and
labels online and request pickups as well. In fact, you can do all of your packing
and shipping from the comfort of your own home, as long as you obtain materials online beforehand and are able to print out postage and labels at home.
Coming up with a plan and a system for getting merchandise on its way will
help you avoid the things that usually gunk up this part of eBay selling—travel
time and waiting in line at the shipping office, the unnecessary expenditures on
sometimes costly shipping materials, and the damage to your merchandise that
can result from poor packaging techniques.

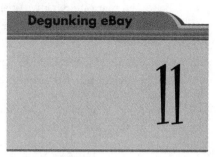

Picking the Right Sales Inventory

Degunking Checklist:

√ Choose inventory while reducing clutter in your own home.

√ Prepare sales items to maximize their marketability.

√ Research items that are most popular on eBay.

√ Locate wholesale items you can sell year-round.

√ Find surplus, overstock, and other cut-rate merchandise.

√ Scour specialty stores for unique treasures eBay buyers love.

It has been said that one person's trash is another person's treasure. But on the other hand, sometimes trash is simply trash. Your job as an eBay seller is to find desirable objects and promote them in a way that makes them attractive. You can't make money, attract bids, or get Buy It Now bidders unless you are able to gather merchandise that people will actually want.

What makes eBay alternatively fascinating and frustrating is the fact that you can't always predict what's going to elicit a flurry of high bids. You don't want to get in the habit of spending your time running around to garage sales when you have a basement or storage area full of junk you could be selling. Make sure you start at home. Don't also fall into the trap of spending many hours more per week going to garage and estate sales than you ought to: do some planning beforehand to determine which sales are the best to attend. This chapter presents some steps you can take to find sales merchandise more efficiently and to develop a system so you can come up with a steady stream of items to sell. I'll help you degunk your approach to selecting items for sale and you'll get more effective at attracting buyers and making more money.

Pick the Right Sales Inventory

When you're first starting out on eBay, it's relatively easy to choose things to sell. You likely start looking around your own home as most of us do. You look for antiques or personal possessions that are obviously valuable, such as jewelry, watches, fur coats, old toys, old dolls, and other things that show up on antiques television shows and get high appraisals. After you sell a few of these obviously desirable pieces, the challenge begins: you start rummaging through boxes and drawers; you ask your immediate family for items they might want to sell; after that, you're left to either go shopping or try to find wholesale items to resell. Shopping at estate sales, garage sales, and flea markets can be fun up to a point. After that point, looking for items can become time-consuming and tiring. To help you degunk your approach to picking the best items to sell, I've developed a five-step process that you'll want to put into practice right away. Putting this system into practice will help you find unique merchandise in a way that maximizes your time.

Step 1: Clean and Purge

I have a friend with several children who is methodical about cleaning. And I'm not talking about the weekly dusting and vacuuming. When the seasons change each year in the spring and autumn, she designates a week to tear everything apart. No corner of the basement or attic is safe from her scrutiny.

She looks over everything she comes across and makes a decision as to whether to put it in the garbage, give it to charity, store it, or continue to use it. We could all really benefit by being disciplined like this and putting a regular system in place for cleaning and purging.

The other important alternative when you come across an item is to consider selling it on eBay. If you haven't used something in five years and nobody you know would like it either, it may be just the thing to help you grow your eBay sales. How many episodes of *Antiques Roadshow* have featured a lucky recipient of an inheritance or a trash picker with a really good eye who came across something in a dumpster or a garage sale that turned out to be worth thousands of dollars? Don't laugh. It could happen to you. The first step is to set up a schedule for cleaning and to add eBay to the list of alternatives for what to do with what you find.

Step 2: Organize Your Clutter

Some people are into computer databases. Others love to keep journals. Still others are into note cards. Whatever your method, your job is to create a system out of chaos. I, for example, like to travel. Just yesterday I noticed I was wearing a hat I fell in love with in Mendocino, California, a jacket I bought with great glee in Ann Arbor, Michigan, and shoes I needed when walking up and down the uneven sidewalks of Washington, D.C. So far, I keep all those facts in my head, but it would be even better if I got into the habit of writing down every object I find in an antique mall or retail store, listing how much I pay for it and what the previous owner knows about its history, in case I ever decide to resell it. I also recommend dividing your objects into various categories and subcategories. Dishes, for example, should be inventoried as to their condition, era, and maker. That way, if you find a collector who is interested in one piece, it's likely that you'll be able to sell other pieces of a set as well. Sites like OrganizedHome.com contain sections on how to get organized, along with tips on reducing the clutter in the home (**www.organizedhome.com/content-3.html**, shown in Figure 11-1).

Step 3: Decide What to Sell

You can't always decide what to throw out and what to sell on eBay. Nobody is objective about their own possessions. A piece that you're in love with because it was a gift from a long-lost friend might be of sentimental value only to you. Or it might be worth far more than you realize because you're stuck on its associations and not being objective about its marketability.

Figure 11-1

Don't be afraid to turn to Web sites for instructions on organizing and reducing clutter.

If you find yourself attached to many of your possessions, consult your friends: call in relatives and friends who can see your sales items and tell you if they seem noteworthy in some way. But make sure you get objective, sensible opinions about what to put online and what to keep.

Step 4: Decide When to Sell

Here, again, a little organization goes a long way. If you're selling consumables, make sure the expiration date doesn't make them unusable. Otherwise, it's wise to do a little variation on the buy low/sell high concept in the form of buy out of season/sell in season. I know someone who spends his summers scouring resale shops, flea markets, and rummage sales looking for wool coats, down jackets, and warm parkas. He cleans, labels, prices them, and then packs them into his van. Off he goes to Alaska in autumn to sell them in the dead of winter.

Being able to store items is of particular value when you're dealing with secondhand children's clothes. A child's size and color preferences from one season to the next are often unpredictable, but a lot of folks will buy last season's mode. After all, who wants to pay full price for a coat that is going to be outgrown in a matter of months? Again, the trick is to have the item available when the need is there.

TIP: *Set aside shelves in your basement, one for each season. Pack clothing in boxes and place each on the appropriate shelf. That way, just a few weeks before the start of the season, you can pull out the things you've been saving and list them on eBay. List your winter clothes in or October or November, your spring garments in March or April, your summer items in May or June, your fall clothing in August or September.*

Step 5: Clean and Prepare

If you see something that's getting a little faded or frayed around the edges, your first instinct might be to fix it up. But before you leap into renovation, learn about the most likely recipient of your object. Let's say you have an original kerosene lamp. It might be logical to conclude you should use your electrical skills to wire it for a light bulb. But that would not be a good idea if it's truly a museum piece that would have more value in its original condition. When antiques are concerned, don't go overboard with cleanup. A light wiping with some Soft Scrub or just plain water might be good enough. For objects that aren't so collectible, make sure the dust is off and any wrinkles have been ironed out.

NOTE: *You obviously should be aware, in terms of storage, of the need to keep items clean and dry. That may mean investing in a temperature-controlled facility or getting the services of an exterminator to make sure unwanted pests don't invade your space.*

Research What Bidders Want

Once you've started to make order out of chaos around your home, you'll probably find yourself scratching your head and wondering, "Will people really bid on this stuff?" You can't predict it with absolute certainty, but you can improve the odds by doing a little research beforehand. By looking around eBay and around the Web, you can get some tips on the kinds of things that are sure to sell on the auction site. Let's look at some actions you can take to fine-tune your process of selecting items that eBay buyers really want.

Is It Hot or Not?

eBay gives you a number of resources for figuring out whether something is desirable or not. You can, of course, scour the thousands of listings that end every day to see how much they've sold for. A more efficient alternative is to check out the What's Hot list in eBay's Seller Central (**http://pages.ebay.com/sellercentral/whatshot.html**). Click the What's Hot heading and you'll get several types of lists. To help you plan ahead for the seasonal sales mentioned earlier in this chapter, you'll find suggestions of items that are sure to sell in the near future: at the time this was written, the holiday season was in full swing and the What's Hot page bore several lines' worth of recommendations for holiday gifts. Most were obvious: computers, cameras, cell phones, movies, video games. But click on one of the links and you can view a detailed report that provides you with information that's not so obvious, including brands, and model numbers of the types of items that have actually sold well on eBay. Listings for digital cameras and other photo equipment are shown in Figure 11-2.

Figure 11-2

The What's Hot link leads you to lengthy and detailed reports of products that have sold well on eBay.

Along with seasonal recommendations, you'll also find Hot Items by Category. Click this link and another detailed report appears. Instead of a short list of items in various categories, you get a report as long as 42 pages. You get lists broken into categories and divided into designations including Hot, Very Hot, and Super Hot. Browsing through these reports can give you some ideas of what to look for if you want to have good sales results on eBay:

√   Wholesale lots of books are Hot, but audiobooks are Very Hot.

√   Optometry equipment is Very Hot, but metalworking and construction supplies are Super Hot.

√   Movie Projectors are Hot, but vintage cameras are Very Hot.

You may be an expert collector in a particular field, but you still need to know what kinds of merchandise do best on eBay at a given moment so you know which ones to acquire for resale.

GunkBuster's Notebook: Using Amazon.com to Check Sales Ranking

If you are planning to sell items such as books, music CDs, and even power tools, you should consider using Amazon.com as a research tool. Amazon.com includes a useful ranking system that provides a sales rank for the different items it sells. The items are ranked according to how well they sell for a particular category, such as fiction books, nonfiction books, power tools, DVDs, and so on. If you have a specific item you are thinking about selling on eBay, you can look up the sales ranking on Amazon.com to see how well the item is selling overall. The lower the number listed, the better the object is selling.

Suppose you do a search on eBay for a book called *Degunking Windows*. You find the title of this book in a set of search results and you view the book's page on Amazon.com. Scroll down to the heading Product Details (see Figure 11-3). You find that this book is ranked number 10,699 (at least, it was when this was written). This might not sound very high, but when you look at other books and discover that the list reaches into the hundreds of thousands, it's really quite good. At the very least, you can compare the sales ranking of the book you want to sell on eBay to similar books and get an idea of the demand for it.

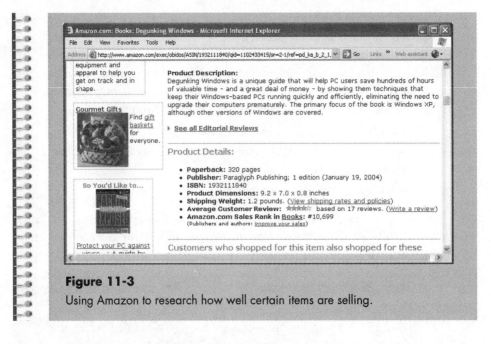

Figure 11-3
Using Amazon to research how well certain items are selling.

Collectors' Price Guides

Printed guides to all kinds of collectibles crowd the shelves of bookstores and antique stores. These books have great value for collectors, but they can also help you decide what to sell on eBay. Rather than doing the research all yourself, scouring lists of completed auctions and hot lists, you can look through price guides whose contents have been compiled by collectors drawing on years' worth of experience. The guides are also useful because they contain detailed lists of model numbers along with photos of selected varieties.

Price guides can also help you prepare more informed descriptions. Rather than saying that something is simply in "excellent" or in "near mint" condition, you can employ terms that are widely recognized as standard ways to grade an item. For example, coins can be described as "proof," "mint," "near mint," "very good," and so on.

Once you have decided what to sell, fall back on price guides to provide you with the essential background data you need to create a good description. If you are trying to determine the value of an old record, for example, you might get an idea of the price from eBay's completed auctions. But you'll get the background on the record as well as any distinguishing marks from a book like the *Official Price Guide to Records* (see Figure 11-4), which is now in its sixteenth edition and edited by a man known as "Mr. Music." *Antique Trader Antiques and Collectibles* contains thousands of photos that can aid you with identification. You can find these and other price guides on Amazon.com as well as in your local bookstore.

Figure 11-4
Printed price guides provide photos and model numbers that can help you evaluate your own merchandise.

Specialist Magazines

Selling on eBay isn't just about profits. For many collectors, it's just one of many venues they visit in order to pursue their passion. If you have a passion and you want to buy and sell collectible items on eBay, you can still get a level of information from specialty magazines that you can't find on eBay's discussion boards.

Consider the example mentioned in the previous section: record price guides. What kind of information can you get from a magazine like *Goldmine* or *Record*

Collector? You can find out about fairs and swap meets where you can meet other collectors. You can read stories about rare 45 RPM records or posters. And you can scan the classified ads at the back of each magazine to get an idea of the kinds of things collectors crave. You can use such ads to determine the rarity of the records you have to sell; you also might be able to buy a large quantity of records at one time so you can then resell them gradually on eBay.

Find Wholesale Items

Previous chapters have mentioned the importance of finding a reliable source of wholesale goods that you can sell year-round. A supply of wholesale items is an integral part of many full-time eBay businesses. Often, the way to find a good wholesaler is by word of mouth: you ask someone who knows someone, and they refer you to the seller. But if you don't have a network of people who are "in the know" to draw upon, what can you do? Some options are described in the sections that follow.

Shop for eBay-Approved Wholesalers

The obvious place to look for wholesalers is on eBay itself. Here's one suggestion. Send an e-mail message to an address that was publicized on eBay's weekly Internet radio show, eBay Radio: **productsources@wsradio.com**. When you do, you'll get a list of wholesale sources that have been "approved" by eBay. The list I received included the following URLs:

√ **http://pages.ebay.com/catindex/catwholesale.html**: This is eBay's own Wholesale Lots category. It's described in the section that follows.

√ **www.thomasregister.com**: This link takes you to the Thomas Register, a directory of wholesale businesses. You can do a search for the type of item you want. When I searched for "figurines" (a popular type of wholesale item sold on eBay), I received a list of 68 wholesale suppliers.

√ **www.dropshipsource.com**: This link leads to Worldwide Brands, a wholesaler that advertises on eBay Radio. This site gives you a set of directories containing contact information for traditional wholesalers (wholesalers that ship items to you) and drop shippers.

√ **www.liquidation.com**: This wholesaler (another eBay Radio advertiser) auctions off hundreds or even thousands of cut-rate items so you can resell them.

√ **www.ustreas.gov/auctions/customs/index.html**: The United States Department of the Treasury regularly auctions off items it has seized as part of customs inspections, including boats, jewelry, carpets, and electronics items.

√   **http://gsaauctions.gov/gsaauctions/gsaauctions**: Another agency of
the U.S. government, the General Services Administration (GSA) auctions
off surplus, seized, and forfeited property through this Web site.

Before you bid on any wholesale items sold through government or other
auctions, make sure you do a search of completed auctions on either eBay or
Andale (**www.andale.com**) to make sure you'll be able to make some profit
on what you've purchased.

Shop on Wholesale Lots

One area on eBay has been designated as the place where people can buy and sell
multiple pieces of merchandise as a group, known as a *lot*. It's a place where
manufacturers and wholesalers can sell off excess or surplus inventory at bargain
prices and resellers can sell it for a profit on eBay or other venues. The Wholesale
Lots area of eBay (**http://pages.ebay.com/catindex/catwholesale.html**, shown
in Figure 11-5) is filled with business and industrial equipment. But you can find
small, easily transportable items that you can sell to individuals at auction, too.

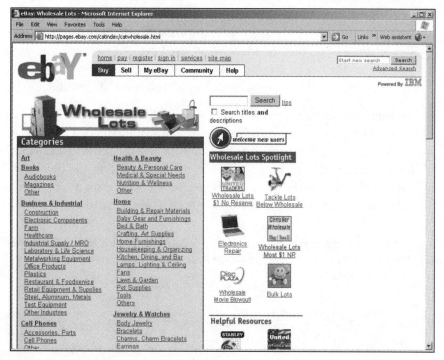

Figure 11-5
If you buy on Wholesale Lots, you can take advantage of eBay's safeguards for
buyers.

A scan of the categories in Wholesale Lots indicates that many of the items offered are the very same ones listed as Hot Items in eBay's Seller Central (see "Is It Hot or Not?" earlier in this chapter). These include audiobooks, healthcare equipment, tools, jewelry, and sporting goods. There is a Collectibles category within Wholesale Lots in which you might find the entire inventory of an antiques store or a large lot of Department 56 miniatures.

When you look for a wholesaler on eBay, you have the advantage of being able to examine that seller's feedback comments. You can (and should) also e-mail the seller to get referrals from satisfied customers. If the wholesaler fails to live up to their part of the bargain, you can use eBay's system of buyer protection, including insurance, negative feedback, and reporting the seller to the Rules & Safety area (see Chapter 13).

Start a Network of Hunters

Shopping for inventory by yourself is time-consuming and inefficient. You can easily exhaust yourself spending hours driving, waiting in line, doing frenzied buying at an estate sale, and hauling everything home. It's much more efficient to develop a team of people to help you. You can develop a network of friends who hunt for merchandise in their local neighborhoods. Those friends can then either sell you the items so you can resell them or consign them to you so you can sell them for a fee. You can also pool your resources and divide up the job of preparing sales descriptions so you can share in the profits.

An entrepreneur who did just that is Stella Kleiman. She is the creator of foundvalue.com (**www.foundvalue.com**, shown in Figure 11-6). She started out selling the items that cluttered her home. Once she gained some experience selling for herself and for her friends and family, she formed a network of salespeople. They serve as agents, finding people who want to sell their goods online but don't want to take the time setting up their own online presence.

TIP: Don't overlook old-fashioned ways to find people who have merchandise to sell on eBay. Put up notices in your local supermarket or library, and consider taking out an ad in your local newspaper.

GunkBuster's Notebook: The Lure of Drop Shipping

When it comes to ways to streamline selling on eBay, you can't get much better than drop shipping—at least in theory. Most wholesale suppliers make you purchase, store, and ship the items you buy from them: you purchase the wholesale goods and

Figure 11-6
Develop a network of merchandise hunters so you don't have to do all the gathering yourself.

physically own them until you can sell them online. Drop-shipping is different, and many sellers find it a very attractive option because you don't actually have to physically own or touch what you sell.

The theory works like this: You sign an agreement to resell merchandise from a wholesale supplier called a drop shipper. A drop shipper is a supplier that sends products directly to your Internet customers for you, one product at a time. Rather than sitting in your closet or basement, the wholesale stock stays at the shipper's warehouse. The shipper packs and ships the products for you. You pay a wholesale price for the products and charge your customer your retail price. You never have to touch the product or spend money to fill your garage up with products that you might not sell. If you don't have a lot of money to start with, drop shipping is an attractive way to get a new business off the ground. You don't have to pay for an item until it sells, and your customer pays you, so your personal cash outlay for the product is zero. You don't have to handle or store the merchandise, either. You don't have to sign up with just one drop shipper; you can arrange to sell different items supplied by more than one company.

The problem is that many companies that advertise themselves as drop shippers aren't actually reputable. You have to check references thoroughly. Some (though not all) require you to pay a setup fee to get started and obtain a tax ID number. And if you like to be in control of inventory, you won't have it if you work with a drop shipper and don't actually have the products on hand. If someone orders an item from you and the drop shipper informs you that it will be out of stock for several weeks, you have no choice but to tell the customer to either wait or take a refund. And don't expect much in the way of customer service from drop shippers if a customer expresses dissatisfaction with what was purchased. In addition, because the drop shipper is paying to stock the merchandise as well as ship it, you don't make as much in the way of profit as you would with items you stock yourself. You might want to consider starting with a drop shipper and moving on to a more traditional wholesaler later on.

Find Cut-Rate Inventory

You probably think you have to focus on antiques, collectibles, or items that are old or used in some way when you first start hunting for merchandise to resell on the auction site. It's natural to think about collectibles, but don't overlook new items that are sold by discount stores in your local area, too.

Warehouse Stores

My daughters love to visit Sam's Club, Costco, and other warehouse stores because they get to gobble up free samples as they peruse the latest and greatest in objects. I consume my share of tasty treats, but I'm more interested in the loss-leader attractions. In other words, each week there are items featured at far less than the going rate. They are designed, I know, to get me into the store so I'll also purchase plenty of regularly priced merchandise. But if an item is hot and I can get it at a fraction of the price, I can resell it on eBay for a healthy profit.

Surplus and Overstock Stores

You've probably got an army surplus store or a store that sells overstocked merchandise somewhere in your area. You might be able to find cut-rate household goods on the cheap at such stores and resell them on eBay.

Sometimes, the big chain stores that deal in this type of merchandise offer selected resources online. The Big Lots chain of stores has a Web site (**http://biglotswholesale.com**) that offers wholesale items. You have to register to view prices, but registration is free and, if you use a specially designated "junk e-mail" account, you won't get any unwanted promotional notices in your primary e-mail inbox, either. Overstock.com has a relatively new auction area (**http://auctions.overstock.com**) where you can potentially buy new merchandise at cut-rate prices. The key here, as elsewhere, is to do research beforehand: search eBay's database of completed auctions to see how much an item is likely to fetch before you place a bid.

Dollar Stores

My daughters earn small sums of money for doing odd jobs and then they go to the local dollar store, where they can walk away with a big bag of treasures for just a few hours of work. This is also their favorite place to shop for the holidays because they can actually use their own money to pay for something they know their favorite aunt will just love. I admit to liking pop culture, and not only what's trendy today. I get even more excited about a ceramic figure, for example, of a cartoon character from my childhood. This is a place where you can often find possessions for pennies that you really can resell for the big bucks.

Advertising Locally

It seems to be common knowledge that you spend the first half of life accumulating stuff and the last half trying to figure out what to do with it. How many people do you know who are downsizing from a big old house to a modern condo and would actually pay someone to carry away things that are just too good to put in the garbage? Whether you live in a big town or a small town, it pays to become known as the go-to person when others are on the move. Sometimes the technique can be as simple as putting up a notice in the supermarket to tell people that you are a PowerSeller or Trading Assistant and are looking for things to sell on eBay.

Find One-of-a-Kind Treasures

Some things will always sell well on eBay. These are collector's items: things that are pursued avidly by collectors because they are especially scarce models. When the weather gets too cold or inclement to drive to garage sales, take a trip to one or more of the stores in your area that specialize in reselling other people's castoffs.

Goodwill Stores

There is a nice feeling when you're shopping in a Goodwill store that, in a way, you're supporting a charity. There is also the advantage that the folks working there probably don't know too much about the value of the objects. You can take your time in examining dishes or furniture, for example, and be very picky about what you buy. You can usually get cooperation in buying a large piece and keeping it there on hold until you bring back a truck and packing materials to haul it away.

TIP: You can find a Goodwill store near you on the Goodwill Industries Web site (http:// locator.goodwill.org/). You'll also find a link to Goodwill's online auction area, where you might be able to find additional bargains.

Resale Shops

The thing about resale shops is that they deal in volume with a high rate of turnover. Stock changes every day. So if you can find a vendor who is likely to carry the merchandise that interests you, it is worth your while to find out when stock is replenished and get there before it gets picked over. If you are a frequent customer, you might even get the owner to call you when a large shipment is expected or to let you know that something in your specialty has just arrived.

Flea Markets

Here you are dealing with folks who may, in fact, know something about their product. They've acquired it from a source in the first place, put it in a truck or van, transported it a distance, and are now sitting under the sun hoping to not have to take it back home again. So although the prices of some items are firm, you're likely to be able to make a deal if you approach them in the right way. I suggest bringing cash and only showing a bill of a denomination slightly less than the asking price. Try to get to the flea market as early as possible: the best merchandise is often sold in the first hour. Another trick that works for me is to offer to buy a combination of objects for less than the marked total would be for all of them. It's also true that the more interest you show in a piece, the higher the price is likely to be. For that reason, I often work with a friend. I scope out the items I want, asking questions and examining them in detail. Then my friend wanders in and makes an offer without seeming to pay too much attention to what the objects really are.

Garage Sale Tricks of the Trade

With garage sales, you go straight to the horse's mouth. There is no intermediary. Nobody has pre-screened the merchandise that's available. Chances are there has been a death or a person is moving. They are highly motivated to sell. There are two strategies here. The first is to get there an hour before the sale officially starts and skim the cream off the surface. The second is to arrive at closing and make a deal for pretty much everything that's left. In any case, you're likely to get a really good price on items, especially if they are obviously of value and the owner has no clue that they are worth anything at all.

Most of the eBay sellers I know attempt to select sales carefully (you can't go to every sale, after all) and get there extremely early. Some actually hire high school or college students to stand in line for them at 5 or 6 A.M., long before the sale actually begins, so they can be first in the door. Just before the sale starts, the real sellers arrive and take the student's place. It's also helpful to have two or three people at a particularly good estate sale simply because such sales can be so crowded and competitive.

Summing Up

This chapter presented a step-by-step approach to organizing and clearing out the clutter in your own home and selling selected merchandise on eBay. The steps (clean and purge, organize, decide what to sell, decide when to sell, and prepare your items) all lead to the ultimate goal of building eBay sales while uncluttering your own residence. Once you clear out the clutter, you need to find new sources of sales merchandise. You learned about different options for researching items that bidders want on eBay, including hot lists and specialty price guides. You also learned about finding wholesale items you can sell all year-round. Finally, you learned about sources (resale shops, wholesale outlets, and other secondhand stores) of collectibles or other items you can find close to home and then resell on eBay.

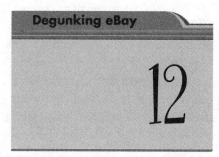

Degunking and Ramping Up Your eBay Business

Degunking Checklist:

√ Find products that you can sell all year.

√ Plan ahead for sales during seasonal holidays, such as Halloween and Christmas.

√ Find a wholesaler and establish an ongoing relationship.

√ Focus on selling merchandise that you have an interest in.

√ Encourage visits by repeat customers by offering discounts for multiple purchases and cross-sell offers.

√ Keep sales online longer by creating an eBay Store and catalog and by using your own Web site.

√ Boost profits by analyzing your sales on a monthly basis.

All of the techniques for maximizing sales and building profits that you've investigated elsewhere in this book lead naturally to some daring and exciting thoughts. Once you begin to get the hang of selling on eBay, you begin to count on the occasional checks you receive from sellers. Once you develop a system for receiving some checks every week, you begin to realize that you can sell on eBay on a regular basis. You begin to think, "Could I sell on eBay full-time and quit my day job? Could I make a new career out of selling stuff on eBay?" The answer, quite simply, is yes! Thousands of individuals generate full- or part-time income selling on eBay. But getting there isn't easy, and like any self-employed person, you need a new level of commitment to succeed. In this chapter, you'll learn some business techniques to scale up your eBay revenues.

Build Year-Round Sales

It's safe to say that tens of thousands of individuals now sell products on eBay as a full-time job. One instructor at eBay's own traveling school, eBay University, told attendees that as many as 430,000 full-time eBay sellers exist (**www.fredericksburg.com/News/FLS/2004/102004/10162004/1537887/ printer_friendly**). Some of those are individuals who never ran a business before. Others are experienced business owners who use eBay sales to supplement or even replace a traditional offline business. There's a seller who is reported to make $5 million per year selling brand new pool tables on eBay. eBay's own newsletter, *The Chatter,* regularly profiles small business owners, such as the wholesale shoe vender shown in Figure 12-1, who resurrected a flagging business by selling on the auction site.

NOTE: *eBay is enthusiastic about the idea of selling part-time in one's off hours or even starting a full-time business through eBay. As one eBay employee reported (**www.alpern.org/weblog/stories/2003/07/07/ myFirstDayAtEbay.html**), many eBay employees are auction sellers themselves.*

How do you make the leap from selling once in a while on eBay to depending on eBay sales for all or part of your monthly income? It doesn't happen overnight. I don't recommend that you quit your "day job" and try to become a full-time eBay seller without some careful planning. Suppose your sales pattern is like this:

√ You sell three things one week after hitting the garage sales.

√ You've got family obligations, and you sell nothing the next week.

√ You go early one Saturday morning to a good flea market, and you are able to sell nine new acquisitions in the subsequent week.

√ Your uncle brings you some baseball cards and some other knick-knacks to sell on consignment, so you sell five things the next week.

Figure 12-1
There's no shortage of success stories involving full- or part-time eBay businesspeople.

You don't sell on a year-round basis because you depend on estate sales, flea markets, and relatives with closets to clean out. If those sources of merchandise aren't available, you don't sell anything that week. There's nothing wrong with this picture if you are looking to eBay to provide some extra "pocket change" for yourself and your kids. But if your goal is to count on a regular income from eBay, you will need to degunk your current sales activities. You'll need to learn how to get focused and develop a steady stream of sales each week, whether or not the weather is good, and whether or not your family gives you some items to sell. Some suggestions for turning a sporadic hobby into a part-time or full-time job follow.

Focus on Holiday Sales

All experienced eBay sellers know that the busiest time for sales is November and December. With that in mind, full-time sellers often spend 9 or 10 months of the year preparing for the busiest 2 or 3 months at the end. First, they purchase decorations and holiday gift items when they are cheapest—in late December or early January. They spend the rest of the year keeping one eye out for merchandise they can sell during the holidays.

Lots of forward-thinking consumers like to buy ornaments, wrapping paper, ribbons, and other holiday-related items well before the holiday season, and the place to put such items up for sale is an eBay Store. See the section "Open an eBay Store" later in this chapter for more details. Items that are used at the end of the year during the holidays, such as old Christmas tree ornaments, are very popular and can be found at resale shops all year round. Reproductions of classic ornaments can be found through wholesalers and sold through much of the year, if not all year round.

The end of the year is the hot time on eBay for buyers and sellers alike. Objects that you've been saving or that are "orphaned" pieces of larger sets might sell well at holiday time. Examples include single pieces of china or Victorian silver. The holidays are the best time of year to unload celery forks or other specialty items. After the holidays, consider selling the following items you might be saving up throughout the year:

√   January: exercise equipment

√   February: vintage Valentine's Day cards

√   March/April: Easter collectibles, Fabergé eggs

√   May: Graduation cards and gifts

√   June: Bathing suits, beach toys, beach towels

√   August: Back-to-school supplies

NOTE. *If you want to be a full-time eBay seller, you need to vary your sales activities with the season. In the summer, you won't be able to sell as much, so that's the time to take a break from selling or to offer your overstock or leftover items at a cut rate. Throughout the year, collect items that can be sold at a particularly busy time: Buy Halloween leftovers in November and save them for the next year, buy Christmas decorations in January and save them for the following November, and so on.*

Find a Wholesaler

What exactly is a wholesaler? It's a company that provides large quantities of merchandise for resale at discount prices. If you want to know the kinds of things you can obtain from wholesalers and sell on eBay, you only need to look around on eBay and see what the PowerSellers are selling. Here are some examples:

√   PowerSeller sweet*beans sells gourmet flavored coffees and foodstuffs sweetened with the herbal sweetener Stevia.

√   chezgems, the founder of the PowerChicks eBay Group, sells handcrafted jewelry, holiday gifts, and much more in her eBay Store.

√   topshelfantiques specializes in antique glassware, but it also sells black lights and other items such as ski suits.

√ tradrmom sells new Mary Frances handbags and purses with dog and cat illustrations on them.

√ eclecticdealer-paula loves to find and sell Oriental art and antiques, but she also stocks her eBay Store with porcelain figurines.

Many of these are objects that the PowerSellers have obtained from wholesalers, who provide a steady source of merchandise that can be sold year-round.

Where do you find a wholesaler? It's important to shop around and not just go with the first one you find. Some wholesalers are just interested in getting your money and not in providing you with a regular supply of quality products. Get references from other satisfied customers—such as other sellers on eBay with whom they work. Make sure the wholesaler stocks objects that you yourself like and will be eager to promote. If you are excited about their figurines or dolls, for example, it will be easier for you to describe them in a positive way. Look for wholesalers on Yahoo or other Internet directories. The business-to-business yellow pages is also a good source.

The logical place to search for wholesale suppliers is eBay's own Wholesale Lots category (see Figure 12-2). The actual Wholesale Lots page (**http://pages.ebay.com/catindex/catwholesale.html**) is a collection of subcategories that are drawn from many of eBay's main categories. There are so many categories that you can easily get overwhelmed. Take this step-by-step approach:

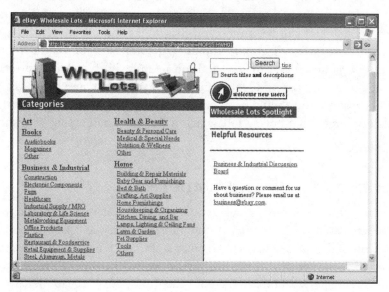

Figure 12-2
You'll find plenty of potential suppliers in the Wholesale Lots area.

1. Look for items you are interested in yourself and that you would be interested in buying.

2. Use the eBay feedback system to evaluate the supplier's reputation.

3. Be sure to ask for references from eBay sellers with whom the supplier has worked: e-mail some of the individuals who have left feedback comments recently.

4. E-mail the wholesaler and ask if they would be interested in striking up an ongoing relationship. Ask to receive a sample of the merchandise. This will give you a chance to evaluate how responsive the person is and how well you might get along.

TIP: *Use the PowerSeller boards in the eBay Groups area (http://groups.ebay.com/ index.jspa?categoryID=123) to find suggestions of suppliers, too. Many of the groups in this area are intended specifically to help members grow an eBay business.*

Focus on What You Love

If you pick merchandise that you're interested in yourself, you'll be that much more inclined to talk about them in sales descriptions or e-mail correspondence. Enthusiasm is contagious. After all, you're trying to convince a potential buyer that you have something wonderful to offer and that you are the vendor they should do business with. The more your descriptions sparkle with your love and knowledge of what you're selling, the more you'll communicate to customers that you can be trusted and that you're the one with whom they should seal a deal. They'll also be impressed if you have a long track record of dealing in a particular type of item, and you are more likely to build up a record if you enjoy selling it. And if you want to turn your eBay business into a full-time occupation, you should be interested in what you're selling; if not, it will quickly become just a boring job, which is definitely something you want to avoid!

Develop Repeat Customers

There are lots of reasons why online businesses failed in the e-commerce bust of the early twenty-first century. A common scenario was this: Businesses attracted lots of shoppers with deep discounts and clever promotions. Those shoppers made a single purchase and got a great deal. But they never returned to the site because there was nothing there for them other than cheap merchandise, which in many cases they could get from other vendors.

eBay has succeeded because it turned this scenario on its ear and promoted customer loyalty. eBay is known for one-of-a kind things you can't find anywhere else. Its members get lots of benefits other than the ability to shop, such as the ability to make friends in the community, to open a store, to find a trading assistant, to start up their own eBay Group, and much, much more. Your goal is to build your customer base—to convert those one-time, single-purchase shoppers into repeat customers.

Provide Incentives for Multiple Purchases

The more special you make your customers feel, the more likely they'll return to you in the future. Experienced eBay sellers do everything they can to put a smile on their buyers' faces:

√ They write personal notes and place them in the box along with the items they've sold.

√ They thank customers for shopping with them in their e-mail correspondence.

√ In their sales descriptions, they make a point of mentioning that they'll be happy to ship two or more items purchased in the same box to save on shipping costs.

√ They personally let their customers know when they have items to sell that their customers might be interested in.

√ They will always go the extra mile in trying to help a customer if a problem emerges.

How do you do it? Simple: In your auction description, near the end of the description with your shipping and payment details, include a statement like the following:

```
I'll be happy to ship multiple items in the same package and pass
along the savings to you.
```

Such offers work best when you sell things that are complementary: bedsheets, pillowcases, and duvets, for instance. Don't be reluctant to point out to buyers that you sell similar merchandise. A cross-promotion of the sort described in Chapter 9 will do the trick, and it has the extra advantage of being free.

Provide Discounts on Cross-Sell Purchases

It's up to you to determine how much you want to cut back on your profits, but you'll ramp up your sales nicely if you offer discounts on multiple-item purchases. Instead of hoping that someone will buy that baseball glove along with that bat and cap, be a salesperson and create the following cross-sell opportunity:

If you like this glove, you'll love the baseball bat and cap, all of
which date from the same period and came from the same household.

The "money sentence"—the one that will seal the deal—is the following:

For every multiple-item purchase you make, I'll knock $1 (or $2 or
$3) off the total purchase price.

You could preface this statement with the phrase "But that's not all!" (heard in
infomercials and commercials all over the airwaves), but I'll leave that extra
touch up to you.

Hire Support Staff

Hiring support staff can really help you improve your operations, but this step
comes with its own set of challenges. If you're the independent sort, a real do-
it-yourselfer, then you are used to tackling challenges all by yourself. You go on
your merry way for a few weeks or months at a time, hauling boxes up and
down the stairs, lugging stacks of boxes into the post office on a handcart,
sitting in front of two computer screens at once, trying to find one special
something amid many crowded shelves full of inventory. You stand by yourself
in a long line waiting to get into an estate sale at 6 A.M., and then you rush
around inside, madly reaching for items and wishing you had four hands instead of two.

These are the kinds of things that happen when you try to do everything on
your own. How do you straighten out the mess so you have more energy to
focus on what you love, whether that is shopping, selling, or preparing sales
descriptions? Here are some suggestions:

√ Turn to your spouse or significant other. Normally, it's risky working with
   the person you live with. But chances are you got together in the first place
   because you share the same interests. Hitting the garage sales and driving the
   back roads looking for sales is a perfect shared activity for many couples.

√ Find a young relative or a high school or college student. Young people
   don't mind carrying around boxes for a few extra bucks. They might also
   have the computer expertise needed to take digital photos or prepare
   auction descriptions.

√ Turn to your neighbors. Chances are you know some people who live right
   down the street and who have some time on their hands. They can run over
   on short notice and help you with packing or shipping, among other things.

CAUTION! It's especially important to find people to help you if you have a day job and you can only do your eBay sales work after hours. If you can accumulate inventory on weekends and prepare some initial sales descriptions, your employee can help you get the listings online during the week, when you're not available, or help you get merchandise to the shipper in a timely fashion when you can't get to it right away.

There are two other issues with hiring support staff that I should mention: salary and management time. The salary for the staff will come right out of your profits. If the person you hire is motivated and can work independently, they will free up time for you to find and list more products to sell—and therefore increase your sales volume. This is an ideal situation. If this person will need your guidance every step of the way, then this person's salary will just become a drain on your profits. Keep in mind that all staff requires management time. It will be essential that you clearly lay out what your employee is to be doing. If your assistant is responsible enough to carry out their duties without a lot of supervision, you will see your sales activities increase. It will also help if this person is an eBay fan because then they will be able to contribute ideas and reinforce your enthusiasm for your business.

Open an eBay Store

Many of the problems that tend to gunk up sales on eBay are reduced when you open an eBay Store. Instead of having to create new sales descriptions every week, you are able to maintain an inventory of dozens or even hundreds of items and keep them online a long period of time—specifically 30, 60, 90, or 120 days, or even indefinitely. Once you have reached a feedback rating of 20 or more, you should consider opening a store. An eBay Store helps degunk and improve your eBay sales efforts in the following ways:

√   Reduced listing fees. When you sell exclusively at auction, these fees can pile up. If you sell 100 items a month and you have a listing fee of $.25 for each one, you pay $25, which can add up to hundreds of dollars a year. In contrast, with an eBay Store you pay only $.02 each 30-day listing period per item and $.01 for each Gallery photo.

√   More cross-promotions. As described in Chapter 9, cross-promoting sales can steer customers toward related items you have for sale. Having an eBay Store makes cross-promotions easier to control: instead of having eBay automatically decide which items should be cross-promoted on a listing page, you can create a custom category within your store and have the cross-promoted items be drawn from it.

√ Better sales tracking. If you only sell at auction, it's pretty much up to you to analyze which of your items sells best. When you operate an eBay Store, you get access to monthly reports that tell you what you've been selling, who's been buying it, and more.

Perhaps the best thing about an eBay Store is that it gives you another way to reach potential buyers. Your eBay sales listings automatically include a link to your eBay Store in the Seller information box. And your store can include links back to your current auction sales.

Creating a Sales Catalog

One of the many advantages of selling through an eBay Store is the ability to create an online catalog—a set of Web pages that present the merchandise you have to sell. The degunking aspect of having a catalog should be obvious. Instead of using one Web page at a time to sell many different items, you can divide those items into more specific and focused category pages. Together, the different category pages make up your online catalog.

Shoppers like online catalogs. A catalog enables them to choose items with one click, place them in a shopping cart, and check out with a few more clicks. Stores give you the ability—and additional responsibility—of organizing what you have to sell. You can organize your merchandise in any way that suits your style of doing business:

√ By type of item

√ By order of importance

√ By sales price (one category for your high-ticket items, one for your more moderately priced items, a category for specially reduced merchandise, and so on)

Be sure to include plenty of details with your store's catalog items. Shoppers crave details from a catalog, the same as in an auction listing. But first you have to actually create your store. You do that by going to the eBay Stores main page (**http://stores.ebay.com**) and then following these steps:

1. Click Open a Store.

2. Sign in with your User ID and password.

3. Click I Accept the User Agreement when prompted to do so.

4. Begin to fill out the Build Your Store pages.

First, you are asked to select a graphic design called a *theme* for your store (see Figure 12-3). After that, you provide a short description of your store and what you want to sell in it. Then you pick the type of store you want to run. Chances

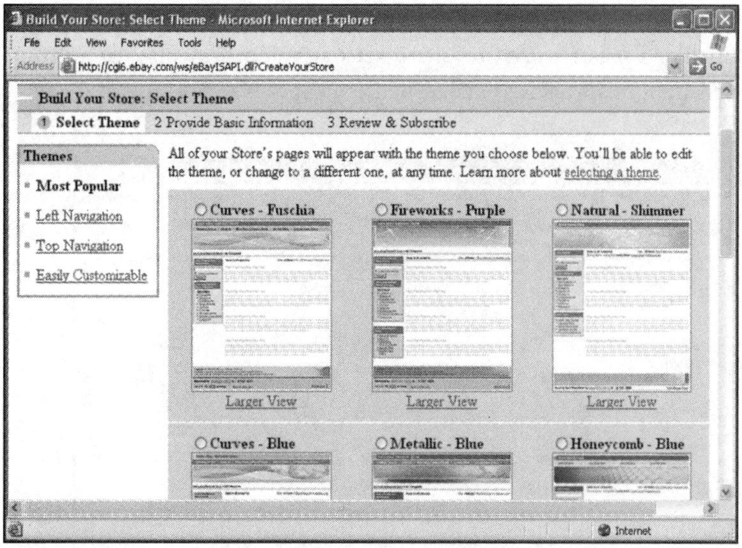

Figure 12-3
You begin by choosing a design called a theme for your eBay Store.

are that when you're first starting out, you'll want the Basic Store, which costs $9.99 per month.

The forms you fill out to create your eBay Store are pretty self-explanatory. The process will be less gunky, though, if you write down some notes beforehand and give some thought as to how you want to describe and organize your store.

The forms with which you are presented in order to create a store have some quirks. The process will proceed more smoothly if you know things like the following:

√   Category. In which of eBay's sales categories do you want your store to be listed? When in doubt, choose the catchall category, Everything Else.

√   Description. Which 300 characters best describe your store? You don't have 300 *words* in which to describe your store; you only get 300 *characters.* Type your description in a word processing program and count the characters before you fill out the form.

√   Uniqueness. What makes your store unique and sets it apart from other eBay stores?

It also helps if you have a logo or other graphic image to use with your store. Once you've specified the basics of your store, you can manage it: you arrange your merchandise into separate sales categories, specify your preferred shipping method, create sales descriptions, and choose a default view.

eBay Store items can be displayed in two different ways: in a list of titles that looks just like a set of search results, a set of category listings, or a group with thumbnail images and prices called Gallery View (see Figure 12-4).

Figure 12-4
Gallery View lets shoppers focus attention on a small number of items.

In my opinion, Gallery View is less gunky because the two-column view sets it apart from the rest of the pages on eBay. It doesn't overwhelm shoppers with 20, 30, or more items on one page. Rather, you see 6 or 8 listings, each with a photo and a price—everything a person in a hurry needs to make a snap decision.

Arrange Your Display

When I worked in a drugstore, I spent a lot of time arranging displays. Because most of the store's traffic came in off the street and we couldn't afford expensive display ads in newspapers, the way items were arranged in the front windows and the shelves made a lot of difference. In the same way, you can adjust the way your eBay Store's inventory is arranged:

1. Choose the order in which you want your items to be arranged: lowest prices first, highest prices first, ending soonest first, or ending latest first.

2. Create a custom home page. If you are experienced with creating Web pages, you can design a custom page that visitors will see when they first connect to your store. This step is optional, but if you have the time and you're familiar with HTML, it adds a professional look to your store.

3. Choose your store's color scheme. eBay presents you with some preselected color combinations in the Build Your Store pages you fill out when you first create your store.

4. Choose a banner graphic for your store. This is a banner that goes at the top of your store's home page.

The graphic identity of your store might seem like a secondary consideration, but if you want to stand out from the many other stores on eBay, it pays to take a few minutes to choose a graphic look that establishes your identity clearly and uniquely.

GunkBuster's Notebook: Visit an eBay PowerSeller Store

eBay Stores can bring both immediate and long-term benefits to sellers. For PowerSeller Kimberly King (User ID: sweet*beans), her store Higher-Groundz (**www.higher-groundz.com**) is a place where she can list items that didn't sell initially at auction. That's the immediate benefit: a store can be a place to relist items and keep them up for sale for several weeks at a time.

In the long-term, though, an eBay Store isn't just a place to relist items that are initially unwanted. A store is a place where a seller can do business around the clock on eBay. King always has hundreds of coffee and sweetener items for sale in Higher-Groundz.

"If someone in my family is sick and I can't prepare any auction listings that week, I still have merchandise up for sale in my store. It's not like I've completely 'closed my doors.'"

Initially, King ran a Basic eBay Store, one of the three types of store levels available (Basic, Featured, and Anchor). But she upgraded it to the Featured level, which includes a monthly sales report, traffic reports, and the ability to participate in the eBay Keywords program. "I LOVE it!" she says of the new store. It's easy to see why: King estimates that her eBay Store is responsible for 55 to 60 percent of her gross sales on eBay.

Managing Your Store

Managing an eBay Store requires a bigger commitment than just selling occasionally at auction. The only key to success is to devote time and energy to keeping the store up-to-date, change merchandise on a regular basis, promote your store, and have lots of different things for sale.

Stores work best when they have many dozens of items for sale. It makes the seller look busier, more professional, and more competent. So does a relatively high feedback rating—perhaps 100 or more is a good rating to start with.

Make a commitment to visit your own store every single day and change something on it—update a sale, reduce a price, or get a new item online. Also consider upgrading some of your sales to give them more attention. Table 12-1 lists the upgrade fees, which are virtually the same as the upgrade fees for eBay auctions.

Table 12-1 eBay Store Listing Upgrades

Upgrade	Cost Per 30 Days of Listings
Gallery	$.01
Item Subtitle	$.02
Listing Designer	$.10
Bold	$1.00
Highlight	$5.00
Featured in Search	$19.95

NOTE: *You can also get more attention for your store by upgrading it to a new level. eBay Stores come in three levels: a Basic Store ($9.95 per month); a Featured Store ($49.95 per month), which gives you a link to your store from the store's category page and a random link on the eBay Stores main page (http://stores.ebay.com); or an Anchor Store ($499.95 per month), where you have your store logo rotate with others on the eBay Stores main page. Your logo can also appear randomly on the eBay home page.*

Sell on Your Web Site

I've said elsewhere in this book that your eBay auction sales and eBay Store sales will be more successful if they include references to one another. Your sales will speed up even more if you are able to make these two sales venues work with a Web site. When it comes to Web sites, you have two general options:

√   An About Me page: A page that eBay lets you create for free and that is hosted by eBay itself (in other words, the pages are posted on eBay's servers).

√   A Web site you create yourself and that is hosted on another site, such as a site belonging to your own Internet service provider or another Web hosting service.

The simplest, quickest, and least gunky alternative for creating a Web page is eBay's About Me feature, which is free and gives you a great deal of flexibility for assembling a simple Web page that describes who you are and what you sell.

An About Me page should tell shoppers who you are and why you are qualified to sell what you sell. If you're in a highly competitive area of business that includes many different individuals, your About Me page can set you apart and give shoppers a reason to buy from you. Suppose you sell something that is commonly found on eBay, like refurbished computer equipment. If your About Me page tells people that you worked for 10 years in the service department of a big-time computer store and you have built computers from scratch for many of the bigger businesses in your area, the chances are good that you'll lure purchasers away from the competition because of your qualifications. Maybe you are in a family business that has been around for decades; maybe you learned what you know at the feet of a master; maybe you provide a money-back guarantee for everything you sell. Whatever the case, your About Me page is the place to blow your own horn.

How, then, do you go about creating your page? Before you start filling out the easy-to-use forms on eBay's site, put on your thinking cap and come up with some preliminary information. Come up with a name for your page, write a subtitle to go beneath the heading, and write a paragraph that describes who you are and what kind of eBay business you have. Take one or more digital photos of yourself, if you wish. Then follow these steps:

1. Go to My eBay, log in, and click Personal Information.

2. Click the link change to the right of the About Me page heading.

3. When the About Me login page appears (**http://members.ebay.com/ws/eBayISAPI.dll?AboutMeLogin**), click Create Your Page.

4. When the Choose Page Creation Option page appears, leave "Use our easy Step-by-Step process" selected and click Continue.

Follow the pages displayed in order to create your About Me page. The steps are pretty self-explanatory. The process of selecting a layout for your page (see Figure 12-5) depends on the type of contents you want to present.

If you want to address a variety of separate topics (your family, your eBay Store, your Web site), choose the two-column arrangement shown in Layout C. Choose the newspaper layout (Layout B) if you have different bits of information about a single subject, such as the items you like to buy and sell. Choose Layout A if you want to present a short bit of text about yourself and a small photo as well.

Maximize Profitability

The formula for maximizing profitability is simple: cut costs and increase sales volume. After you've found an affordable photo host, reduced your insertion fees by keeping starting bids low, and found an affordable wholesale supplier for

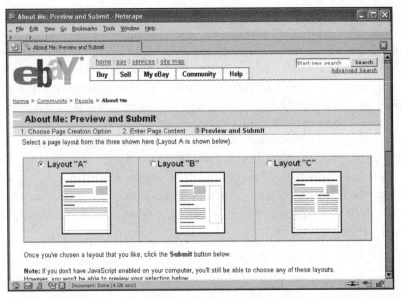

Figure 12-5
Choose a layout option that matches your desired About Me page content.

the merchandise you want to sell, focus on ways to boost sales, such as opening a store, advertising your sales through the eBay Keywords program, or simply finding merchandise that's more desirable.

Analyze Your Most Profitable Products

One surefire way to ramp up sales is to calculate your profits, examine which items are most profitable, and adjust your sales accordingly. First, you need to prepare your own P&L (Profit & Loss) statement—a report that measures your expenses against your revenues. If you are able to break down your costs and revenues by the type of activity you perform on eBay, you'll find it that much easier to focus on areas where you aren't as efficient as you should be. Maybe you're spending too much on postage or spending too much on advertising, for instance. Break down your income by categories such as these:

√   eBay auction sales

√   eBay Store sales

√   Trading Assistant commissions

√   Advertising (this includes advertising revenue your Web site attracts)

√   Consulting (this includes any eBay classes you teach)

Expenses can be broken into categories such as these:

√ Salary costs (for your assistants)

√ Purchasing (the amount you pay to acquire merchandise you can resell)

√ eBay fees (insertion fees, Final Value Fees, listing upgrades, and so on)

√ Postage

√ Shipping supplies

√ PayPal fees

√ Mileage and other automobile expenses

√ Telephone costs

√ Advertising

√ Computer and office supplies

Once you put your income and expenses into categories, you can focus in on the ones that are most relevant. Your income from auction sales is an obvious example. Suppose you put 50 items up for sale last month. You take a look at the end of the month, add up your expenses and income, and determine that you only made about $50 in profit for all that work. What's going on? You look at your sales for the month:

√ One item of clothing, $15 profit

√ Two pairs of shoes, $10 profit

√ One antique lamp, $3 profit

√ One baseball bat, $2 profit

√ Twelve sporting goods items that didn't sell at all

It looks like your best bet is to forget selling sporting goods and focus on clothing. This kind of analysis can help you use your time to your best advantage.

TIP: Auction services such as HammerTap (www.hammertap.com) can provide you with programs like DeepAnalysis that can suggest the most profitable categories and products.

Claim Your Tax Deductions

As everyone knows, taxes can be extremely gunky. You may not be able to change the tax code, but you can make tax time less stressful by ensuring that you deduct all the expenses you can that are associated with running a business on eBay. It's a matter of keeping good records and taking all the permitted deductions.

Think about the things you deduct (if you do itemize your deductions) when you file your personal taxes, possibly including the following:

√ Your mortgage interest

√ Insurance and other house expenses

√ Charitable contributions

When you run a business on eBay and generate income from that business, the range of deductions you can claim expands dramatically. The deductions are, in fact, one of the biggest advantages of running your own business online. You can deduct everything you use to create your auction listings and run your eBay business:

√ Your digital camera

√ Your computer equipment

√ The eBay insertion fees and Final Value Fees you pay

√ Gas and other expenses associated with traveling to buy merchandise to sell

You need to keep records of all of these expenses so you can record them at tax time. In My eBay or Selling Manager, you get access to a record of the basics: how much you've sold and how much you've paid to eBay in fees. But you need to keep records of the rest. How do you do it? Follow these steps:

1. Choose an accounting method. The two alternatives are cash-basis and accrual-basis accounting. The simplest is the cash-basis method: you report income when it comes in and record expenses when paid. The other method requires you to record expenses when services are rendered, not necessarily when you make the payment. Consult a professional accountant for more details on these categories.

2. Come up with a system for keeping records. A big manila envelope into which you throw all receipts is better than nothing. A spreadsheet prepared in a program like Quicken or QuickBooks is much better; such programs can also help you fill out your tax forms. Setting up an Excel spreadsheet where you list your monthly expenses and income will work just fine as well, just as long as you keep all your receipts in one place.

3. Record your revenue. Make sure you write down the date of the transaction, the type of payment you received, how much you were paid, and who your high bidder or buyer was.

4. Depreciate your equipment. Estimate the value of your digital camera or computer and spread out the cost over what you project to be its useful life. You can then deduct the result every year at tax time. Keep records of the purchase date and price of your equipment, too.

5. Record your expenses. Make sure you can cite the date of the expense, the name of the person or company you paid, and a brief description of what the payment was for.

Don't forget to charge sales tax when applicable. The Internet Tax Freedom Act expired in 2003; it called for a freeze on taxes related to Internet commerce. Unless you live in states that don't collect sales tax at all (Montana, Alaska, Delaware, New Hampshire, and Oregon), you need to collect tax from customers who live in the same state where you live. Keep in mind that most states require merchants to charge sales tax on shipping and handling charges as well as the purchase price. (Find out more from your own state tax agency; you'll find a set of links at **www.tannedfeet.com/state_tax_agencies.htm**.)

TIP: *After you start selling on eBay regularly, preparing your taxes on your own becomes more difficult. Take it from me: you'll be better off hiring an accountant to do the heavy lifting for you. A professional can tell you how much you have to pay in quarterly taxes (something you may have to do if you have self-employment income) and provide you with the paperwork to file the taxes on time. And of course, a qualified tax accountant can help lower the amount of taxes you have to pay in the first place.*

Summing Up

When you buy and sell on eBay as a source of regular part-time or full-time income, your level of commitment needs to be higher than if you're just an occasional seller. By following the strategies described in this chapter, you'll go a long way toward degunking your eBay business and ramping it up. The key is to come up with a system for finding inventory and making sales all year around and keeping your products on the site as long as possible. With the help of wholesalers, you can also build an inventory of items to sell at holidays such as Halloween and Christmas. Additional steps that will make your business run more smoothly are opening an eBay Store and finding a supplier of wholesale merchandise that you can sell all year. You should also continue to sell items on your own (non-eBay) Web site. Once you build up a steady revenue stream, you should consider hiring help to prepare your sales, manage inventory, and ship out items. This chapter also discussed how to encourage repeat business, when to offer volume discounts, how to analyze your monthly profitability and provided suggestions on taking all your allowable tax deductions—all tactics that are part of ramping up your eBay business.

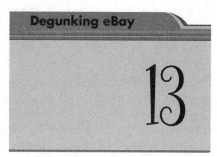

Degunking Problem Transactions

Degunking Checklist:

√ Recognize warning signs so you can avoid transactions that go sour.

√ Protect your eBay user account to avoid fraud.

√ Keep an eye out for suspicious bidding patterns.

√ Avoid sellers who make offers that seem too good to refuse.

√ Take steps to get non-selling sellers to respond to you.

√ Take advantage of eBay and PayPal buyer protection.

√ Follow the Unpaid Item dispute process for non-paying bidders.

S ometimes, the best way to speed up or streamline tasks is simply to take steps to avoid potential problems. In addition to knowing how to automate and speed up your eBay transactions (which was described in other chapters), you also need to be prepared for what can go wrong and avoid trouble whenever possible. Then even if a problem occurs, you'll be able to reach a resolution more quickly and effectively.

Whether it's due to a mistake or caused by intentional fraud, there are many potential trouble spots that plague eBay transactions. You're not alone in dreading non-paying bidders, non-selling sellers, unwise purchases, and shipping snafus. There are plenty of people who've dealt with such problems before you, and you can learn from them. No matter how clean you try to keep your nose, you probably won't be able to avoid every problem that can come up, either. My job is to lead you through the steps that will enable you to resolve difficulties when they occur so you can return to profitably using eBay as quickly as possible.

Reduce Clutter: Degunking for Buyers

I have a friend who came to me with a confession. She had an eBay addiction. Her problem was not obsessively shopping or having trouble finding things; she had no problem finding objects to purchase. Her problem was buying the first items that came along without thinking about whether she really wanted it, what she would do with it, or where she would put it. As a result, her apartment became crammed with crazy hats, lamps, books, and other things. When it came time to move, she really had a task on her hands. Let's look at some ways to avoid this next.

Learn to Not Bid Compulsively

My most recent purchase on eBay was a pair of shoes. I knew exactly what I wanted: they cost $144 new at the local store. When I found them new on eBay for $89, I thought I had a great buy on my hands, so I pushed the Buy It Now button without even trying to bid. When the shoes arrived, they fit just fine, but there were some obvious flaws in the color and finish of one shoe: essentially, they were different colors. I could have complained; I could have demanded a refund; instead, I polished the shoes up and they looked passable.

The moral, in my opinion, is that sometimes it's better to buy things in person from your local vendors than depend on eBay to shave a few dollars off the wholesale or retail price.

Set a Bidding Budget

Some of the worst gunk you can encounter is found on the credit card bill you receive at the end of each month. If you start seeing too many charges from PayPal due to purchases on eBay that you don't even remember making, it's high time you set a budget.

When you only use eBay to purchase personal items or gifts, setting a budget is simple. When you're purchasing on eBay to obtain merchandise to resell, you've got to take measures like these:

1. Calculate your operating costs. Keep track of the cost of shipping supplies, postage, toner and paper, and gasoline, and include the salary you pay to yourself or to assistants in your operating costs.

2. Calculate your gross income. This is your income from sales on eBay. It probably fluctuates quite a bit each month. Take an average over six months or so.

3. Subtract your operating expenses for one month from your average gross income for one month. The resulting net income should be your top limit for purchasing for a month.

4. Calculate the monthly profit you'd like to make. Don't lose sight of the reason why you started a business on eBay. The selling isn't an end in itself. (At least, it shouldn't be.) You need to make a profit.

5. Subtract your desired profit from the net income amount you came up with in step 3. Alternately, you can pay yourself a salary and add this to your expenses. The result should be your budget.

To make this even clearer, you'll find a sample budget in Table 13-1.

Table 13-1   Sample eBay budget

Item	Monthly Amount
Average monthly income	$6800
Your own salary	$3000
Your assistant's salary	$1200
Shipping and computer supplies	$175
Gas and travel expenses	$75
eBay fees	$200
Total expenses	$4650
Income minus expenses (purchasing budget)	$2150

If you find yourself continually going over budget, enlist the help of any eBay buddy or a real-world friend whose job it is to nag and cajole you into following your budget and business plan when you exceed your self-appointed limits.

Prevent Trouble from Occurring

Buyers tend to be more susceptible to fraud than sellers on eBay. Sellers, in most cases, have used eBay for a while as buyers and are familiar with how the site works. They tend to know what kinds of dangers to look out for. Buyers, on the other hand, are often less experienced. When they are just starting out on eBay, buyers need to learn lots of new procedures. They need to register, learn how to bid, set up a PayPal or other account, and build up positive feedback. This chapter describes a step-by-step process for buyers that will help you avoid trouble with fraudulent sellers, with other bidders, and with criminals who are out to get your money.

Follow these steps to prevent problems before they occur:

1. Ask questions. I, personally, make it a point to ask questions of just about every seller I deal with. Be sure you know everything about an item before you bid.

2. Get more photos. If you don't see an item clearly photographed from a number of different angles, ask for more photos. Most sellers will be happy to send them to you on request. If they won't send you more photos, consider this a sign that the seller is less than totally responsive and you should probably move on to another seller.

3. Review feedback. It's easy to look at someone's feedback number but not really take a close look at negative and neutral comments that have been left for the individual.

4. Look at other sales. Review the way the seller presents merchandise in other sales currently on eBay or in an eBay Store to determine whether the person is reputable.

You can't always predict whether someone is going to behave in an untrustworthy way or not. But your goal is to observe safe bidding practices and reduce the amount of trouble you encounter as much as you can.

Create Strong Passwords

Do you write down the PIN to your ATM card? On the contrary, you've probably memorized the number to prevent someone from stealing it. And chances are you shield the keypad with your hands when you enter the PIN in a store to make a purchase. You should protect your eBay password as well because it's your first line of defense on eBay.

It's easier to describe what a strong password isn't than what it is: it isn't a recognizable name in the dictionary, such as *password*; it isn't your own name; it isn't the name of one of your pets; it isn't the word *administrator*; it isn't your initials. Such passwords are all relatively easy for a criminal or a hacker to crack, especially if they have other personal information to go on.

A strong password consists of the following:

√   At least six to eight characters—the more characters the password contains, the harder it is to crack

√   A mixture of characters and numerals.

√   A mixture of upper- and lowercase characters.

The trick is to choose a password that's relatively complex, but not so complex that you can't remember it by heart. One trick is to think of a phrase you can easily recognize and turn that into a password. Here's an example:

1. Think of an advertising slogan, such as "Do It eBay."

2. Turn this into an acronym using the first letter of each word: DIeB. (I added the letter *B* to make the acronym longer than just three characters. I also kept the letter *e* lowercase to create a more secure phrase.)

3. Add some numbers before and after. Pick some numbers that are easy to remember: the numbers in your address, the last four digits of your telephone number, or your birth date. Here's an example: 1442DieB65.

The result is a strong password that can be difficult to crack. If you think of longer phrases, you can create even stronger passwords. A song title such as "There's No Business Like Show Business" (TNBLSB), can be turned into a strong password like 49TnBlSB1962, for instance.

TIP: *Software is available that can store your passwords in encrypted format on your computer. Each password is assigned a number so you can retrieve it easily: you only have to remember the number, not the whole password. Look into Password Officer, a program by Compelson Laboratories (www.compelson.com/pofi.htm). You can download a free version of the program or buy more full-featured versions for $29 or $59.*

Guard Your Personal Information

Once you have created a strong password, the next step is to protect it. It's not difficult; you only need to follow two steps:

1. Don't write your password down.

2. Don't ever give your password out, for any reason, no matter how plausible it seems.

It's been said elsewhere in this book, but it bears repeating: Along the way, you may well receive e-mails that claim to be from eBay and that give you a reason why you need to submit or "verify" your personal information. Often, a security-related reason is given. No matter what the reason is, don't respond to such messages. Remember that eBay will never request your personal information in an e-mail message. Forward such messages to spoof@eBay.com, an e-mail address that eBay has established especially for investigating such spoofs.

TIP: Be sure to log off eBay when you're done. It's all too easy to simply leave a browser window open for hours at a time when you're not at your desk. This makes it easy for passersby—primarily your children or your co-workers—to see what you've been doing on eBay. If you leave your password written on a sticky note affixed to your monitor or in plain sight on your desk, someone could conceivably place a bid as a prank using your User ID and password. Try to memorize your password or write it down in a well-hidden location.

Recognize Bidding Problems

You're probably already aware of potential problems with people from whom you buy on eBay. But you might not be as familiar with problem bidders. One way to avoid trouble and make your transactions proceed more smoothly is to recognize bidding patterns that are suspect:

√   **Bid siphoning.** This occurs when someone tries to lure a bidder away from one item and convince them to purchase another one at a lower price. The siphoner tries to convince the buyer that they have decided not to put the cheaper item up for sale in an eBay auction for a legitimate-sounding reason. Instead, you get the exclusive chance to buy the item yourself at a bargain. Don't believe it. Remember that if you agree to buy the item in a private sale outside of eBay, you can't take advantage of any of eBay's buyer protection provisions.

√   **Shill bidding.** This takes place when two or more people bid against one another, placing unnaturally high bids and counterbids in order to hike the price required to win the item. It can be hard to distinguish shill bidding from legitimate bidding on a very desirable item. The important thing is to do research beforehand so you know what an item is worth; if the bids go far above the item's value, bow out and wait for another, similar item to come along.

√   **Bid shielding.** Someone places a high bid on an item. This person stands to win the sale until, at the last moment, the bid is withdrawn. The original bidder then places another, lower bid using a different User ID and thus wins the auction. Hopefully, you won't see much of this type of activity because eBay prevents bids from being retracted when 12 hours or fewer are left before the end of a sale. But it's good to know that it can occur.

√ **Fake escrow services.** An escrow service is a company that accepts payments on behalf of sellers as a protection for buyers. Payment is released by the escrow company only when the item purchased has been received and approved by the buyer. One of the best-known is Escrow.com (**www.escrow.com**). However, this escrow service and others have been faked by criminals who are able to make them look legitimate. A fraudulent seller sends the buyer an end-of-transaction e-mail message with a link to an escrow service. The service looks legitimate, but the money really goes directly to the seller, who disappears along with the merchandise that was supposedly purchased.

Also be aware of bidders with little or no feedback. Everyone's got to start at zero, so you can't say all bidders with zero feedback ratings on eBay are automatically suspect. But you can do some investigation into their recent bidding activities, which can give you a clue as to whether they are participating in a shill bidding scam. Suppose you bid on an auction in which six other individuals have placed bids. Five of the six either have zero feedback or very low ratings, such as +1 or -1. Follow these steps to research that bidder's history:

1. Click the bid number next to History (in this example, you would click on the link 7 bids).

2. When the Bid History page appears for the auction, click the feedback number next to one of the bidders. (For instance, in the User ID byte-writer (12), you would click the number (12).

3. When the eBay Member Profile for the selected member appears, scan it to see how long the member has been on eBay and what kinds of feedback comments the member has received. An example is shown in Figure 13-1. (Pay special attention to any negative comments.) You can also click About Me to view the member's About Me page, or ID History to see how frequently the member's User ID has changed (if it has changed frequently or very recently, that can be a warning sign).

4. Click Advanced Search to do a little more research into the member's bidding history.

5. When the Advanced Search page appears, click Items By Bidder.

6. Enter the member's User ID, click the button next to "Even if not the high bidder" (shown in Figure 13-2), and click Search.

7. Scan the member's bid history. If the individual has a habit of bidding on many items but never winning, you may be a potential victim of shill bidding or bid shielding. If you find that the person has never won any auctions and just joined eBay, that's a warning flag.

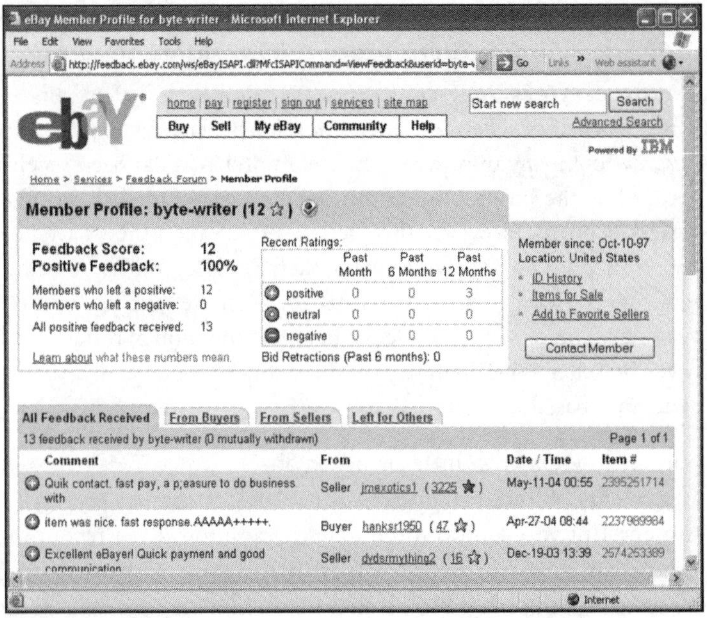

Figure 13-1

Research bidders to determine if fraudulent bidding might be taking place.

Figure 13-2

Research a bidder's behavior in other sales to judge whether fraudulent bidding might be taking place.

8. If you are suspicious of this bidder, report the sale to eBay: click the link Security Center at the bottom of any eBay page.

9. When the Security Center page appears (see Figure 13-3), click Report Problem to connect to the Contact Us form.

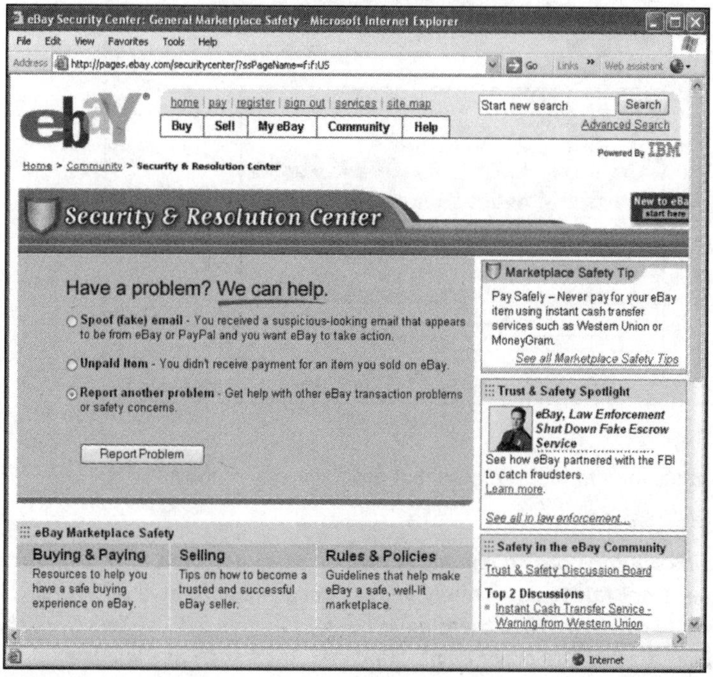

Figure 13-3
Turn to the Security Center when you need to report a problem to eBay.

10. When the Contact Us form appears, select options in the form's boxes to specify the problem you're seeing. For this example, you would select "Report problems with other eBay members" in the box labeled 1, "Selling Offenses" in Box 2, and the appropriate option in Box 3 (see Figure 13-4 for options). You might choose "Seller is bidding on his or her own items" in Box 3. While you don't know this for sure, keep in mind that you're only reporting a potential problem; it's eBay's job to determine whether an offense has actually occurred.

11. Click Continue, and follow the steps shown in subsequent pages to report the problem to eBay.

After you file the report, you'll receive a confirmation from eBay stating that your report has been received. For privacy reasons, you probably won't receive a report stating how the situation was resolved. You can revisit the auction later on to see if it was ended, however.

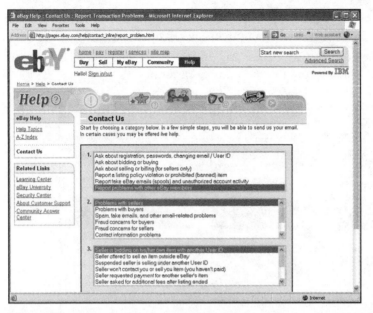

Figure 13-4
Use this contact form to report a potential problem sale to eBay.

CAUTION: Certain countries are commonly known on eBay as home to fraudulent sellers. It's perhaps not fair to paint every seller from Singapore as a potential cheat, but it's also good to be aware that there have been problems with sellers from that country, as well as Nigeria and other Pacific Rim countries such as Malaysia.

Recognize Selling Problems

Sometimes, sellers behave in a way that should immediately raise warning flags for experienced users. If you encounter one of the following situations, move on to another sale and consider reporting the seller to eBay at **http://pages.ebay.com/help/contact_inline/index.html**:

√ **Wire fraud**. If a seller requires you to send a wire transfer to an overseas location (or any location, for that matter, but overseas locations are more common), end the transaction there and then. You have absolutely no protection if you send a wire transfer by Western Union or through a bank.

√ **Second chance offers**. A Second Chance Offer is a legitimate offer that sellers can make. But it can be misused in the following way: you didn't win the auction, but the seller extends a Second Chance Offer to buy that item (often, an item that is expensive and hard to find). The catch: you have to pay not through eBay but via Western Union. To overcome your skepticism, the seller tempts you with an extremely low price. The item that sold for $899 can be yours for only $549, for instance.

NOTE: *Western Union wire transfers are common scams on eBay. However, other services provided by Western Union, such as money orders and the popular BidPay auction payment system (www.bidpay.com), are not scams. Don't shy away from obtaining money orders from Western Union; it's the wire transfer system that is suspect.*

Deal with Problems If They Occur

You can't avoid trouble on eBay all the time. Sometimes, all the safeguards in the world can't prepare you for a transaction that just goes sour for one reason or another. The seller might change their mind; the merchandise might be damaged; the shipper might lose the item in transit. Even if you learn how to anticipate trouble, it is likely to occur at least once, and you can resolve the situation more quickly by following the options presented next.

If the Seller Doesn't Sell

The biggest worry for buyers on eBay is that, after they pay their money, the seller will run away with it and they'll never get what they purchased. This does happen. But there's a series of steps you can follow to degunk such situations should they occur:

1. Realize all the protections you have. eBay has its own set of buyer protections, which are explained in the next section, "eBay Buyer Protections." You are also protected by the Federal Trade Commission (FTC), as detailed in "Fall Back on the FTC" later in this chapter. You can point out such protections to the seller when you are trying to get them to ship what you have purchased. And you can call on these two agencies if the shipment never does occur.

2. Buy with a credit card. All the major credit card companies offer their customers some form of buyer protection for online purchases. If you are defrauded, you can file a claim with your company and hopefully get a refund. Don't, however, fall into the trap of using a debit card and think that the debit card will give you the same protection as a credit card. When you use a debit card, the money is immediately taken out of your bank account, and once the transaction occurs, you won't have any recourse. Debit cards are a bad idea and you should avoid using one when you are purchasing products online.

3. Look carefully at all the URLs of the payment- and auction-related Web sites you visit. Make sure the URLs are legitimate. If you go to Escrow.com, for instance, make sure the page you visit has the URL **www.escrow.com/ cgi-bin/form.cgi** rather than one that has a subtle difference and is thus fraudulent: **www.escrowe.com/cgi-bin/form.cgi** or **www.escrow.net/ cgi-bin/form.cgi**.

4. In your e-mail communications with the seller, refrain at all times from being profane and abusive. Realize that there may be reasons, initially, why the seller fails to respond to you. After perhaps a week to 10 days of no response, you can request the phone number and street address of the seller and call them directly on the phone.

5. Fall back on outside agencies. Rather than giving up or threatening the other party, file a complaint with the dispute resolution service SquareTrade (**www.squaretrade.com**).

If you have tried all of these options and still haven't resolved the situation, you should turn to eBay's own buyer protection system.

eBay Buyer Protections

eBay begins its Buyer Protection Program Web page (**http://pages.ebay.com/ help/confidence/isgw-fraud-protection.html**) with a series of steps it wants you to pursue *before* you approach eBay to resolve a dispute with another member. In fact, you can approach eBay at any time to report trouble. But there is a two-step sequence you need to follow, and it begins 30 days after a sale ends if the seller has failed to deliver what was purchased:

1. Between 30 and 60 days after the end of the sale, file a fraud alert with eBay at **http://cgi.ebay.com/aw-cgi/ebayisapi.dll?crsstartpage**. This tells eBay you have a problem transaction and that you may be eligible for eBay's fraud protection insurance of up to $200 (less a $25 processing fee).

2. If you are found to be eligible for fraud protection (both you and the seller have to be in good standing on eBay; read the full requirements at **http:// pages.ebay.com/help/confidence/isgw-fraud-claim- requirements.html**), you'll receive a link to a Protection Claim form. After you file the fraud alert, but before 90 days from the end of the sale, you need to file the Protection Claim form if you still haven't heard from the seller. Fill out the form at **http://pages.ebay.com/help/confidence/isgw- fraud-claim-instructions.html** to file the Protection Claim.

3. You also need to file, along with the claim form, proof that you paid for the item, a denial of reimbursement from your credit card provider, and, if you received an item and it was substantially different than described, a letter of authenticity from an independent authenticator. You need to mail or fax all of this information to eBay.

4. Wait for an eBay claims administrator to contact you within 45 days. The administrator will contact you and the seller during the investigation. Eventually, the administrator will tell you whether or not you are eligible for reimbursement.

NOTE: *For items that cost more than $200 that were purchased on eBay with a credit card, you should apply to your credit card provider for insurance under its buyer protection program. There's no guarantee that you'll be reimbursed, however. You can find out about eBay's Customer SafeHarbor at **http://pages.ebay.com/help/ confidence/problems-support.html**.*

PayPal Buyer Protection

PayPal, which is eBay's official auction payment service, has its own set of buyer protections. If a seller has a feedback rating of at least 50, is a verified PayPal member, and has positive feedback of at least 98 percent, their sales are eligible to receive PayPal Buyer Protection status (there are other listing requirements; see **www.paypal.com/cgi-bin/webscr?cmd=_pbp-info-outside** for more). If a buyer pays for an item using PayPal and never receives it, or the item is "significantly not as described" (to use PayPal's words), the buyer may be eligible for up to $1000 in reimbursement.

In addition, PayPal buyers can enter into a Buyer Complaint Process with PayPal. PayPal will investigate the situation and attempt to resolve it. "If our investigation determines that you are owed money by the seller, we will make every effort to recover funds for you," says PayPal at **www.paypal.com/cgi-bin/ webscr?cmd=_protections-buyer-outside**.

Fall Back on the FTC

The Federal Trade Commission has a set of Prompt Delivery rules. These rules require shipment of something you have purchased to be sent to you within 30 days from the time a sale is made. That rule applies whether the sale is online or off, or whether the sale is an auction or a fixed-price sale. If the seller does not comply, they must refund your money.

The Federal Trade Commission rules also require sellers to disclose all relevant information about something you buy. If you aren't told about a flaw or some aspect of an item that does not match the description, you can file a complaint at **www.ftc.gov** or call toll free 1-877-FTC-HELP (1-877-382-4357). The FTC, however, emphasizes that it "does not resolve individual consumer problems." Rather, complaints help the FTC investigate types of fraud in general. Don't look to the FTC to get your seller to ship what was purchased, in other words.

TIP: *You can find out more about the FTC's buyer protection provisions at **www.ftc.gov/ bcp/online/pubs/alerts/intbalrt.htm**.*

If the Merchandise Arrives Damaged

Things are simple when you purchase through a brick-and-mortar store—or even a store's e-commerce Web site. If something arrives with a crack or flaw, or if it doesn't function the way it should, you have a well-defined set of options: You send it back to the manufacturer for free warranty repairs; you get a refund; you exchange it for another item. In any case, you have the reputation of the store or the manufacturer to rely upon.

On eBay, the system works in a similar way. But the burden is on you to fully understand the seller's terms of sale. You can't fully rely on a seller to resolve problems with merchandise you've purchased. If damage occurs, you can file a claim with the shipper. In addition, if you or the seller obtained insurance for the item (always a good idea), the burden is on the buyer to file the insurance claim.

Degunking for Sellers

The experienced sellers on eBay that I've talked to don't run into Non-Paying Bidders (NPBs) very often. But on occasion, someone will turn up who writes a bad check or fails to respond to your initial requests. It can be difficult to not get impatient or irritated, especially if you are in a hurry to complete a sizeable number of transactions. You need to make every effort to remain professional and courteous at all times, if only to preserve your own good reputation. There's always a chance your buyer fell ill or was called out of town unexpectedly and couldn't respond for a period of time. And there's always a chance that a check bounced inadvertently and the buyer is embarrassed about it.

Pre-Approve Your Bidders

If you're tired of running into Non-Paying Bidders, you have more control over your shoppers than you probably realize. If you are suspicious, or if you just want to offer an item to customers who have already purchased from you, you can pre-approve bidders and buyers. Pre-approval means that you have the ability to assemble a list of eBay members who are allowed to bid or purchase your item. Anyone who's not on the list must e-mail you for approval before they can bid. To create such a list, go to the eBay Pre-Approve Bidders page (**http://offer.ebay.com/ws/eBayISAPI.dll?PreApproveBidders**), click Add a new item with pre-approved bidders, and fill out the form that appears.

Each pre-approved bidders list applies to only one item, so you can restrict bidding or buying on one of your listings without changing the others. You can add and delete pre-approved bidders/buyers until your listing ends. Find out more at **http://pages.ebay.com/help/confidence/know-buyer-preapprove.html**.

TIP: You can also block a buyer if you feel the person is untrustworthy. Find out more about blocking buyers at http://pages.ebay.com/help/confidence/know-buyer-block.html.

If the Buyer Doesn't Pay

Before anyone places a bid on eBay, they have to confirm their bid. They are presented with the page shown in Figure 13-5, which spells out in no uncertain terms what their responsibilities are as a buyer.

Figure 13-5

Buyers are reminded that their bids are binding contracts before they actually place a bid.

Nevertheless, it frequently happens that a buyer either never responds to the e-mails from you and from eBay or responds but fails to pay. You're not alone in this situation, so there's no reason to take it personally. Try to contact the buyer by e-mail and phone; if that doesn't work, you enter into eBay's Unpaid Item Process, which is detailed at **http://pages.ebay.com/help/policies/unpaid-item-process.html**. The basic steps work like this:

1. File an Unpaid Item dispute form with eBay. You need to do so up to 45 days after the end of the transaction using the form at **http://feedback.ebay.com/ws/eBayISAPI.dll?CreateDispute**.

2. Wait for eBay to contact the buyer with a reminder to pay as a result of the Unpaid Item form being filed. eBay's message appears in a pop-up window if the buyer signs on to eBay within 14 days of the form being filed, in fact. The buyer is urged to contact you and resolve the dispute.

3. If the buyer fails to respond within seven days after you file the Unpaid Item form, you have the option of closing the dispute. (You need to close the dispute, in fact, in order to obtain a refund of your Final Value Fee from eBay.) You do so in your Dispute Console, which you access at **http://feedback.ebay.com/ws/eBayISAPI.dll?ViewDisputeConsole**.

You need to close the dispute within 60 days of the end of the sale or you won't receive a Final Value Fee credit. If you do close the dispute in time, not only do you get your refund, but the buyer receives an Unpaid Item "strike" against their User ID.

GunkBuster's Notebook: Don't Be Cheated by a Buyer

You probably know that, as a buyer, you have to beware of being cheated by a seller. Here's a variation: *You* should never end up sending a check to one of your own buyers. It sounds unlikely, but it happens: a con artist wins an item on eBay.

Let's look at an example. Assume that you have an auction and the winning bid is $1000. The buyer lives outside the U.S. The buyer explains to you that they know someone in the U.S. who owes them a large sum, such as $3000, and will instruct the debtor to send a cashier's check to you for the full amount owed—$3000. All you have to do is deposit a cashier's check for the balance (in this example, $2000). Not only that, but your check must be sent by FedEx overnight. You do receive the cashier's check for $3000, and you deposit it and send the buyer the balance, as requested. Later, your bank informs you that the cashier's check was fake. It was made on a high-quality color copier. The bank demands that you reimburse them for the total of $3000. Not only did you lose a large amount of money, but you have lost the merchandise you sold!

Set a Schedule for Getting a Response

It can help to keep your own record of non-paying bidders and draw up a schedule. That way, you won't forget about the need to file an Unpaid Item dispute form or to close the dispute at some point so you can obtain a refund. The schedule might include dates such as these:

√ End of transaction:

√ Buyer's User ID: [fill in the blank]

√ Date of first e-mail reminder

√ Date of second e-mail reminder

√ Date of Unpaid Item dispute form

√ Date on which Unpaid Item dispute must be closed: 1/14/06

Drawing up a schedule makes the dispute seem like more of a business matter (which it is) than a personal affront or attack (which it is not). Once the dispute has been closed and you have obtained a refund of your Final Value Fee, you should file negative feedback for the buyer. But here, too, professionalism is key. Don't sink into personal attacks and name-calling that makes you look as bad as the other person. Simply report the facts, such as "Buyer failed to pay after reminders from me and from eBay." This tells another member all they need to know about the situation.

Degunking Problems with Shipping

Unfortunately, within every system that exists is a way to be ripped off. Even if your buyer pays up, you can still run into problems at the shipping stage of the transaction. Suppose you are a seller and your buyer demands a refund on an item that was shipped. It's important that you examine that object carefully upon your return. The buyer may complain that the item was not in the condition you mentioned in your original eBay description or that a piece was missing from the item or that it was damaged in transit. When the item is returned, you discover that a piece has been removed and replaced; the buyer is a collector who took the piece from your item in good condition and replaced it with a piece of their item, which was not in such good condition.

Hold on to Your Photos

In the world of collectible magazines and newspapers, for instance, collectors have been known to take a ripped and yellowed page from their valuable publication, exchange it for the page that's in better condition from the item they just bought, and demand a refund. If you have kept the original photos to prove that your item was in a condition other than the buyer is claiming, you don't have to comply: you can turn to SquareTrade to have your dispute mediated.

Obtain Tracking Numbers

You can also prevent buyers from falsely claiming that a package has been lost by obtaining tracking numbers from your shipper of choice. When you use, for instance, the USPS's Delivery Confirmation with a confirmed tracking number, you can send the link with the tracking number to your buyer. That way, the buyer and you can see specifically when the item is coming and will know right away if it was misdelivered or lost. Many sellers do this now with even fairly small purchases. The service is available if you purchase Delivery Confirmation for a nominal fee with the USPS's Priority Mail service.

TIP: Something I stated in Chapter 10 that bears repeating here is that the extra expense of obtaining delivery confirmation as well as insurance is better than being forever uncertain that your item was really lost in transit as the buyer claims. The insurance can provide you with some compensation in case the item is really lost or damaged by the shipper (though it can take a while to get reimbursed). The delivery confirmation gives you evidence that your item reached its destination.

Summing Up

This chapter examined a variety of step-by-step processes for dealing with inevitable problem transactions that occur on eBay. By following a few simple, commonsense precautions, you can avoid trouble before it rears its head. First, you can avoid taking a hit to your checking account or credit card file from spending too impulsively on eBay. By learning to regulate your bidding and observing a budget, you can keep unwanted clutter out of your living area. By protecting your personal information, you guard against fraud. As a buyer, you can also get to know the types of suspicious behavior that signals the presence of disreputable buyers or sellers. As a seller, you'll occasionally run into non-paying bidders. But if you maintain a professional demeanor and follow eBay's process for handling Unpaid Item disputes, you'll at least get a refund of eBay's Final Value Fee so you can relist the item, and the seller will get a black mark against their record in the form of an unpaid item strike.

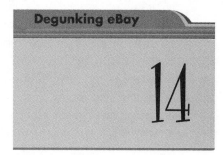

Degunking eBay

Degunking Tips from eBay's PowerSellers

Degunking Checklist:

√ Improve your buying strategy by discovering new items as soon as they are listed, and buy quickly if you can.

√ Eliminate overpaying and get better deals by returning on a regular basis to sellers you already know and trust.

√ Sell merchandise you already know and love.

√ Be prepared to go the extra mile with customer service.

√ Make friends with other eBay sellers who can provide support.

√ Use smart techniques like offering free shipping to make your customers really happy.

√ Learn to always pay yourself first so you benefit from your work.

Often, it's not what you know on eBay. It's *who* you know. When it comes to solving problems or streamlining procedures on eBay, experienced buyers and sellers know exactly where to turn. You might think they would turn to writers like me, but in fact, they turn to their eBay friends for help. They post questions on one of the eBay Groups they've joined or post a message in the discussion forums, chat rooms, or the Answer Center. These experts have been buying and selling on eBay for a long time and they really know how to degunk their eBay activities, make or save money, and cut through all the clutter.

As PowerSellers and other longtime eBay merchants know, the best people to ask for degunking help are other PowerSellers. (They not only have more extensive day-to-day experience than many eBay support staff people, but they'll probably get back to you more quickly, too.) I've been lucky enough to get to know a number of PowerSellers over the years, and in this chapter, I want to pass along some of their best degunkng procedures and strategies for making eBay work better for you.

By now, you should have an arsenal of degunking techniques you can put to work to streamline your eBay activities, get organized, be more successful, and save valuable time. We'll finish off by discussing some buying and selling degunking techniques that you can easily put to work. On the buying side, you'll learn how PowerSellers know how to work eBay to sort through the myriad of auction listings and find the best deals. Some of the techniques they use are similar to techniques that we've discussed earlier in this book, but with all their experience, PowerSellers know how to do things a little differently, as you'll learn here. On the selling side, you'll learn how PowerSellers apply masterful degunking techniques to the art of improving customer service by going the extra mile and making friends on eBay.

Learn PowerSeller Degunking Tips for Buyers

In almost all cases, PowerSellers started out on eBay as buyers. They continue to shop on eBay, for their own pleasure and to obtain merchandise they can resell. Over the years, competition has grown among shoppers on the auction site. It's become more and more difficult to find true bargains, and that's why it is important to learn the degunking techniques presented in this book so you know how to work through all the clutter. PowerSellers still have some degunking tricks up their sleeves when it comes to buying on eBay. Let's look at some of these tricks next to see how they can help you improve your buying process.

Pounce Quickly

By default, you search and browse eBay's auctions in such a way that the sales that end in the shortest amount of time appear first. Savvy shoppers, however, know that a steady stream of merchandise is being listed on eBay at any one time. They focus their searching and turn around the default browsing order by choosing "Time: newly listed" from the Sort by drop-down list that appears at the top of a set of search results or a category (see Figure 14-1).

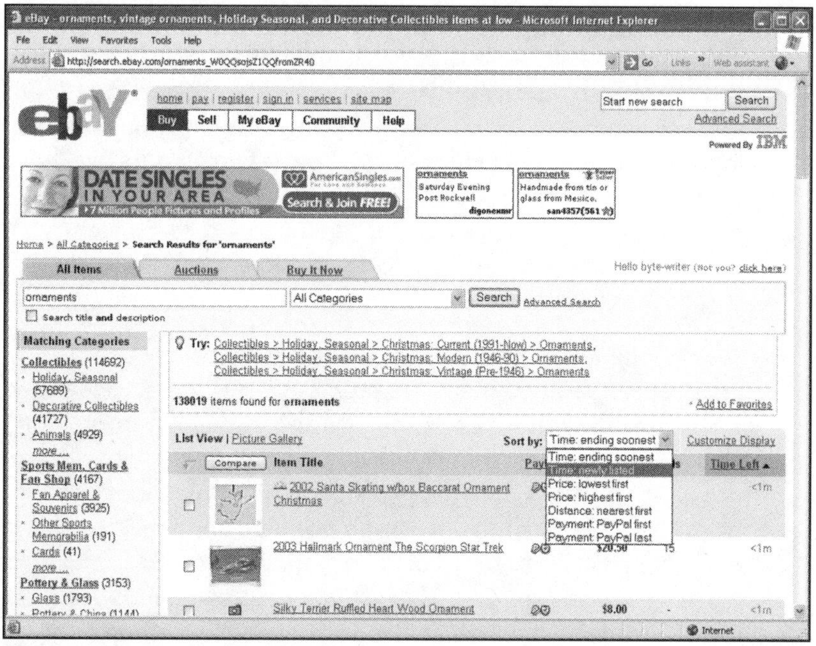

Figure 14-1

Search by newly listed items to get them at a Buy It Now bargain price. Get them the minute they are listed.

Any items that show up with a Buy It Now (BIN) option near the top of the Time: newly listed search results are ones that you can buy immediately and that probably haven't been seen by too many others. This is a good way for you to narrow down your searching and focus on a smaller list of items. You may need to act quickly if you see something that you recognize as especially desirable that is offered with a BIN option and no reserve price; the BIN option disappears as soon as the first bid is placed, and some eBay shoppers take delight at "killing" BIN prices by placing a bid on such sales. (They hope to save money by purchasing the item at auction.) If you want to avoid such "BIN killers," you have to act quickly. Of course, always take a close look at the BIN price and do your research to make sure that you really are getting a good deal.

GunkBuster's Notebook: Manage Your User IDs Wisely

You already know that your identity and reputation matter on eBay. If you have a high feedback number or a PowerSeller icon next to your name, your customers will feel they can trust you more. Your User ID matters, too. On the one hand, having a User ID that people come to know well will result in more bids. But in some ways, your User ID can be a liability and actually gunk up your buying and selling. If you change your User ID often, buyers might get suspicious. Keep in mind that anyone can research your User ID by clicking Advanced Search, clicking Find Members, clicking User ID, and then clicking Search. If they discover that you've been a member of eBay several years but have changed your User ID six times in the past two months, they might draw the conclusion that you're trying to conceal your identity for some reason. It's far better to settle on one User ID and stick with it for as long as you can.

There's one more thing to consider when selecting User IDs. In the past, some eBay members took out User IDs that they used solely for the purpose of posting on the discussion boards and chat rooms. Most of these User IDs had feedback ratings of zero. However, in 2004 eBay limited User IDs with feedback ratings of less than 10 to only 10 message postings per day. If you hang out in the chat rooms and like to converse with others for hours at a time, you need to use a User ID that has some feedback associated with it or you'll be limited in how much you can post.

A User ID that has a high feedback number and a PowerSeller icon can actually attract more bidding than you want. If buyers see that a PowerSeller is trying to buy something, they'll realize that it's valuable or a good buy and drive the price up by counterbidding. For that reason, some PowerSellers use a different User ID when they shop on eBay. That way, they don't let other bidders know that they're interested in something. Other PowerSellers avoid bidding whenever possible and try to make purchases at Buy It Now prices as soon as items are listed; in this case, it doesn't matter what User ID you use.

For more tips on setting up a User ID, see Appendix A.

Don't Be Afraid to Ask Questions

If you're absolutely certain an item is worth purchasing and is available with a Buy It Now option, it pays to pounce and buy it quickly, as described in the previous section. If, on the other hand, you are bidding on something that is available only to bidders, you have to wait. While you're waiting for the sale to end, be sure to ask questions about the item. Asking questions gives you a chance to evaluate the seller's responsiveness. Put on your detective hat and see what you can really find out. Here are some of basic questions that you'll want to get answered for most items:

√   What is the age of the item?

√   What is the real condition of the item? (Try to dig a little deeper and get beyond the basic "new," "almost new," and "used" descriptions that sellers often use. Take the time to find out how "new" the item really is.)

√   Is the color shown in the photos accurate? (Often, poor lighting results in the color being lighter or darker than it really is.)

√   If the item is used, does it have any defects, scratches, or cracks?

√   Are there any significant shipping issues that you might not be aware of?

√   Is there any documentation available for the item? (This could be really important if you are purchasing a rare or valuable item.)

√   Does the seller have more of the item or other items that you might be interested in?

√   Does the seller provide insurance, or is that up to the buyer?

The level of detail and courteousness can indicate whether you can really trust this person. Consider which of the following responses to the question about the color of an auction item is likely to lead to a gunk-free transaction:

√   "Color is as depicted. Only serious inquiries please."

√   "Thank you for your inquiry about the item I'm selling. I took a look at the image on my own computer and compared it to the real life object and the real one is slightly lighter in color. But basically the color is accurate. Please don't hesitate to ask further questions."

Basically, the two responses say the same thing. But the way the response is phrased makes a difference. Someone who takes the time to address your concerns and obviously pays attention to what you are asking is likely to pay attention to problems that turn up after the sale.

TIP: Try to ask the seller a question early in the sale so they have time to respond. A question asked early on also gives you more of an opportunity to decide whether to bid or not.

One question you should not be afraid to ask is this: Can you send me more photos? Frequently, items that are large are difficult to photograph in their entirety. Yet, it's essential to get photos from all angles to check for damage. For example, if you're thinking of bidding on a car or other vehicle advertised in eBay Motors, you need to be sure there aren't any dents hidden on the passenger side, for instance. If the vehicle isn't photographed from all angles, ask for an image of the side that's not depicted. If the seller fails to respond or sends a photo that is dark or blurry, better wait for another car on which to bid. If you have some specific concerns, you might want to send the seller an e-mail to ask them to provide you with photos from specific angles and sides. Don't be shy here. It's your money that you are spending.

GunkBuster's Notebook: Stick with Your Favorite Sellers

As you probably know from shopping in brick-and-mortar stores, there's a difference between coming into a place for the first time and shopping at the same location every week, or perhaps every day. After a while, the clerks get to know you and they greet you by name. As a regular customer at a big retail store, you may be eligible for special promotions that other customers don't get. They might even send you special mailings or call you to inform you about merchandise they are offering only to their best customers. Some stores even offer "special preview" days when their preferred customers get to come in and look things over before the general public can.

The same sort of advantages apply on eBay, but arrangements are less formal. In fact, they vary depending on the individual seller. Once you find a seller who deals in items that you like, it makes sense to return to that person on a regular basis, even if you could conceivably save a dollar or two by shopping around and buying at auction. Why? As the seller gets to know you, they are likely to offer you deals on special items or suggestions of new items that have just come in. There may even be a special Web site for their preferred customers that you can visit to learn more about what the seller has to offer.

As a preferred customer, you can also suggest combining several purchases to save on shipping costs. Suppose you see some related items from the same seller—a common occurrence, especially in an eBay Store. If you purchase two items separately, such as a set of screwdrivers and a box of screws, you might have to pay $6 to ship each. But by asking the seller to ship both at the same time, you might have to pay, say $8. You save a couple of dollars, and the seller saves the time and materials required to pack one item: it's a classic win-win situation.

Building a special arrangement with a seller might also help you when the seller has new items to sell. Because the seller will get to know what your interests are, they might contact you when they have new items before they auction them off to the general public. Smart sellers will do this because they can save time and money by not having to write up product descriptions and pay auction fees. If you purchase items from a seller who actually makes custom merchandise, don't be afraid to ask the seller if they will make custom items for you.

Capitalize on Sellers' Mistakes

If you specialize in an area, take advantage of your knowledge and experience to turn up some items that have been incorrectly described by sellers. In Chapter 3, you learned about misspellings and how they can help you uncover bargains that have been overlooked by others. I'm continually surprised by the number of auctions in which the seller has made errors such as these that you can turn to your advantage:

√   The incorrect date or model number

√   The incorrect manufacturer

√   An item that is not valuable in itself but that contains a valuable part. I see this in fountain pens that have replacement nibs: sometimes, the pen is worth only a few dollars, but the nib is by a more famous manufacturer and is valuable to collectors.

The key to finding such mistakes is taking the time to read through descriptions thoroughly and browsing through lots of sales. Bargains that turn up due to misspellings aren't the well-kept secret they once were. But if you're having a hard time finding a good buy in your area of interest, scrounging for other errors in the description can help you turn up a "gold nugget" among all the "fool's gold."

Shop Close to Home for Large Merchandise

Finding bargains is all about finding things that other buyers overlook. One thing that frequently gets overlooked on eBay is the item that's hard to ship. Things that are heavy, such as couches and appliances, don't attract a lot of bids because they are expensive to ship. However, they can be a bargain if you happen to live close to a seller and can pick them up in person. (Many sellers will, in fact, specify that they will sell only to someone in their immediate geographic area.) Follow these steps to search for something close to home that you can pick up yourself:

1. Connect to the Advanced Search page by clicking the <u>Advanced Search</u> link that appears near the top of nearly all eBay pages.

2. Enter your search terms.

3. Scroll down the page to the heading "Items near me." Enter Your zip code in the Zip Code box.

4. Choose a distance in miles from the drop-down menu list labeled "within." The distance you choose (see Figure 14-2 for examples) represents the distance you are willing to travel in order to make the pickup. The higher the distance, the wider the range of search results you'll get.

5. Click Search.

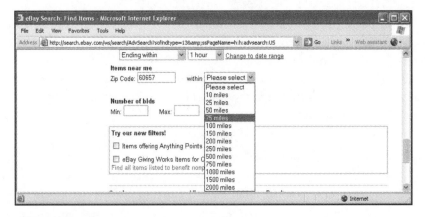

Figure 14-2
You can win large items others aren't willing to bid on if you search for them in your local area.

The search results you receive should list items in your geographic area. You'll probably still have to pay a deposit to the seller before you make the pickup. But you'll have the extra satisfaction of being able to pick up your object in person and hand over the payment at the same time. When the object in question is a car or other motor vehicle, an in-person pickup can be a memorable and rewarding experience. You might get to learn about the vehicle's history first hand or possibly even see photos of the vehicle in its "younger days."

TIP: You might find a heavy object that is not in your area but still turns out to be a really good deal. Don't be afraid to take the time to research what the shipping costs might be. Heavy objects are shipped around the country all the time. I know of a person who lived on an island in Maine and purchased many of his household belongs on eBay and had the items shipped, including even a custom golf cart. The key is that you need to get a good enough deal on your eBay purchase so that you can afford the shipping costs. Buying merchandise this way still might get you a better deal than buying your items from retail stores.

Learn PowerSeller Degunking Tips for Beginning Sellers

When it comes to security, sellers on eBay have some advantages over buyers. They can wait for a check to clear before shipping out something that has been purchased, for instance. But there are disadvantages, too: they can fall victim to credit card fraud and have their time wasted by buyers who won't pay up (see Chapter 13 for more information on such transaction troubles). But in this chapter, the focus is on getting off the ground and building regular sales on a weekly basis. Some PowerSeller degunking tips are arranged in an easy-to-follow plan next.

Step 1: Focus on What You Know and Love

The first step is one of the most enjoyable you can take: deciding what you love and what excites you in terms of collecting, buying, and selling. When you become an eBay seller, you don't have to sell the same things you collect your-self—but it helps. If you love what you're doing, your enthusiasm will spread to others through your product descriptions, you'll enjoy the buying and selling processes, and you'll welcome the chance to trade in those same types of items on eBay. You can look around for wholesale items that aren't part of what you collect, and you can and should sell a wide range of items, too. But if you have a core set of items you especially love, your time will go much faster when it comes to the tedious and tiring aspects of selling—packing, driving to the post office, responding to questions, and so on.

Step 2: Don't Overlook Oddball Items

As I write this, the news media is buzzing with a story about a woman who put a ghost up for sale on eBay in an effort to calm her son, who was afraid of being haunted by the ghost of his grandfather. She told a good story about her father (the boy's grandfather) and how he might have seemed scary to her son due to an illness that proved fatal. The ghost was purchased by a magic company for $75,000. Just a few weeks before this sale, a woman in Florida was able to auction off a portion of a 10-year-old grilled cheese sandwich that allegedly bore the face of the Virgin Mary. This unlikely item actually sold for $28,000 to an online casino that reportedly planned to put it on display during a "world tour."

The moral: Don't be afraid to auction off things that are unusual and even downright weird. Before you throw out that strange item you found in the basement, put it on eBay and see what happens. I once wrote about a PowerSeller who found an artificial leg at an estate sale. He put it online as a joke and it ended up selling for $100. A woman found a beer can in the crawl space of her home, where it was perfectly preserved from the elements; it sold for $19,000 (you can read an article about it in eBay's community newsletter at **http:// pages.ebay.com/community/chatter/2003Feb/Sub2.html**). Buyers shop on eBay in the hope of discovering something strange and unusual. No matter how ugly or oddball the object you have, try selling it online.

Step 3: Take Time with Your Descriptions

You've already learned in this book that one of the most important degunking activities involves sprucing up your auction descriptions. The better you get at writing descriptions, the more successful you'll be. You probably know all of the things you should do (make your copy clear, provide plenty of details, be honest, and so on). But writing great copy also involves putting your imagination to work. With all of the items being sold on eBay, something that catches the interest of eBay buyers will go a long way, especially because eBay buyers can easily get bored reading the same descriptions over and over.

Let's look at an example. I just mentioned the woman who sold a ghost on eBay. Why did this sale (in which the seller offered only the old cane that had been used by the grandfather who allegedly haunted her young son) attract several people who were willing to bid thousands of dollars?

It was the story the seller told, of course. Perhaps you can read the entire story shown in Figure 14-3. If not, I'll just quote the first two paragraphs here:

> My 5 year old son believes the ghost of my father haunts our house (which was once my fathers house.) My son knows I sell on ebay and asked me to put my dads ghost up for auction. Since he wants to make sure someone gets the ghost he wants me to put his cane up so he goes with it.
>
> Ever since my father died my 5 year old son has been afraid to go anywhere in the house alone whether it be day or night! I always thought it was just normal kid fears until a few months ago he told me why he was so scared. He told me "Grandpa

Figure 14-3
This seller won thousands of dollars for a son who was haunted by his grandfather's ghost.

> died here, and he was mean. His ghost is still around here!" He then brought up the couple of times my dad tapped him with his cane and how mean his grandpa looked when he yelled at him. so up for auction is my dad's ghost along with his cane he used for getting around and hurt my 5 year olds feelings with.

The seller went on to explain that the grandfather had lung cancer and medications were making him irritable. She was obviously sincere and honest, and this resulted in substantial bids from more than a dozen individuals and companies. No matter what you have to sell, you'll get more attention if you can engage someone's imagination. Tell the prospective buyer how they might use the object or how it might make them feel. Tell a story, if you can; it's been proven time and again that they reach eBay buyers on a personal, one-on-one level.

Step 4: Go the Extra Mile

I'm impressed over and over again by hearing about successful sellers who do things that aren't necessary for buyers—things I would, frankly, never have thought of doing myself. An extra bit of goodwill will not only defuse problem situations, it'll make your time on eBay pass more enjoyably. A few suggestions are described next; you can probably learn about others on eBay's discussion groups.

Send a Goodwill Gift

Experienced retailers know that it's important to reach prospective buyers at every stage of a transaction. The last stage at which you have contact with someone is the moment when the buyer opens the package you have shipped. You don't have to insert more than a straightforward, businesslike invoice with your package. But if you have some extra gifts lying around, add them. One seller adds an extra surplus item such as an antique postcard, a holiday card, or a Christmas tree ornament with each of her sales. Even if you add only a simple note card that thanks the buyer for their patronage, you'll spread goodwill and increase the chances of a return purchase by the same person later on.

Be Liberal with Refunds

I realize that it's easy for *me* to tell you to offer your customers refunds. It's not my money, after all. But you might discover that a liberal return policy pays off in the long run. Consider the following examples from PowerSellers I've interviewed:

√ Despite her best attempts at careful packing, a delicate item arrived broken in two pieces. The seller refunded part (not all) of the purchase money. The buyer didn't ship the item back and didn't complain; the situation was resolved happily.

√ A buyer reported that the item just wasn't exactly what she wanted; the seller decided to provide a full refund. The buyer was so pleased that she made some subsequent purchases from the same seller and didn't return the items.

Some PowerSellers who are confident enough in their ability to gain regular income from eBay sales specify in their descriptions that they guarantee customer satisfaction and will refund purchase money for any reason. You may not want to adopt a global return policy yourself, but if you can be generous with your customers on a case-by-case basis, you'll leave them with a positive feeling, and you'll get positive feedback, too.

TIP: Many sellers promote multiple purchases by offering to combine shipping costs. They include a notice in each sales description to the effect that, if someone buys not only this item but others they have for sale, they will take a dollar or two off of subsequent purchases. It's a great way to encourage shoppers to buy many different items from you.

Give the Buyer a Break on Shipping Costs When You Can

Shipping costs are something that everyone hates to pay. You can really make a repeat buyer and important customer happy by giving them a break on the shipping charges now and then. (It's especially easy to save money on shipping if you sell on Half.com, as described in the next section.) For example, if you have a buyer who purchases multiple items from you but the extra items won't really add much to the shipping costs, you might want to tell the buyer that you will ship all of the items together, which should save the buyer money on shipping. This is something that can really make a buyer's day. They likely will tell all of their friends and other eBay shoppers they interact with.

Save Time by Selling on Half.com

It's especially easy to give buyers a break on shipping costs if you sell on a part of eBay known as Half.com (**http://half.ebay.com**). Half.com, which started out as a marketplace separate from eBay, was purchased by eBay in 2001. It's a place where sellers can easily put books, CDs, DVDs, videotapes, sporting goods, and other items up for sale at a discount price. One of the big advantages of selling on Half.com is the fact that you get reimbursed for part of your shipping costs. It's an effort to promote the site and to ensure that sellers make a profit from selling low-cost items. For instance, if you put a used textbook up for sale on Half.com for $19.99 and it is purchased, you make a profit in the following way:

1. The buyer pays you $20.41 (the purchase price of $19.99 plus $1.42 for shipping by USPS Media Mail, the shipping method that sellers are encouraged to use by default on Half.com).

2. Half.com charges you a 15 percent commission on the $19.99 sale price, or $3.00.

3. Half.com reimburses you $1.94 for shipping because this is a paperback book.

4. Half.com directly deposits the result, $18.93, in your checking account.

TIP: Half.com has an elaborate system for reimbursing sellers for shipping. The amount of the reimbursement depends on the type of item you are selling. Find out more at http://half.ebay.com/help/index.cfm?helpsection=fulfill#5.

I know one eBay seller, Andy Noise, who keeps his customers satisfied when they purchase music from him on Half.com. Andy charges them for Media Mail shipping (a bargain rate). But he sends the merchandise by First-Class Mail. It uses up most or all of his shipping reimbursement, but customers are happy because they get the item faster than they expected; in this way, he encourages repeat business. One of Andy's sales is shown in Figure 14-4.

Half.com is a great place to sell books, music, video games, or other items if you're in a hurry and you don't want to go through the effort of creating a sales description and managing an auction. You enter the ISBN or UPC product number for the item (if there is one), you set a price, you describe the item's

Figure 14-4

Half.com gives you another option for selling books and entertainment items quickly.

quality (New, Like New, Good, Fair, and so on), you put the sale online, and you're done. The item remains in your online sales "inventory" on Half.com until it is sold or until you remove it; there's no time limit for how long a sale on Half.com can last. For that reason alone, it's a good place to relist items you don't sell the first time around at auction.

Degunking Tips for Full-Time eBay Businesspeople

PowerSellers know all about running full-time businesses on eBay. By following the example of sellers who know how to build consistent sales over the long haul, you can boost your income and your feedback level whether you're currently a PowerSeller or not. Here's a step-by-step degunking program for those who want to sell on eBay full-time.

Step 1: Develop Contacts with Other Sellers

No matter what you want to do on eBay or what sorts of problems you encounter, you'll be better off if you have real live eBay sellers you can contact for support. Like anything on eBay, sources of "gunk" change all the time. Although

I've tried to describe as many tips and options as possible in this book, the PowerSellers who frequent eBay Groups and the discussion forums will be able to help you with current problems that others might be encountering too.

Step 2: Find Some "Listing Buddies"

Don't go it alone. Again and again, PowerSellers tell me they lean on their eBay friends for help. Melissa Sands, who is profiled later in this chapter, says she depends on her "listing buddies" to encourage her to create at least 10 new sales descriptions every day, no matter how tired she is or how much other household activities press in upon her.

"One time I went through the day and I was very busy, and I didn't get any sales online," says Sands. At 10:00 that night, I got an e-mail from my listing buddy, encouraging me to get my sales online."

Step 3: Pay for a Logo

Many PowerSellers create a graphic identity by paying a few hundred dollars to have a logo created by a professional graphic designer. It might seem like an outlandish expense at first, but you'll be able to use your logo for years to come and in many different venues: your eBay Store, your business card, your Yellow Pages or newspaper ads, your eBay classes, and much more. It's a very cost-effective option; in other words—one that will pay off for years to come.

A logo, of course, is only one part of creating an effective business Web site. By launching a Web site, you gain the ability to publicize your sales in another online venue. You also gain credibility for your overall sales operation, which will foster trust among your eBay customers.

Step 4: Make a Commitment

The word *commitment* is overused and can mean many things. When it comes to selling on eBay on a regular basis, it means being committed to do something on eBay every day, and whether you're busy or not, whether you're feeling totally energetic or not. Make the time to check e-mail and respond to questions from current and prospective customers.

If you feel like you're putting pressure on yourself to do your eBay work and create a certain number of sales listings every day, maybe that's not such a bad thing. A little pressure can be a good motivator, whether it comes from your listing buddies or from yourself. "I think there's a little bit of pressure that comes along with it in wanting to maintain your PowerSeller status," comments Melissa Sands." I put pressure on myself to keep that status. I feel I have to list a certain amount of items and be there for people constantly. You have more people you are helping. That's my goal: to be able to spend more time on my business, to take it seriously, and do it well."

You should also take the time to review your listings while your auctions are taking place. Read over your descriptions and try to put yourself in your buyers' shoes. Look for ways in which you can improve your descriptions and photos the next time around. If you have items that don't perform well, try to take the time to do a postmortem and see if there are some mistakes that you are making. You might also want to have other people you know who are successful at running businesses and selling items review some of your material. A few fresh and good ideas can go a long way in helping you to improve your selling approach.

GunkBuster's Notebook: Pay Yourself First, PowerSeller Advises

Like many eBay sellers, Melissa Sands manages to fit eBay business activities around raising her three children (ages 11, 3, and 6 months) and other responsibilities associated with her suburban Detroit home. She doesn't do it alone. She turned to her sister for help with creating listings. She also hired a straight-A high school student to help with the packing of merchandise after school.

"It's a great job for him; he comes here from 2:00 to 5:00, he knows how to work the computer, and he can print out invoices, too."

That's one of several tips Sands has for budding sellers. Another is one that many sellers overlook: although she spends anywhere from 40 to 60 hours a week on eBay, she always remembers to pay herself a salary of $25 per hour first. What's left over goes to the student, to eBay, to advertising, and to acquiring merchandise to sell.

"You've got to give yourself an hourly wage," she says. "Should I do a $6.50 packing job? I hire someone else do to that. Then I can work 'close to the money,' doing the actual buying and selling."

Some of what's left over after the salary also goes to the auction service Marketworks, which helps her keep track of orders and paperwork. "Marketworks is a nice program; it keeps all of your activities in one place. It helped me increase gross revenues from $5 to $7000 per month to $9 to $12,000 per month."

Sands has been a member of eBay since April 1999. "I had a "real" job at a Detroit area accounting firm which I hated. I discovered eBay because my husband used to sell comic books and sports cards at local shows and we had a ton of stuff lying around. I wanted to dispose of it, and my brother had asked me if I had heard of eBay. The first things I sold were a bunch of old Promo cars–cars that were given away in the 50s, 60s, and 70s and that were scale models of the car you actually bought. I decided to try to sell these things and laid each one flat on my scanner, uploaded the picture, and wrote a description. I had tons of collectors e-mailing me for more and I learned all about them. Some of these cars sold for between $150 and 200! Needless to say, I was hooked. I realized that if I could learn about these and sell them and make a big profit, I could sell other things. Pretty soon, I was obsessed."

Sands became a PowerSeller within that very first year. She began to scour garage sales and antique stores, looking for items to resell on eBay. In March of 2000, she was able to quit her job to work full time. At first, the move was "scary," she admits.

"I spent every minute doing eBay so I could prove to my husband we had made the right decision and, more importantly, my long-term goal was to have him be able to quit his job, too. So I looked at this as an investment into our future.

Sands passes along a list of five tips she has done to be successful on Bay: She educated herself about antiques and collectibles; hired an assistant; signed up with Marketworks; decided to use UPS to pick up at her house, and Endicia to print postage; and installed an oversized mailbox in front of her house.

"I don't have to take 20 padded envelopes to a big blue mailbox anymore," she explains. "Now it's just a giant sized one and my mailman likes it because when I receive a package he doesn't have to bring it up to the door any more."

Step 5: Open an eBay Store

Most of the PowerSellers I know have an eBay Store. Once you meet the minimum feedback requirement, you should set one up yourself. Typically, they make up anywhere from 40 to 60 percent of a seller's income. An eBay Store also gives you the ability to sell merchandise for several months at a time or even indefinitely. Find out more about creating your own store in Chapter 12.

NOTE: *Make sure you devote the time and attention required to make an eBay Store a success. You need to keep creating auction sales because each contains a link to your eBay Store.*

Step 6: Develop Contacts with Wholesalers

I've already written about finding wholesalers in Chapters 11 and 12, so I won't belabor the point here. You don't have to sell large quantities of wholesale merchandise year round, but the fact is that most of the PowerSellers I have interviewed feel such items give them a useful supplement to one-of-a-kind collectibles. They make the overall eBay selling experience go more quickly.

Step 7: Hire Staff People to Help You

The last step is actually one of the most important, and one you might consider early on in your eBay sales "career." Don't try to do everything yourself on eBay, in other words. It does take a certain amount of work to find employees to help you, but it will make your life easier in the long run. If you are less stressed out and have more time to devote to taking lots of good photos and writing good descriptions, you're bound to sell more.

The last tip I have to convey is more of a mental attitude than an "action step": think positive, and plan for success. Buy the best computer equipment you can, compile a steady stream of inventory to sell, put plenty of items up for sale, and respond quickly to your customers. Don't rest on your laurels, either; always think of ways to take new photos, save a few dollars on photo hosting or other options, and otherwise improve your new eBay business.

Summing Up

This chapter provided a roundup of degunking tips and strategies I've gleaned from eBay PowerSellers over the years that can help you degunk your eBay activities. PowerSellers tend to be responsive and generous with their time and knowledge (a lesson you can take to heart), and you can learn from their experience. If you can learn to shop wisely on eBay, you maximize profits and increase the chances that you'll sell merchandise that buyers actually want. When it comes to selling, you need to take some time with your descriptions and go the extra mile with your customer service, and your chances of success will increase that much more.

Appendix A

Avoiding Registration Gunk on eBay

To do just about anything on eBay, you need to register and sign in first. Registering and then using the User ID and password you obtain as a result of registration is a process that should definitely not be gunky. But you can run into speed bumps that can slow you down. This appendix runs through some strategies for keeping your registration and sign-in operations gunk free so the rest of your activities on the auction site run more smoothly.

Pick Good Registration Data

Chances are you plan to be a member of eBay for a long time. You can change your User ID at any time, but it's worth giving some thought to choosing the right User ID and password the first time around. Why? A User ID is part of your identity on eBay, just as much as your eBay Store or your feedback rating. A password is an essential security tool, and a strong password (one that's hard to crack, in other words) can make it more difficult for unauthorized users to hijack your account.

NOTE: *An account hijack occurs when an unauthorized user takes over someone's account in order to fraudulently buy or sell on eBay.*

Once you create a User ID, you have to wait 30 days before you change it. And even if you change User IDs, your old ones can still be traced by anyone who does a search for you by entering your current User ID in the User ID History area of the Find Members form. Here are the steps for creating a new User ID:

1. Go to the Search: Find Items page.

2. Click Find a Member.

3. Click User ID history.

4. Enter the User ID, and click Search.

Choose a Good User ID

Your User ID is the identity with which you greet other members on eBay. Like an alias in a chat room, a User ID can convey something about you or your interests. If you are interested in buying or selling effectively, I suggest you choose a nonoffensive, bland User ID that doesn't make you seem silly or frivolous. Try to choose a User ID that's short and easy to remember and conveys something about your business: button_dealer, coin_lover, cosmeticsboutique, and moms-toyshop all fit the bill.

Of course, it is a good idea to try to put some thought into how you plan to use the User ID over time. For example, let's assume you start out on eBay by selling toys and creating a User ID something like BestToys4U. Then, six months later, you expand your business and you start selling all kinds of other household items. You might find that the User ID no longer fits with what you are doing. It's difficult to always know how your business will change, but try to think of your User ID as a company name or a business logo and make it specific enough to fit your business but also general enough to give you room to grow. (See Chapter 14 for more on managing your User ID.)

CAUTION: Don't use a well-known trademark as part of your User ID. eBay probably won't allow it, and you just might get an angry e-mail message from the trademark owner telling you to stop using it.

Create a Strong Password

The other part of your eBay registration information is your password. A good password is one that you can remember easily, yet is complex enough that an unauthorized user won't be able to guess it. Pick a password that is at least six or seven characters long, contains a mixture of numerals and letters, and is not a word in the dictionary. But even the best password can be undone if you give it out yourself to someone who claims to need it. The most important piece of advice about choosing a password, then, is to keep it to yourself and never give it out.

TIP: *If you run into problems with choosing a User ID and password, or with other aspects of registration, you can turn to one of eBay's discussion boards to ask other members for advice. The Registration board is at http://forums.ebay.com/ forum.jsp?forum=78.*

Verify Your PayPal Account

PayPal, eBay's official payment service, is used by many eBay members. Your PayPal User ID and password should be different from your eBay User ID and password. It's also a good idea to verify your identity so you appear reputable.

To verify your identity, check your bank account just after registration and note the two small deposits made by PayPal. You can also respond to the reminder e-mail message that PayPal sends if you need to verify your information. Once you have recorded the amount of the deposits, go to the PayPal site (**www.paypal.com**), log in with your PayPal User ID and password, and click My Account. When the Account Overview page appears, click the link Un-verified. When the next page appears, enter the deposit amounts and click Submit.

Adjust Your Browser Preferences

As described in Chapter 2, you have to configure your browser to accept cookies in order to avoid having to sign in to eBay repeatedly. In my experience, if I set Internet Explorer so that it doesn't accept cookies, I can't sign in at all; every time I click the Sign In link, I keep returning to the current page rather than moving to the sign-in page. You can also customize your browser's links or personal toolbar to contain links to eBay Web pages you visit frequently. Plus, you can set up bookmarks or favorites to those same pages. See Chapter 2 for more information.

Ignore Requests to "Update" Your Data

As I write this, the biggest and most commonly reported security threat affecting eBay members is that of fraudulent e-mail messages that trick members into giving out their account information or other information such as credit card numbers. It's been said many times, but not often enough, that *eBay will never ask you for your personal information by e-mail*. The fraudulent messages attempt to instill fear and anxiety: You are going to be suspended if you do not confirm your registration. Someone has hijacked your account and you need to provide your accurate information. Other reasons are given as well. Ignore such e-mails and, instead, forward them to the e-mail address eBay has set up for such spoof messages: **spoof@ebay.com**.

The practice of spoofing members by sending out e-mails is actually called *phishing*. Not only does this occur with eBay accounts, but it is becoming a widespread practice for bank accounts, credit card accounts, and so on. If you are interested in learning how to protect yourself from scams like this, I suggest you pick up a copy of *Degunking Your Email, Spam, and Viruses* by Jeff Duntemann (Paraglyph Press, ISBN 1-932111-93-X).

Avoid "Free" E-Mail Accounts

Some eBay members who have e-mail accounts with free (or almost free) providers such as Yahoo!, Juno, NetZero, and Hotmail have reported that they were unable to register with eBay. eBay, so the reports go, prohibits registrations that include e-mail addresses from ISPs that are supposedly free, even though virtually all such services charge fees for e-mail service now. You may have to change your e-mail address to one that isn't one of the "free" ones.

Verify Your ID

On the Web, no one knows for sure who you really are. eBay's ID Verify program (**http://pages.ebay.com/services/buyandsell/idverify-login.html**) goes a long way toward ensuring your identity to the buyers and sellers you meet. By verifying your ID, you eliminate the need to register a credit card with eBay. In return, you receive a special icon that appears next to your User ID and feedback number and adds a bit of trustworthiness to your reputation.

Appendix B

Troubleshooting eBay with Degunking Techniques

This appendix briefly presents a group of tried-and-true tips to help you use eBay more effectively. Those listed first are for buyers, and the ones that follow are for sellers, but all will be of interest to anyone who wants to degunk their eBay business. In most cases, you can find more details about each technique elsewhere in this book. This appendix is intended to be a quick review of the main degunking approaches you can implement right away.

Set Up Favorites

Don't waste time searching through page after page of auctions or worrying about sellers you are dealing with for the first time that have low feedback numbers. After you have searched eBay for a while and made some purchases, you'll be able to identify favorite sellers, categories, and searches in My eBay so you can connect to them more quickly in the future. Once you've listed your favorite sellers, categories, and searches in My eBay, you can access them from the bottom of eBay's home page. (Find out more about this and other ways to navigate eBay more quickly in Chapter 2.)

Do Your Homework Before You Bid

Try to avoid impulse purchases. Many of the problems that arise when you are trying to win an auction can be avoided by researching what you want to buy before you click Place Bid or Buy It Now. By comparing prices, you can determine for yourself the value of what you want to purchase. You can compare prices from a number of sources:

√ eBay itself. You can do an advanced search of eBay's completed sales (**http://search.ebay.com/ws/search/AdvSearch**) to access sales for the past two weeks or so.

√ Andale (**http:/andale.com**) lets you search for completed auctions on eBay for several preceding weeks.

√ Froogle (**http://froogle.google.com**) provides price comparisons for new consumer items.

Once you have determined a reasonable price for a product, you can decide how much to bid. By doing this, you can avoid getting caught up in bidding wars. If the bidding goes beyond the price you have already identified as a fair amount, it's usually wise to wait until another, similar item comes along.

Use Buy It Now

I'm a big proponent of sales with a Buy It Now (BIN) option. While it's sometimes true that Buy It Now prices are higher than you would pay at auction, it isn't *always* true. I've followed auctions that started out with a Buy It Now price that was quickly "killed" by someone who placed a bid. The bidding ended up soaring higher than the original BIN option.

BIN prices might be higher than auction prices, but you do get the certainty of knowing that you have purchased something and you don't have to worry about competing with last-minute bidders who can beat you. For highly desirable collectibles, BIN prices provide a level of comfort and certainty that's hard to match.

Tailor Your Bidding to the Type of Sale

Once you've been on eBay for a while, you get to know the basic types of sales: reserve and standard auctions, Dutch auctions, and fixed-price sales. For each type of sale, there's a type of bidding technique you can use. For a standard (no reserve) auction, sniping or placing high proxy bids can help you win. For reserve auctions, "nibbling" away at the reserve with small bids can help reveal how much is required to win. For a standard auction with a BIN price, a small bid to kill the BIN price might help you find a bargain. For a Dutch auction, a bid that keeps you off "the bubble" is important. Find out more about each of these strategies in Chapter 4.

Choose the Right Items to Sell

If you want to make money on eBay as a seller, finding the best items to sell is one of your most important considerations. You need to learn what items eBay shoppers will bid on and buy. One option is to pick an area of specialty, get to know it well, and then try to buy items at a bargain and resell them for a profit. You can also find a wholesaler that can give you a steady supply of low-cost merchandise that will attract a steady stream of buyers. Some other selling tips are provided in the sections that follow.

Degunk Your House

One of the common reasons people start selling on eBay is not to make a profit but to clear the clutter out of their attics, garages, and other storage areas. Start by organizing, cleaning, and evaluating the extra junk in your house. Look up each item on eBay and try to determine if there's a market for it.

If you have multiple items that are similar, such as a shelf full of books or a box of videos or DVDs, you might not even have to take photos or get fancy with your auction descriptions. In fact, books and other items with ISBNs can be sold in a fill-in-the-blank format. Choose 6 to 10 items such as audio books, self-help tapes, movies, DVDs, books, or record albums and put them up for auction. Don't overwhelm yourself by trying to sell 50 or 100 separate objects at first. Start small so you don't get overwhelmed, and build up your experience and confidence gradually.

Do Your Research

Do your homework on what's hot and what's not. Collectors' price guides such as those published by the Kovels (**www.kovels.com**) can help you determine value and also supply you with dates, model numbers, and other background information about what you have to sell. Also scour magazines and special interest publications for collectors or hobbyists to find out what's rare and desirable in a field, whether it's antique furniture, dinnerware, figurines, coins, or other items. The more detailed information you can present about something you have to offer, the greater the interest you'll inspire in shoppers who see that item on eBay.

Write a Good Auction Description

Shoppers who look for merchandise online don't have a salesperson to consult, nor do they want one. They are independent sorts who want to learn about items for themselves. They hunger for every little detail about an object, and they want to look at images showing items from every possible angle. While photos are important, the way you describe an item makes a difference as well. If you are enthusiastic about something, you can inspire the same level of interest in prospective customers. Be sure to use good adjectives when you create descriptions. The right choice of words will make an item sound more interesting. Here are some examples:

√   Antique

√   Vintage

√   Classic

√   NIB (New in Box)

√   MIB (Mint in Box)

√   Rare

On the other hand, be sure to avoid cliches that don't add anything to a description, such as LOOK, L@@K, or HOT.

Tell a Good Story

I once wrote about a seller who had a gift for telling stories about the things he sold. He told a story about someone stealing a camera he took to the seashore; he was selling the leftover instruction manual. His story was so heart-wrenching that a fellow collector later returned the manual to him—along with a

replacement for the lost camera. Here's another example:

> This and many other items we currently have at auction come from a Columbus, IN, estate that has been untouched since the 1930s. The woman who last resided in the home was the sole survivor of a family in which her father and brother were tragically killed in a 1931 train accident. Her mother was pregnant with her when the accident occurred so she never knew her dad or sibling. The home was where her grandparents and parents resided. It is full of unique and interesting pieces! Keep us on your watch list because we'll have some terrific items listed and at great, low opening bids.

Such a description is sure to build additional interest in the items being sold. Try to include the most compelling details about an object in the first sentence or two because many Web surfers are impatient and not willing to read through long descriptions.

Embed Lots of Keywords

You'll help buyers locate your merchandise if you take care to add some relevant keywords in the body of your descriptions. A *keyword* is a term or phrase that someone enters in order to search for something. If your description contains the keywords your customers are likely to enter when they do a search for merchandise on eBay, your sales will turn up more frequently in the search results.

For instance, if you are selling a Trek bicycle, you might enter keywords such as these:

```
bicycle mountain bike Trek 10-speed lock lights
```

This will cause the description to turn up in search results for "mountain bike," "mountain bicycle," "Trek," and "10-speed bike."

CAUTION: *Don't do keyword spamming, which is the practice of inserting keywords that don't apply to the item you have to sell. (For example, "Acme bicycle NOT Trek Gary Fisher Schwinn.") And don't insert musical clips into a sales description; they slow down browsing and turn off potential buyers.*

Emphasize Good Customer Service

The kinds of basic sales practices that are second nature to experienced businesspeople aren't obvious to amateurs who are selling for the first time on eBay. Remember that buyers are anxious: they don't get to meet sellers in person, and no matter how often they buy on eBay, there's always a worry that a transaction will go sour. Respond to your e-mail as quickly as possible, and make every effort to accommodate buyer requests such as faster shipping options. You'll not only ensure positive feedback, you'll spread goodwill and increase the possibility of repeat business.

Draw Up a Sales Schedule

To boost sales, you need to get more sales online and process more transactions in a systematic way. You can accomplish both goals by scheduling your sales activities to fit your own needs and the habits of your customers.

The first step in a sales cycle is finding merchandise to sell. If you are like many eBay sellers, you scour yard and estate sales and flea markets, which typically occur Thursdays through Sundays. As anyone who attends such sales knows, the good material is available early in the day. It makes sense to set aside Thursday, Friday, and Saturday mornings for purchasing products and bringing your inventory home.

After that, you should make sure your sales go online during the following week. eBay itself reports that activity on its site peaks *every* day at 3 P.M. and 8 P.M. Exactly when you get your sales online depends on when you want the sales to end. If you choose the popular seven-day auction format, you should get your sales online Friday, Saturday, and Sunday so those sales end on the weekends when the most bidders/buyers are available.

TIP: *eBay's Sell Your Item form and software (such as Turbo Lister) give you the ability to schedule when your sales start and end. You can prepare dozens of sales in advance, during the work week, and schedule them to start and end on Sunday, for instance.*

Create Multiple Ways to Sell

People who shop online don't stick with just one favored venue. They tend to skip around from one e-commerce site to another, looking for the best options or the lowest prices.

Open an eBay Store

An eBay Store is a surefire way to boost your sales on eBay. Selling at a fixed price in a store is simple compared to conducting multiple auctions. The fee for running a Basic Store is only $9.95 per month. Items can be listed from 30 to 120 days. You can promote your store in your auction listings and on your About Me page. (You can find out more about opening and operating eBay Stores in Chapter 12.)

Create a Web Site

As described in Chapter 6, a Web site that you create to promote yourself, your interests, or your business is a good complement to your sales on eBay or an eBay Web page. If you have products to sell, you can advertise them on your site. You can also make links to your sales in your store or at auction. By simply creating a few Web pages on which you display your knowledge about what you buy and sell and provide information about your background and interests, you can build trust in your expertise and present a good appearance for your potential customers. Find out more about linking a Web page to your eBay sales in Chapter 6.

TIP: *You can also make some extra money and boost your feedback rating by selling on consignment for friends and family or by being designated an official Trading Assistant by eBay. Find out more about the Trading Assistants program in Chapter 6.*

Don't Overlook Packing and Shipping

The most worrisome and important part of a transaction (from the buyer's point of view, at least) is the part that comes at the very end: the fulfillment of the sale, when the item is to be delivered. The better you can pack and ship your items, the better your feedback will be and the fewer complaints about damaged goods you'll receive. Here are some packing and shipping tips to observe:

√   Clearly spell out shipping options in your auction description. Include a shipping fee, if possible.

√   Double-pack fragile items. Objects that can break easily should be insulated with Bubble Wrap or other material and double-boxed for extra protection.

√   For extra-valuable or odd-sized objects, use a shipping service.

√   Pay attention to packaging. For example, if you are selling an old quilt, add in extra quilt squares or a vintage pincushion. If you are selling little Asian figurines, package them in Chinese takeout containers.

√   Add a personal touch. Many sellers add a personal thank-you note or extra gift. Even a short note that says "I hope you enjoy this as much as I did" can leave a lasting and positive impression on customers.

For more tips on packing and shipping, see Chapter 10.

Treat eBay As a Business

If you depend on eBay as a part-time or full-time source of income, treat it as a business rather than a hobby. Draw up a schedule and make yourself stick to it. If you already run a business, make eBay a part of your overall sales strategy. You can use eBay to sell off your overstock, or you can sell specials on eBay and use the auction descriptions to direct visitors to your business Web site so they can buy more products from you directly. Research products that are likely to be profitable on eBay: search the Top 10 Lists in Seller Central's newsletters, which also contain reports on what's hot in a particular area. Remember that the most desirable items on eBay are likely to be small, easily transportable, and hard to find or one of a kind. Even if they're not one of a kind, they should be things that appeal to a small, niche market. Find out more about picking the right inventory in Chapter 11.

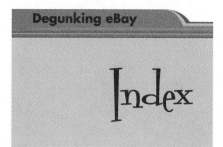

searching for, 52
sharing, 67

V

Value, assessing, 152
Vendio, 22

W

Warehouse stores, locating inventory in, 198
Watch Alert button, using, 121
Web browsers, receiving Bid Alerts on, 119–120
Web crawlers, 79
Web sites
    business, creating, 101–104
    fake, avoiding, 21–22
    selling on, 216–218
Web spiders, 79
Western Union
    Auction Payments section of, using, 144
    wire transfer scams on, avoiding, 232–233
What's Hot List, viewing, 190–191
Wholesale Lots
    category for, using, 207–208
    link for, 195–196

shopping, 195–196
Wholesalers
    contacts with, developing, 257–258
    locating, 206–208
    selecting, 194–195
Windows, using multiple, 58
Wire fraud, understanding, 232
Wireless devices, bidding with, 90–91
Wireless messages, signing up for, 89–90
Workshops
    locating, 84–86
    older eBay, listings of, 86

Y

Yahoo! Small Business program, using, 101–102

Z

Zeitgeist Web page, 163
Ziesche, Suzanne, 130
Zip codes
    search results for, 37, 50

Degunking Your Mac

By Joli Ballew
ISBN 1-93211-94-8
280 pages
Available Now!
$24.99 U.S.

Make your Mac run faster and better than ever!

Degunking Your Mac covers the latest operating system (OS X Panther) and earlier versions, including OS 9. It provides the essential tips and tricks to help you bring your Mac up to top performance. All of the crucial degunking tips and tricks are in the book, including how to degunk Macs that run dual operating systems, how to better manage hard drives that get gunked up with all types of media files, how to properly optimize the desktop, how to manage fonts properly and get rid of unneeded "font gunk," how to properly get rid of the extra stuff that OS X installs, and much more.

Degunking Your PC

By Joli Ballew
ISBN 1-933097-03-5
340 pages
Available: March 2005
$24.99 U.S.

Are all the connections to your PC and peripherals all gunked up?

Are you tripping over a viper's nest of cords and cables at every turn? Do you have printer drivers installed that date back to the Eisenhower administration? Is it impossible to vacuum under your desk? Still using dial up? Having trouble syncing your PDA with your PC's address book? If so, you have PC gunk! *Degunking Your PC* will show you the way to get out of the rat's maze of cables and old plug-and-play devices and onto the road of clean and neat PC organization. Joli Ballew, the co-author of the bestselling book Degunking Windows, will show you simple, fast, and effective ways to manage your PC hardware so that everything works seamlessly and efficiently. Degunk your PC and get rid of those cables once and for all!

Degunking Linux

By Rod Smith
ISBN 1-933097-04-3
350 pages
Available: April 2005
$24.99 U.S.

Get Linux set up and running the way you want!

Linux has a great reputation for stability, but it also has a reputation for being difficult to set up and use. It also can collect more gunk than an oversized garage. After all, it is an operating system, and all operating systems get gunked up after a few months of use. *Degunking Linux* will help you get your Linux configurations working efficiently by providing you with a proven, time-saving 12-step program to get rid of clutter and organize everything from user files to system upgrades. This is the only book that is completely focused on helping Linux users clean up their OS and getting it running smoothly and efficiently. It will show you how to perform tasks ranging from degunking user files and applications to improving account management, security, process management, and more.

Degunking Microsoft® Office

By Christina Palaia and Wayne Palaia
ISBN 1-932111-95-6
320 pages
Available: April 2005
$24.99 U.S.

Make Microsoft Office run like a dream!

Battling constant mishaps with Microsoft Office? Does PowerPoint hog your memory? Does Excel or Word crash without warning? Do these applications load at a glacial pace? Are temp files running rampant? Do you have problems finding the really important documents that you need? If these problems are frighteningly familiar, you need to degunk your Microsoft Office applications and files! Having a gunked up system with Office can really impact your productivity, especially if you don't have a method to keep everything organized and clutter-free. The solution is to use *Degunking Microsoft® Office* to streamline all your Office applications, better organize your data files, and take advantage of the applications' built-in time-saving features.

Degunking Your Personal Finances

By Shannon Plate
ISBN 1-933097-02-7
320 pages
Available: April 2005
$24.99 U.S.

Free Yourself of financial burdens starting TODAY!

Do you worry about having enough money to pay your bills, cover unexpected expenses, provide for the future, or even take a vacation? Do you know how much you spend and where the money goes? Are you uncomfortable with your level of credit card debt? You don't have to win the lottery to improve your financial status. *Degunking Your Personal Finances* will give you a simple, proven, 12-step plan to help you get out and stay out of debt. This unique book will help you create a workable and enjoyable lifestyle, and get you to organize your finances, save money, and really put your money to work for you.